Fritz Breuss (ed.)

The Stability and Growth Pact
Experiences and Future Aspects

SpringerWienNewYork

Univ.-Prof. Dr. Fritz Breuss
Europainstitut, Wirtschaftsuniversität Wien

Financial supporting was given by *Bundesministerium für Bildung, Wissenschaft und Kultur,* Wien

Printed in Austria

SpringerWienNewYork is a part of Springer Science + Business Media
springer.com

Typesetting: Camera ready by editor
Printing: Ferdinand Berger & Söhne Gesellschaft m.b.H., 3580 Horn, Austria

Printed on acid-free and chlorine-free bleached paper
SPIN: 11497004

CIP data applied for

ISSN 1610-384X

ISBN-10 3-211-27964-4 SpringerWienNewYork
ISBN-13 978-3-211-27964-9 SpringerWienNewYork

SpringerWienNewYork

European Community Studies Association of Austria
(ECSA Austria) Publication Series

Volume 10

Herausgegeben von der
Österreichischen Gesellschaft für Europaforschung
(ECSA Austria)

SpringerWienNewYork

Preface

On March 10-11, 2005, the European Community Studies Association (ECSA) Austria and the Europainstitut at the Vienna University of Economics and Business Administration organized a conference on *"The Stability and Growth Pact: Experiences and Future Aspects"*.

Shortly after the conference took place, the Ecofin Council and the European Council agreed upon a revision of the Stability and Growth Pact (SGP). After being confronted with many practical problems concerning the implementation of and the adherence to the SGP the Commission started with suggestions to reform the pact in its Communication on *"Strengthening economic governance and clarifying the implementation of the Stability and Growth Pact"* on September 3, 2004. Then, on March 20, 2005 the Ecofin Council reached a political agreement on a revision of the SGP. The substance of the agreement is laid down in a report on the *"Improving the implementation of the Stability and Growth Pact"*. In parallel, the Council prepared, on the basis of a contribution of the Commission services, a revised Code of Conduct including specifications on the implementation (the content and the format of the Stability and Convergence Programmes) of the SGP (endorsed by the Ecofin Council on October 11, 2005). On March 22, 2005 the European Council endorsed the Ecofin report, stating that it updates and complements the SGP and invited the Commission to bring forward proposals for amending the Council Regulations (EC) No 1466/97 (on the strengthening of the surveillance of budgetary positions and the surveillance and coordination of economic policies – the *"preventive arm"*) and No 1467/97 (on speeding up and clarifying the implementation of the excessive deficit procedure (EDP) – the *"corrective arm"*). These proposals were submitted to the Council and simultaneously to the European Parliament. The amending Regulations were finally adopted by the Council on June 27, 2005, published in the Official Journal of the European Union on July 7, 2005 as amended Council Regulations No 1055/2005 and No 1056/2005, respectively. The SGP 'mark I' consisted of the Resolution of the European Council on the "Stability and Growth

Pact" of June 17, 1997 and of the two Council Regulations No 1466/97 and No 1467/97, respectively. The revised Stability and Growth Pact (in short, the SGP 'mark II') encompasses also the Ecofin Council Report of March 22, 2005 plus the two amended Council Regulations No 1055/2005 and No 1056/2005.

The *major changes of the SGP 'mark II'* can be summarized as follows (see also "Public Finances in EMU 2006", published by the European Commission in European Economy 3/2006):

(I) The legislative changes concerning the *"preventive arm" of the SGP*:

(i) *Medium-term budgetary objective (MTO).* In addition to existing MTO obligation of "close-to-balance-or-in-surplus" the MTOs should now be *differentiated across countries* and may diverge from the requirement of a close-to-balance or in surplus position. The MTOs should provide a safety margin with respect to the 3 percent of GDP reference value, ensuring rapid progress towards *sustainability* and allowing room for budgetary maneuver. The consideration of sustainability plays an important role in the definition of the MTOs (in the Stability and Convergence Programmes) and in the long-term budgetary projections when evaluating the implications of age-related expenditures (for an extensive discussion see "Public Finances in EMU 2006"). *MTOs for euro area and ERM II Member States are set between* -1 percent of GDP and balance or surplus (in cyclically adjusted terms, net of one off and other temporary measures).

(ii) *Adjustment path towards the MTO.* In the SGP 'mark I' there were no provisions. Now, Member States should take active steps to achieve the MTO. The annual minimum adjustment (budgetary improvement) for *euro area and ERM II Member States* which have not yet achieved their MTO is 0.5 percent of GDP of their structural balance. The effort should be higher in "good times", and may be more limited in "bad times" (correcting pro-cyclicality or pursue a *counter-cyclical* fiscal policy as a norm).

(iii) *Early policy advice.* In addition to the previously Early Warnings addressed by the Council, upon recommendation of the Commission, the Commission can now issue direct *"early policy advice"* to encourage Member States to stick to their adjustment path.

(iv) *Increasing the focus on debt and sustainability.* Whereas there were no provisions in the old SGP for sustainability, the debt criterion, and in particular the concept of a debt ratio "sufficiency diminishing and approaching the reference value at a satisfactory pace" will be applied in qualitative terms in the revised SGP.

(v) *Provisions on structural reforms.* In the SGP 'mark II' reforms will be taken into account when defining the adjustment path to the MTO and may allow a temporary deviation from it under the following conditions:

- Only major reforms (direct/indirect impact on sustainability) like a multi-pillar pension reform (cost and benefit analysis of major structural reforms);
- Safety margin to the 3 percent reference value is guaranteed;
- The deficit returns to the MTO within the programme period;
- Detailed information is provided in the Stability and Convergence Programmes.

(II) The legislative changes concerning the *"corrective arm" of the SGP*:

(i) *Report under Article 104(3) EC Treaty.* Until now there was no obligation to prepare a report. Now, under the SGP 'mark II' the Commission will always prepare a report in case there is a deficit above 3 percent of GDP. It will be examined whether the exceptions in Article 104(2) apply and whether the deficit exceeds government investment expenditure ("golden rule") and all "other relevant factors" (which are precisely defined).

(ii) *Severe economic downturn.* Until now this was given in case of a fall of real GDP of at least 2 percent in one year. The Member States could not invoke the exception of an excessive deficit procedure (EDP) when growth was above -0.75 percent. Past experience showed that this definition is much too restrictive. In the SGP 'mark II' an economic downturn may be considered "severe" in case of a negative growth rate or accumulated loss of output during a protracted period of very low growth relative to potential growth.

(iii) *Other relevant factors (ORF).* The SGP 'mark I' included no specific definition of "ORF" and their role in the EDP. In the SGP 'mark II' "ORF" play an important role. The Commission report under Article 104(3) will take into account several factors (e.g., developments in the medium-term economic and budgetary position; any other factors, which in the opinion of the Member States, are relevant in order to assess the excess over the reference value). "ORF" will be considered only in cases where the excess over the reference value is temporary and the deficit remains close to the reference value.

(iv) *Systemic pension reforms.* These are now treated like an "ORF", but under strict conditions also with a role in abrogation. Consideration to the net cost of the reform will be given regressively for the initial five years after a Member State has introduced the reform (or five years after 2004).

(v) *Extending deadlines for taking effective action and measures.* Deadlines are extended: (a) for a decision under Article 104(6) – from 3 to 4 months after notification; (b) for taking effective action following 104(7) – from 4 to 6 months; (c) for moving to 104(9) – from 1 to 2 months; (d) for taking action following a notice under 104(9) – from 2 to 4 months.

(vi) *Minimum structural effort.* There were no specific provisions in the SGP 'mark I'. Now, countries in excessive deficit are required to achieve an annual structural effort of at least 0.5 percent of GDP as a benchmark.

(vii) *Initial deadline for correcting the excessive deficit.* The rule of the SGP 'mark I' remains: the excessive deficit has to be corrected in the year following its identification, unless there are "special circumstances". The SGP 'mark II' allows a possible extension by one year based on "ORF" and on the condition that minimum fiscal efforts have been taken.

(viii) *Repetition of steps in the EDP.* This was not foreseen in the SGP 'mark I'. Now, deadlines for correcting the excessive deficit can be extended if: (a) effective action has been taken by the Member State concerned in compliance with the initial recommendation or notice, and (b) unexpected adverse events with major unfavourable budgetary effects occur during the correction phase (e.g. natural catastrophes).

After one year of *experiences with the SGP 'mark II'*, the Commissions assessment of the functioning of the *"preventive arm"* of the SGP is mixed (see "Public Finances in EMU 2006", p. 18). On the positive side, differentiated medium-term budgetary objectives reflecting country-specific economic fundamentals were set in the context of the 2005 updated Stability and Convergence Programmes. Member States also based their budgetary projections on more realistic macroeconomic assumptions, and the recourse to one-off measures declined. However, the structural fiscal adjustment planned for 2006 by Member States not yet at their MTO falls short of the 0.5 percent benchmark.

The experience with the implementation of the EDP (the *"corrective arm"* of the SGP) is positive. The Commission in its reports initiating the EDP considered all elements relevant for the evaluation whether an excessive deficit exists as foreseen in the SGP 'mark II'. The deadlines for correcting an excessive deficit are realistic. The application of the provisions related to "ORF" confirmed that the SGP remains a rules-based fiscal framework: since the reform, all deficits in excess of 3 percent of GDP have been considered excessive.

It seems as if the intended fortification of the "preventive arm" as a counterbalance of the increased flexibility in the "corrective arm" of the SGP 'mark II' is not (yet) achieved. The reason can be found in the fact that the Commission has no "hard" instruments to discipline the Member States.

Since spring 2005, the Commission and the Council took action on six Member States currently subject to an EDP. The Commission and the Council considered that the Netherlands had corrected its excessive deficit and the Council decided to abrogate the EDP for this country in June 2005. In June 2005 the Council also adopted a decision that an excessive deficit exists in Italy and set fiscal efforts and deadlines for its correction. The same actions were taken in September 2005 for Portugal and in January 2006 for the UK. In light of the fiscal notifications of spring 2006, the Council decided in March 2006 to address a notice to Germany, which has to correct its excessive deficit in 2007. Finally, the Commission and the Council considered that Hungary has not respected the recommendations. Since January 2006, twelve EU countries are subject to an excessive deficit procedure: five euro area Member States, the UK and six new Member States.

In 2005, the budgetary position in the euro area and the EU improved significantly. In the euro area, the government deficit fell by 0.4 percentage point and reached 2.4 percent of GDP. The deficit of the entire EU also improved by 0.3 percentage points and reached 2.3 percent of GDP in 2005. The deficit reduction in the euro area and in the EU reflects better-than-expected economic growth, better than expected revenues, as well as structural budgetary adjustment. It was particularly important in the countries currently subject to an EDP. According to the spring 2006 forecasts of the Commission services, the euro area and EU deficits would remain roughly stable in 2006 and 2007, based on the assumption of unchanged policy. After increasing in 2005 for a second consecutive year, the debt-to-GDP ratio in the EU would fall from 63.4 percent in 2005 to 62.9 percent in 2006.

The proceedings of this conference contain the revised papers. As the authors had time and the opportunity to revise their papers this conference volume has the advantage not only to report and analyze the experiences with the SGP 'mark I' but it offers also a first ex ante assessment of the future aspects of the SGP 'mark II'. The conference volume consists of five parts.

Part 1 deals with the *"Legal Aspects of the SGP"*. *Jean-Victor Louis* describes "The Legal Foundations of the SGP in Primary and Secondary EC Law" and explains the origin of the SGP and its legal evolution up to the revision in 2005. At the SGP conference, *Michael Petite* of the Legal Service of the European Commission gave a lecture on the "Judgement 27/04 of the ECJ: Clarifying the Powers of the Commission and the Council in Relation to the Excessive Deficit Procedure?" (concerning the Ecofin Council conclusions in the EDPs against France and Germany). This paper was discussed by *Angelika Hable* and *Wolfgang Wessels*. Unfortunately, all three speakers were not able to supply a written version of their presentation for this conference volume. Those who are interested in the Judgement C-27/04 of the ECJ of July 13, 2004 may consult the ECJ homepage: http://www.curia.europa.eu.

Part 2 touches some of the *"Economic Problems with the SGP"*. *Paul van den Noord* sees the "Fiscal Policies in EMU at the Crossroads". Looking the experiences with the SGP 'mark I', he diagnoses several gaps in the pact: an incentive gap, a surveillance gap and an enforcement gap. In the spirit of the revised pact he stresses to the importance of long-term (sustainability) issues. *Andrew Hughes Hallett* in his contribution "Fiscal Policy Coordination with independent Monetary Policies – Is it possible?" offers a new approach of co-coordinated policy making in the EMU. In a Stackelberg-like game he proposes a fiscal leadership with an independent central bank. Fiscal leadership leads to improved outcomes because it implies a degree of coordination and reduced conflicts between institutions, without the central bank having to lose its ability to act independently. The paper by *van den Noord* is critically discussed by *André Sapir*, those of *Hughes-Hallett* by *Ewald Nowotny*.

Part 3 asks for *"The Theoretical Basis of the SGP"*. *Wilhelm Kohler* philosophizes "On the Theoretical Underpinning of the Stability and Growth Pact". After a tour d'horizon over possible theoretical justifications for the pact (from the traditional OCA theory over aspects of policy coordination and long-run sustainability) he comes to the conclusion that the specific rules of the SGP and its "numerology" are not well founded theoretically. This paper is commented by *Waltraud Schelkle.*

Part 4 digs into the *"Economic Aspects of the Reform of the SGP". Marco Buti* – one of the architects of the reformed SGP - asks the question "Will the New Stability and Growth Pact Succeed? An Economic and Political Perspective". His answer is in the affirmative because the SGP 'mark II' tackles the following issues: (a) overcoming excessive uniformity, (b) improving transparency, (c) correcting pro-cyclicality, and (d) strengthening enforcement. He sees all this requirements fulfilled. Lastly, however, the new rules can be applied only if they are backed by key players and fully integrated in their national policy framework. The paper is commented by a famous critic of the SGP, *Paul de Grauwe.*

Part 5 concludes with *"Model Simulations of the SGP Fiscal Rule". Fritz Breuss* and *Werner Roeger*, using the Quest model of the European Commission study the specific problem of "Sluggish Growth and the SGP Fiscal Rule: Model Simulations". The reason why France and Germany exhibited an excessive deficit over nearly five years, starting in 2002 was the fact that they were caught in a "protracted period of very low growth relative to potential growth". In such a situation the exception of an EDP could not be invoked under the SGP 'mark I'. Now, the SGP 'mark II' allows for such a constellation. This actual situation of the downturn of the European economy since 2001 is reproduced in the Quest model for simulation purposes. Sticking to the SGP rule would have been advantageous (at least in the long-run) in case of the supply shock interpretation of the downturn. In the case of a symmetric demand shock interpretation the SGP rule would have been neutral over the cycle, although harmful in the very short-run. The paper is commented by applying similar simulation experiments with another world macro model, the McKibbin-Sachs Global Model (MSG2 Model) by *Reinhard Neck* and *Gottfried Haber*.

I would like to acknowledge the generous support by the Austrian Ministry of Education, Science and Culture and by the European Commission DG Education and Culture. Thanks go also to the organizer of the conference, *Roman Puff* and to *Nurgül Özen* who produced the camera ready text.

Fritz Breuss, Vienna June 2006

Table of Contents

Part 1:
Legal Aspects of the SGP

Jean-Victor Louis

The Legal Foundations of the SGP in Primary and Secondary EC Law

I. The Origin of the SGP

The "Stability Pact for Europe" as it was called when the initiative was launched by the German Government[1] (and which is generally related to the Minister of Finance of the time, *Mr. Waigel*) reflects the traditional concerns for stability expressed by the German authorities before and during the negotiation of the Maastricht Treaty, and reflected also in the ratification process in Germany as well as in the "Maastricht Beschluss" of the BVerfGericht of 1993 (Part II, e)[2] and in the position of the Bundesbank. A simple look at the Preamble of the Document of November 1995 and its vocabulary (for example, the reference to the "*Solidar Gemeinschaft*") demonstrates the filiations with earlier German positions. One of the main purposes was, indeed, to reassure the German public that the euro will be as stable as the DM.

---

[1] The Pact received its definitive denomination at the European Council of Dublin, of 13 and 14 December 1996. In addition to the SGP, the European Council in Amsterdam adopted, on 16 June 1997, a Resolution on growth and employment, *OJ* C236/3, 2 August 1997.

[2] Decision of 12 October 2003, BVerfGE 89, 155.

The proposal was based on the will "to permanently ensure budgetary discipline in the final stage", for its own merits but also in order to strengthen "the soundness and credibility of the European monetary union". The main features of the desirable fiscal policy of the participating Member States, as exposed in the original document, did not only bear on fighting deficits and reducing public sector debt but also on limiting public expenses and orientating government spending towards public investment "which helps business and for the promotion of private investment in order to develop the infrastructure and to safeguard Europe's economic future". No specific allusion to the costs of the ageing population, an element which will constantly appear in future documents.

The elements of the Pact roughly described in the initial document submitted to the partners of Germany include the commitment to respect the requirements of stability in the preparation of national budgets. In the medium term, growth rates of public sector spending should be kept below the growth in nominal GNP. A medium-term deficit goal of 1% is suggested in order to ensure a safety margin so that the 3% limit can be observed even in economically unfavourable periods. The 3% limit may only be exceeded in "extreme exceptional circumstances" with the agreement of a qualified majority of the participating Member States. The debt must be reduced "further even below the Maastricht limit of 60%". The most specific proposals concern the sanctions. The German Government clearly wants more automaticity and the recourse straight away to the most stringent sanctions listed in the Article 104c: non-interest-bearing deposits and fines. It suggests considering other sanctions as well, like the restricted access to the structural funds.

The more interesting aspects of the proposal under a legal standpoint are related to the institutional suggestions. Under the Pact, the participants would found a "European Stability Council" "in order to implement and coordinate their binding commitments". This Council will meet twice a year after the deficit data have been presented by the Commission "or upon the request of a member". "The Stability Council will review the main features and goals of the Stability Pact, will report on the implementation of the commitments and decide on exemptions…"

The German Government was adamant that "The provisions of the Treaty will not be called into question either economically or legally. Renegotiating the Treaty of Maastricht is not intended."

The commitments of the participating Member States were meant to be compatible with the existing provisions. In the first presentation of its plan, the German Government did not disclose its ideas on the form of the Pact it suggested, but the idea of what was called an "economic Schengen" promptly circulated and in a further document (of February 1996) more elaborated as far as the legal and institutional aspects are concerned the proposal appears of adopting a "legally binding agreement under international law".

The objectives of the German Government in proposing the conclusion of the Pact could not be met by what it called "a self-binding political declaration of the Member States". Some elements of the Pact should be realised by acts of secondary law (regulations). For the other elements, the insertion of the Pact in the agenda of the IGC 1996 was excluded, perhaps in the fear of opening the famous "Pandora box". An agreement of the Member States binding under international law was the solution.[3] This agreement was "reconcilable with Community law" as it was intended to further the objectives of the EC Treaty. It would not modify or replace the existing procedure, but create a "parallel procedure".

What would be the content of the agreement? It would introduce automaticity where Article 104c (now 104) provided for the exercise of some discretion, lift the exemption criteria which the Commission could take into account under paragraph 2 and establish a Stability Council, either within or outside the Council and with a capacity for making legally binding decisions. In the course of the discussion, the idea of "shifting the burden of proof" was advanced. Sanctions would be adopted when a decision on an excessive deficit would be taken and these sanctions could be lifted by a decision of the Council at a qualified majority. Some ideas in the same direction but taking more into account the lack of automaticity of the Treaty were presented as early as 1997 in the economic literature.[4]

The "legality" of the German Government's proposal was immediately contested by most of the partners of Germany. The compatibility with Community law of agreements parallel to the Treaty either partial ones (among some Member States, here those of the Euro area) or global (among all the Member States) has been recently discussed in relation with the insertion by the Amsterdam

---

3 For an analysis of the motivations of the German Government and the legal basis of the Pact as proposed by it, see *Hahn* (1998) pp. 77-100.

4 See *Gros* (1997) p. 239 et seq.

Treaty of formula's of closer cooperation. The question is now put in the following terms: does the existence of formulas of closer co-operation within the Treaty exclude such cooperation outside the Treaty? Those in favour of the possibility to conclude parallel agreements mention in particular the example of the Schengen agreement. Parallel agreements would only be limited by the primacy of Community law and the pre-emption rule.[5]

In specie, the German Government invoked in favour of the "legality" of a parallel agreement the limited competences of the EC in the field of economic policies which remain under the authority of the Member States, allowing them as a matter of principle to adopt between or among them bilateral and multilateral agreements. They are also free to reach an understanding outside the agreement in order to meet the objectives of the treaty in an even more stringent manner. In other terms, they may agree on the way to use the leeway open by the provisions of the Treaty and to exercise their vote in the Council, as far as deadlines are concerned for example. It was also possible for the participating Member States to create a "Stability Council" which would be, in legal terms, a "Conference of the Representatives of EU Member Governments in the Council".

It is not surprising that such a construction did not convince the legal services of the institutions and most of the other Member States. To be sure, the rejection of the proposed binding agreement by the partners of Germany was at least in part motivated by the political will to preserve the rules on EMU which were discussed at length before and during the Maastricht IGC and constitute a bundle of political compromises but there were strong legal arguments against the arguments presented by the German Government. To accept the conclusion of the so-called "supportive agreement" would have been a dangerous precedent for the Community legal order. It was felt impossible to modify the institutional framework by the creation of a new organ and to change the role of the institutions in a procedure exhaustively settled in the Treaty without recourse to the formal revision procedure, the more so that all the Member States would not participate to the proposed organ. The Opinion 1/76 of the Court on the navigation on the Rhine[6] could be invoked against such a pretension and the case law of the Court ex-

---

[5] See *de Witte* (2001) p. 231 et seq.

[6] See *ECR* (1977) p. 741.

cluding a revision of the Treaty under a procedure not provided by it. A matter settled in every detail by the longest provision of the Treaty would have been governed by a parallel agreement concluded by some of the Member States. There are cases where pre-emption does not derive from secondary law but directly results from primary law, as it was expressly decided by the Court in Ruling 1/78 (under Article 103 Euratom Treaty)[7] on the Euratom Supply regime. One could add that to invoke the limits of the Community competences under Article 103 EC (now 99) of the Treaty in order to justify the proposed legally binding agreement when the stringent rules of Article 104c (now 104) were at stake was particularly audacious.

There was a rapid consensus among the Commission and the Member States on the finality of the Pact and on the opportunity to avoid a revision of Treaty provisions concerning the correction of excessive deficits. The Commission suggested right from the beginning to look at the means of founding the Pact on the Treaty. It was of the opinion to exploit the legal basis in the Treaty, not only Article 104c (104) but also Article 103 (99) for avoiding the necessity to engage in corrective action, i.e. to provide for a better coordination of economic policies, to request from the Member States the elaboration of programmes which would be scrutinised at Community level, to provide for an "early warning system" in case of deviation and to extend the Pact on appropriate terms to Countries which did not participate to the euro. To the corrective or repressive measures proposed by the promoters of the Pact, it added the necessity of a reflection on preventive action. This orientation was rapidly accepted.

Neither the Commission, nor the partners of Germany were favourable to the conclusion of an international agreement. The Pact should be realised "in accordance with the procedures and principles of the Treaty" and contrary to the view expressed by Germany an international agreement could not achieve the prospected results on two points: the automaticity where the Treaty provides for some discretion, and the creation of a Stability Council, parallel to the Ecofin Council. Hence the orientation which was taken towards the drafting of two regulations and a European Council resolution.

---

7 See *ECR* (1978) p. 2151.

The question of the legal basis of preventive action (what was to become Regulation N° 1466/97)[8] was if not uncontroversial at least easy to solve once the objectives of this action had been accepted. Article 103 (99), paragraph 5 clearly allowed the Council to adopt under the so-called cooperation procedure, the modalities of multilateral surveillance. It was considered that a link was to be established between the coordination of economic policies and multilateral surveillance, on the one hand, and the realisation of the objective of "stable finances", particularly important in an economic and monetary union, on the other hand. Article 103 (99), paragraph 4 confirmed the justification of this link in allowing the Council acting against economic policies of a Member States if "they risk jeopardising the proper functioning of economic and monetary union". The coordination and mutual surveillance should contribute to avoid excessive deficits which were conceived as an important risk for EMU. This explains the content of Regulation N° 1466/97 which introduces in secondary law the objective of a budget "close to balance or in surplus" substituting the objective of 1% deficit of the Waigel Plan, which was considered as arbitrary, and provides for some flexibility in its implementation to each Member State. It includes nothing about the debt because it was meant to be superfluous if an effective action against deficit and the objective of balanced budget was promoted. It provides for an early warning procedure and for the elaboration by the Member States of stability (for the *Ins*) and convergence (for the *Outs*) programmes to be submitted to the Council.

The choice of the legal basis was not so easy for the measures concerning the corrective aspects of the Pact which included complements to Article 104c (104). Three points were at stake: the definition of the exceptional and temporary circumstances authorising to exceed the 3% GDP limit of the deficit, the provision of deadlines for the stages of the procedure and the specification of the mechanism of sanctions. The question was: how to use Article 104c (104), paragraph 14 which provides that

> "Further provisions relating to the implementation of the procedure described in this article are set out in the Protocol on the excessive deficit procedure annexed to this Treaty (subparagraph 1). The Council shall, acting unanimously on a proposal from the

8 See *OJ*, L209/6, 2 August 1997.

> Commission and after consulting the European Parliament and the ECB, adopt the appropriate provisions which shall then replace the said Protocol (subparagraph 2). Subject to the other provisions of this paragraph, the Council shall, before 1 January 1994, acting by a qualified majority on a proposal from the Commission and after consulting the European Parliament, lay down detailed rules and definitions for the application of the provisions of the said Protocol (subparagraph 3)"?

The Protocol on the excessive deficit procedure includes the reference values (3% and 60%), some definitions among others, the one of "government" which is capital for the calculation of the deficit,[9] some obligations of the Member States related to the effectiveness of the procedure and the obligation of the Commission to provide statistical data. A regulation was adopted in 1993 for the application of the Protocol.[10]

II. The structure and legal nature of the Pact

A choice was apparently possible among two legal basis in order to adopt the rules that would have to be included in Regulation N° 1467/97.[11] One could replace the Protocol, a possibility provided, as we have seen, under Article 104c (104) paragraph 14, subparagraph 2. This solution which would allow for giving to the new rules a substantial content presented the risk of opening a discussion on the reference criteria, which was meant to be inopportune. On the other hand, to act on the basis of the easier procedure offered by subparagraph 3, which did not require the unanimity in the Council like subparagraph 2, only permitted to give a rather limited content to

---

9 Government means general government, that is central government, regional or local government and social security funds, to the exclusion of commercial operations, as defined in the European System of Integrated Economic Accounts (ESA), a System also referred to for the definition of deficit and investment.

10 Council Regulation of 22 November 1993 on the application of the Protocol on the excessive deficit procedure annexed to the Treaty establishing the European Community, *JOCE,* L332, 31 December 1993, p. 7 as amended by Regulation N° 475/2000 of 28 February 2000, *JOCE,* L58, 3 March 2000, p. 1 and Regulation N° 351/2002 of 25 February 2002, *JOCE,* L55, 26 February 2002, p. 23.

11 See *OJ* N° L209/6, 2 August 1997.

the complementary rules, too limited at least in order to realise the objectives of the Pact.

The solution was found in another direction. The regulation would not replace the Protocol but come in addition to it. Recital 1 of the Preamble of Regulation N°1467/97 is very clear to this effect:

> "Whereas it is necessary to speed up and to clarify the excessive deficit procedure set out in Article 104c of the Treaty in order to deter excessive general government deficits and, if they occur, to further their prompt correction; whereas the provisions of this Regulation, which are to the above effect and adopted under Article 104c (14) second subparagraph, constitute, together with those of Protocol (No 5) to the Treaty, *a new integrated set of rules* for the application of Article 104c."

It seemed to the authors of the text that if the Council could substitute the Protocol by new provisions, it was also able to "enrich" the content of the protocol by a regulation. This act includes the definition of what constitutes an exceptional and temporary excess of a government deficit over the reference value (section 1). It fixes a calendar for the procedure of correction of excessive deficit (section 2: "Speeding up the excessive deficit procedure"). It provides for the conditions of abeyance and the monitoring of the procedure (section 3) and specifies the sanctions to be applied and the destination of the funds (section 4).

There was to be a third constitutive element of the "Stability and Growth Pact", as it was finally coined: a resolution of the European Council.[12] As described by *Martenczuk*,[13] the idea of the addition to the regulations of a resolution of the European Council was presented before the Dublin European Council of December 1996, by the German *Finanzminister*. This resolution would include what this Minister called a "*feierliche politische Verpflichtung*" of the Commission, the Council and the Member States to implement consistently the Pact. The European Council decided to adopt the resolution before the adoption of the regulations by the Council and the content of these acts was discussed at the heads of government level. There is a point (7) where strangely enough the resolution

---

[12] See resolution of 17 June 1997, *OJ* N° C236/1, 2 August 1997.

[13] See *Martenczuk* (1998) pp. 151-177.

specifically refers to an article of Regulation N° 1467/97, not yet officially adopted at the time but which clearly was reviewed at the European Council's level. To adopt a resolution was the most which could be done without revising the Treaty in order to go into the direction of a more automatic implementation of the rules on excessive deficits. Paragraph IV of the Preamble of the Resolution explains the objective and the nature of the Resolution:

> "The European Council solemnly invites all parties, namely the Member States, the Council of the European Union and the Commission of the European Communities, to implement the Treaty and the Stability and Growth Pact in a strict and timely manner. The Resolution provides *firm political guidance* to the parties who will implement the Stability and Growth Pact. To this end, the parties have agreed upon the following *guidelines…*"

The words in italics are similar or at least analogous to those used in Article 4 TEU in order to define the mission of the European Council: "The European Council shall provide the Union with the necessary impetus for its development and shall define the *general political guidelines* thereof." The content of the Resolution appears as the intended way to use Treaty and secondary law provisions in the field. It is not intended to produce legal effects. It has been underlined in the literature that the European Council not being an institution of the Community cannot bind the Council or the Commission.[14] On the other hand, the formulas used in the resolution have been carefully drafted in order to avoid any conflict with the Treaty. The "commitments" are political ones[15] and when the Council is "invited" or "urged" to do something, it is not legally bound by these more or less pressing "invitations". Sometimes, the Resolution only repeats obligations that derived either from the Treaty or from the Regulation. When it requests from the Commission to exercise its right of initiative under the Treaty "in a manner that facilitates the strict, timely and effective functioning of the Stability and Growth Pact", it gives a guideline which does not sub-

---

14 See *Martenczuk* (1998) p. 156 (and note 37) and p. 164.

15 See *Bandilla* (2005). The author underlines the political features of the orientations and commitments in the Resolution but accepts the idea that the institutions are bound by the commitments they took in the Resolution. See *infra*.

stantially add to what the Treaty itself imposes to the Commission, as a general obligation of conduct inherent to its duty of loyalty. If the Commission is asked to and accepted to

> "prepare a report…whenever there is the risk of an excessive deficit or whenever the planned or actual government deficit exceeds the reference value of 3% of the GDP, thereby triggering the procedure under Article 104c (3),"

a reference is made to this same paragraph which allows to the Commission a margin of appreciation of the situation of the Member State. The report has to be prepared "under Article 104c (3)". Another example: in the event the Commission is requested by the Council under Article 109d to make a recommendation for a Council decision on whether an excessive deficit exists under Article 104c (6), the Commission commits itself, *as a rule*, to make such recommendation. Where the Resolution invites or urges the Council "*always* to impose sanctions", "*always* to require a non-interest bearing deposit", "*always* to convert a deposit into a fine", the respective articles 6, 11 and 13 of Regulation N° 1467/97, adopted by the same Council use the expression "*as a rule*", leaving some room for discretion.[16] Analogous reflections can be made as far as the "commitments" of the Member States are concerned.[17] To be sure, it is possible to recognise to some resolutions of the European Council, the nature of an international agreement binding for the Member States. *In casu*, they could have accepted to bind their vote in the Council or to adopt a determinate conduct. But it is very doubtful that it was here their intention considering the accent put on the political features of the text, the lack of political will among the Member States to accept far reaching commitments going farther than what the Treaty provides and the limits imposed by the Treaty provisions. In some cases, the "commitments" are but a solemn repetition of obligations deriving from the Treaty. In other, the Member States are "invited" to do something, like making public Council's recommendations (points 2 and 3). Of course they are under an obligation of loyalty to consider complying with this request but they are not legally bound to implement it.

There is another example of the cautious way the resolution was drafted. In point 7, the Member States

---

16 On this, see *Herdegen* (1998) pp. 9-32.

17 See ibid. p. 165.

> "commit themselves not to invoke the benefit of article 2 (3) of the Council regulation on speeding up and clarifying the excessive deficit procedure unless they are in severe recession; in evaluating whether the economic downturn is severe, the Member States will, *as a rule*, take as a reference point an annual fall in real GDP of at least 0, 75%."

A first question raised by the text is the difference between "recession" and "downturn". The Regulation uses only (three times) the word "downturn",[18] which it associates twice with the adjectives "severe economic" in article 2. In point 7 of the Resolution, the word "recession" is used in the first sentence and the word "downturn" in the second.[19] But the conditions expressed, either in the regulation or in the Resolution, in terms of loss of GDP and the wording of the different linguistic versions are eliminating the potential difference between a "severe recession" and a "severe downturn". On the other hand, the use of the words "*as a rule*" mitigates the stringency of the commitment and underlines that it is a norm of conduct and not a legal rule which is provided by the Resolution. All the subtleties in the wording of the Resolution come from the unwillingness and the impossibility to provide for automaticity where the Treaty leaves a margin of appreciation and to eliminate what could appear as a contradiction between the various elements of the Pact.

In its judgment of 13 July 2004,[20] the Court refers to the Pact in the following terms:

> "*71.* The rules laid down in Article 104 EC are defined more precisely and strengthened by the Stability and Growth Pact, constituted, in particular, by the Resolution of the European Council of 17 June 1997 and Regulation N° 1467/97. *72.* The Resolution of the European Council of 17 June 1997 draws attention to the crucial importance of securing budgetary discipline

---

[18] In French, the Regulation uses three times the expression "*grave récession économique*".

[19] In the French version of the Resolution, the word "*récession*" appears twice.

[20] See Judgment of the Court of Justice in Case Commission/Council (C 27/04). This judgment is analysed by *Mr Petite* in his report. On this judgment, see *Chaltiel* (2004) pp. 509-514; *López Escudero* (2005) pp. 61-89; *Bandilla* quoted in note (15) and *Smits* quoted in note (38).

> in stage three of EMU. In the light of that observation, it solemnly invites the Council to be committed to a rigorous and timely implementation of all elements of the Stability and Growth Pact in its competence and to regard the deadlines for the application of the excessive deficit procedure as upper limits."

And after alluding to two recitals of the Preamble of Regulation N°1467/97, going in the same direction, the Court concludes that

> "*74.* In this context, marked by the importance that the framers of the Treaty attach to observance of budgetary discipline and by the aim of the rules laid down for applying budgetary discipline, those rules are to be given an interpretation which ensures that they are fully effective."

For *Bandilla*, this means that the Pact in all its components – the Resolution and the Regulations – are to be used in the application and interpretation of Article 104 and so have "*Rechtliche Relevanz*". That corresponds for this author to the principle of "*Selbstbindung*" of the institutions by their earlier conduct, in the present case, strengthened ("*erweitert*") by the assumption of commitments, which are laid down in a political text.[21] We should anyway be cautious in accepting the idea of "self binding commitments" by the institutions where the Resolution includes invitations to these institutions by the European Council or commitments taken for the Commission by its President within the European Council. It is noteworthy that while the Court puts at the same level in Points 72 and 73, some sentences of the Resolution and of the Preamble of Regulation N° 1467/97, in its further reasoning, the Court did not refer to the Resolution any more. The Court has taken stock of the Resolution in order to support its views on the necessity to give to the rules their "*effet utile*" (in order to have the rules "fully effective", in point 73) for the realisation of fiscal stability. In other terms, what was important for the Court in its reading of the resolution is the strong affirmation of the objective of fiscal discipline more than specific commitments.

III. Fiscal policy in the Constitution

Before going into the analysis of the reform process and its results, it seems relevant to look at the relatively modest modifica-

---

[21] See *Bandilla* (2005) pp. 538-549.

tions resulting for the "E" of EMU from the Constitution. It can seem as the Convention has not complied with one of the many objectives laid down by the Laeken Declaration of December 2001 which requested to consider the modalities of strengthening the coordination of economic policies. Different views existed within the Convention and among the Member States on the desirability and the modalities of the coordination of economic policies. In this context, it is not extraordinary that the Stability and Growth Pact was not inserted in the Constitution, which means that the legal rules have not been adapted to the political wording of the European Council resolution of 1997. A Declaration N° 17 on Article III-184 was attached to the Constitution by which the Conference reaffirms its commitment to the provisions concerning the SGP "as the framework for the coordination of budgetary policies in the Member States." It confirms "that a rule-based system is the best guarantee for commitments to be enforced and for all Member States to be treated equally" but this system already results from the Treaty itself. Reference is made in parallel to the goals of the Lisbon strategy, and economic growth is invoked next to price stability.[22] A number of objectives are mentioned that could have been included in the objectives of economic policy. More related to the current thinking in relation with the reform of the Pact is the agreement of the Conference on the need to use "periods of economic recovery actively to consolidate public finances and improve their budget positions." The Conference calls for proposals of the Commission and contributions of the Member States "with regard to strengthening and clarifying the implementation of the SGP." And after alluding to the need of taking measures "to raise the growth potential of their economies" and to the support that improved economic policy coordination can bear to this goal, the Declaration ends by the surprising sentence that it "does not prejudge the future debate on the SGP", which once more demonstrates the differences of opinions on the SGP, the opportunity and the content of its reform. From these quotations, it clearly appears that, under the Constitution, the Pact keeps the specific nature we have underlined.[23]

---

22 See the analysis of the Declaration in *Fitoussi/Le Cacheux* (2005) pp. 123-125.

23 For some authors, the Pact was present in its substance in the draft of the Convention but it was implicit. Declaration N°17 to Article 184 has

If the Constitution does not significantly modify the rules on economic policy coordination and budgetary discipline, it nevertheless contains some interesting provisions, but for some of them limited to the Member States whose currency is the euro.

First of all, the main responsibilities in the field of economic policy remain in the hands of the Member States. The accent in Part I lays on their responsibilities more than on the role of the institutions. Under Article I-12, paragraph 3 "Member States shall coordinate their economic and employment policies within arrangements as determined by Part III, which the Union shall have competence to provide." And Article I-15, paragraph 1 in a compromise formula which results from a lot of earlier versions provides that

> "The Member States shall coordinate their economic policies within the Union. To this end, the Council of Ministers shall adopt measures, in particular broad guidelines for these policies. Special provisions shall apply to those Member States whose currency is the euro."

Coordination of employment and social policies are also mentioned in this article. These provisions take the place of Article 4 EC (whose provisions subsist in Article III-177) which provided for an economic policy based on the close coordination of the economic policies of the Member States. An allusion to "an ever-closer coordination of economic policies" is also included in the Preamble of the Protocol on the Euro Group. But the signal is clear; the famous "asymmetry" between the "E" and the "M" of EMU is underlined. At the same time, monetary policy is recognised as an exclusive competence of the Union (for the countries whose currency is the euro) in article I-13.

Second, the powers of the Commission have been *slightly* strengthened both in the coordination of economic policies and in the excessive deficit procedure (EDP).

---

made the link explicit. The draft prepared by the Convention included only the repressive part and the Constitution has reintroduced the preventive one. See *Fitoussi/Le Cacheux* (2005) pp. 105-106. *Le PSC était…bien inscrit dans le projet de Constitution mais sa présence était tue.* For these authors, the convergence criteria were related to the "*convergence préalable*" to the adoption of the euro and the Constitution has "prolonged" the application of the provisions to the participating Member States and the Euro area.

The Commission will have the right, under Article III-179, paragraph 4 (99 EC) to address a warning to a Member State

> "when it is established..., that the economic policies of a Member State are not consistent with the broad guidelines...or that they risk jeopardising the proper functioning of economic and monetary union."

In the present situation, the Commission may only recommend the adoption of a recommendation by the Council. The Constitution makes an interesting but limited step forward.

A modification in the same direction has been introduced in the excessive deficit procedure of Art. III-184 (104 EC), paragraph 5:

> "If the Commission considers that an excessive deficit in a Member State exists or may occur, it shall address an opinion to the Member State concerned and shall inform the Council accordingly."

On the other hand, it will be on a *proposal* from the Commission that the Council will decide under Article III-184, paragraph 6 "whether an excessive deficit exists". But the modification stops there. It will still be on a *recommendation* of the Commission (and not on a proposal, as the Commission requested) that the Council will adopt the recommendation addressed to the Member State concerned "with a view to bringing that situation to an end" (presently, recommendations under Article 104, paragraph 7). The Council should adopt "without undue delay" the recommendations it addresses to the Member State concerned.

Third, the vote of the Member State concerned will not be taken into account anymore for the adoption of all the acts taken by the Council under Article III-184, and only the Member States whose currency is the euro will have the right to vote for all the acts of the Council under Article III-184. The situation where the State concerned could vote on the decision whether an excessive deficit exists will disappear and only the participating Member States will be entitled to vote at the different stages of the procedure. These progresses do not change the fact that this procedure will still be based on peers' control. And, if for some, peers' control represents an inadmissible intrusion in the sovereignty of the Member States, it could more accurately be viewed as a very weak instrument.

As referred to in Article I-15, Part III includes "Provisions specific to Member States whose currency is the euro". This is the title of Section 4 of the Title on Economic and Monetary Policy but it is evident that they are other provisions of the Constitution that only apply to the Euro area. Section 5 on Transitory Provisions is relevant in that respect.

Of Section 4, we will mention Article III-194 and the "institutionalisation" of the Euro Group, which nevertheless does not receive formal decision-making powers, under Article III-195 and the specific Protocol attached to the Constitution. Article III-196 relates to the external representation of the euro area, a subject matter irrelevant to the SGP.

Article III-194 is more to the point. It provides in its paragraph 1 that:

> "In order to ensure the proper functioning of economic and monetary union, and in accordance with the relevant provisions of the Constitution, the Council shall, in accordance with the relevant procedure among those referred to in Article III-179 and III-184, with the exception of the procedure set out in Article III-184 (13), adopt measures specific to the Member States whose currency is the euro: (a) to strengthen the coordination and surveillance of their budgetary discipline; (b) to set out economic policy guidelines for them, while ensuring that they are compatible with those adopted for the whole of the Union and kept under surveillance."

It results from this text that the measures adopted by the Council must be in conformity with the Constitution, a principle also valid for closer cooperation under Article III-416. The article does not offer a possibility of simplified revision for the Member States of the Euro area. The measures have to be taken in accordance with the procedures provided in Article III-179 (coordination of economic policies and multilateral surveillance) and III-184 (correction of excessive deficits), but "the procedure" provided under Article III-104, paragraph 13 cannot be used. That means that the Protocol cannot be replaced or modified by rules specific to the Euro area but we suggest, for the sake of giving some effectiveness ("*effet utile*") to the reference to Article III-184, that the Protocol may be complemented as it was by Regulation N° 1467/97.[24] Under paragraph 2 of Article III-194 only the Member States whose cur-

[24] For another, more literal, interpretation, see the contribution of *Servais/ Ruggeri* (2005) pp. 43-71. If their interpretation is correct, the reference to Article III-184 (ex-104) would be meaningless.

rency is the euro will participate to the vote of these measures. A special qualified majority is also provided.

Article III-195 referred to the Protocol on the Euro Group which lays down the arrangements for meetings between the Finance ministers of those Member States whose currency is the euro. In its Preamble, the Protocol provides for the development of an ever-closer coordination of economic policies within the euro area but the Euro Group remains an informal gathering. It is a place for dialogue and discussion, in particular on topics to be decided by the Ecofin Council, but not for legally binding decisions. The subjects it can discuss are very loosely defined: "(all) questions related to the specific responsibilities they (the ministers) share with regard to the single currency". There is no doubt that budgetary discipline is one of those topics (as it is now already within the Euro Group).[25] The Commission shall take part in the meetings. The ECB shall be invited. The Euro Group will have a president elected, by a majority vote of the Ministers whose currency is the euro, for a term of two and a half years. One knows that a president, Prime Minister and Finance Minister *Juncker*, has been elected in 2005 for two years in anticipation to the entry into force of the Constitution.

IV. Some considerations on the framework of the present reform

The reform process, started officially with the Communication of the Commission to the Council and the European Parliament of 3 September 2004[26] on a mandate of the European Council of 18 June 2004, included in a Declaration on Article III-184 of the Constitution, had different objectives than the one expressed by the German Government in 1995. The Communication puts more focus on debt and sustainability. It advises to take into account the increasingly different economic conditions and the developments in a Europe of 25 and more. The procedure should redefine the exceptional cir-

---

25 See *Bandilla* (2005), observes that the discussion within the Ecofin on 25 November 2003 about the recommendations of the Commission concerning the excessive deficits of France and Germany was short because the "*entscheidende Gespräche*" took place the day before at the Euro Group. The same could be said about the discussions on the reform of the SGP.

26 See *COM* (2004) 581 final. See already *COM* (2004) 425 final, 24 June 2004.

cumstances which can justify an excess over the reference value, in order to consider not only recessions but also protracted slowdowns ("sluggish growth"), and the adjustment path to the medium-term budgetary objective. The enforcement should be strengthened by stronger institutions and better statistics for which European minimum standards should be adopted. The Lisbon strategy should be more taken into account while coordinating budgetary policies and the calendar should be adjusted for more effectiveness on national budgets.

Despite the difference of accents between the *Waigel* proposal and the SGP, on the one hand, and the topics of the present reform, there were similarities between the two processes. Any revision of the Treaty was excluded in the present circumstances, after the adoption of the Constitution, as it was in 1995-1997 when the Pact was discussed. As the talks progressed, it rapidly became clear that the reference values included in the Protocol (which could be modified by a unanimous decision, under Article 104, §14) would most probably be kept unchanged, because apparently a consensus on better ones or on…deleting both or one of them would be very difficult to achieve. The Member States and the Commission were opposed to such move. Contrary to what France and, more forcefully, Germany[27] were requiring, blocks of expenses (Research and development, military, development aid, structural reforms, specific charges like the ones imposed on Germany by the unification of the country, etc.) would not for the same reason be excluded as such from the definition of the "general" budget considered for valuing the deficit. Everybody agreed that sanctions would remain what they are. The debates at the European Convention have demonstrated that there was no consensus for an important reform of the Treaty as far as economic policy, and specifically the excessive budget procedure, was concerned. There was neither the will nor the possibility to introduce a qualitative change in the SGP.

On the other hand, there was a way to adopt some elements of the reform without a revision of secondary law. For example, Article 104, paragraph 3 already permits to the Commission to take into

[27] See the interview of 17 January 2005 of Bundeskanzler *Schröder* to The Financial Times Deutschland as reproduced in http://www.bundeskanzler.de (last visited January 2005). The Chancellor asked for the elaboration of a compulsory list of criteria the Commission should look at before engaging an EDP.

account, in its report on an apparent violation of the reference values, "whether the government deficit exceeds government investment expenditure and … all other relevant factors." The text, as it is, allows for considering the nature of the expenses, the structural or conjunctural aspect of the deficit, the volume of the debt and the rhythm of its reduction, etc. But, for the sake of legal certainty, a revision of the regulations would be thought to be preferable in order to take on board the results of the reform. That would also allow for debating on the reform in the European Parliament[28] and avoiding the situation where another report, resolution or code of conduct would be added to the existing ones on the excessive deficit procedure. This observation seemed especially valid for the preventive aspects of the fight against excessive deficit. But for some elements of the reform of the EDP, a revision of Regulation N°1467/97 was necessary anyway. It is the case for any change in the deadlines, for example. On the other hand, the need for increasing the convergence between the action at Union's level and at national level by associating in a more effective manner national parliaments to the process was obvious. The necessity of national ownership of the rules concerning budgetary policies was repeatedly underlined. But it appeared to be politically difficult to impose common rules in that matter. The debates confirmed that there were opposite views on the content of many points for achieving the consensus.[29] The objective was for the Ecofin to agree on the reform in order to have it adopted by the Spring European Council in March 2005. But the meetings of the Euro Group and the Ecofin on 7 and 8 March were not successful and a new meeting was convoked for 20 March, two days before the meeting of the European Council. After long discussions, the Euro Group achieved an agreement, approved by the Ecofin Council and thereafter by the European Council which met on 22 and 23 March. The Commission was asked to produce rapidly proposals for adapting Regulations N° 1466/97 and N° 1467/97. It presented the proposals on 20 April.[30]

---

28 The so-called « cooperation » procedure under Article 252 EC Treaty applies for the modification of Regulation N°1466/97 and the consultation of the European Parliament is required under Article 104, 14, for the revision of Regulation N° 1467/97.

29 See, for example, *Le Monde,* 18 février 2005: "Le va-tout allemand complique la réforme du pacte de stabilité."

30 See *COM* (2005) 154 final and *COM* (2005) 155 final.

Regulations N° 1055/2005 and 1056/2005 were adopted on 27 June 2005.[31]

V. The main accents of the reform of the SGP: The European Council Resolution and the Council Regulations

It is not our intention to exhaustively analyse the results of the reform as it derives from the eighteen pages report of the Ecofin Council as endorsed by the European Council at its meeting of 22-23 March 2005 and reproduced in Annex II of its conclusions, and the two Council's Regulations, but to limit ourselves to what is necessary for our subject: the legal basis of the SGP.

The text of the Resolution, which becomes an "integral part" of the SGP, comprises both rhetorical declarations and precise rules to be translated in proposals by the Commission. The aim of the reform is stated in the title of the document: "*Improving the implementation of the SGP.*" As the Preamble of the report comments: "The aim is not to increase the rigidity or flexibility of current rules but rather to make them more efficient." But, this objective called for more flexibility because the more stringent rules of the Treaty and the Pact have not been implemented correctly when the political obstacles were too important. With an involuntary sense of humour, the Ecofin Council states under point 3, that "the excessive deficit procedure should remain *simple*, *transparent* and *equitable*."[32] But, "nevertheless, the experience of recent years shows

---

[31] See Council Regulation (EC) N° 1055/2005 of 27 June 2005 amending Regulation (EC) N° 1466/97 on the strengthening of the surveillance of budgetary positions and the surveillance and coordination of economic policies, *OJ* L174, 7.07 2005, pp. 1-4 and Council Regulation (EC) N° 1056/2005 of 27 June 2005 amending Regulation (EC) N° 1476/97 on speeding up and clarifying the implementation of the excessive deficit procedure, *OJ* L174, 7.07.2005, pp. 5-9. Regulation (EC) N° 1055/2005 was adopted with the cooperation procedure (between the Council and the European Parliament, Art. 252 of the Treaty) under Article 99, paragraph 5 and Regulation N° 1056/2005 after consultation of the E.P. under Article 104, paragraph 14. Both proposals have been submitted for consultation at the ECB. See the opinions of the ECB, *OJ* C144, 14.06.2005, p. 16 and 17.

[32] Italics are ours. The Council was obviously so happy with this formula that it added it in the Preamble of Regulation N° 1056/2005 (Recital 5, not included in the Commission's proposal).

possible scope for improvement in its implementation." One can support the view that the procedure was, and still is, neither simple - its is and will remain a complex procedure-, nor transparent - let us only mention the role of the Economic and Financial Committee and of the Euro Group, which both work in a very non transparent manner – and, as it was implemented, one could say that it was not equitable either, while considering the differences of treatment reserved to smaller and bigger Member States.[33]

It is important to underline right from the start of the analysis what the reform does not change. As it could be expected, the 3% and 60 % criteria, called "the two nominal anchors of the Pact" will "continue to be the centrepiece of multilateral surveillance". Under Point 3.1, it is stated that: "The Council and the Commission are resolved to clearly preserve and uphold the reference values of 3% and 60 % of GDP as the anchors of the monitoring of the development of the budgetary situation and of the ratio of government debt to GDP in the Member States". Indirect revision of the criteria through the exclusion of particular budgetary items from the definition of the excessive deficit is also excluded.

The report comprises three parts: I. Improving Governance, II. Strengthening the preventive arm, III. Improving the implementation of the excessive deficit procedure.

In the first section on "*Improving Governance*", the report puts the accent on the necessity for all the authorities involved to act conscientiously. The Commission has to exercise its right of initiative timely. The Council has to exercise responsibly its margin of discretion, the peer support and peer pressure should be effective at every stage of the procedure. The Euro Group receives the mission to make a horizontal assessment of national budget developments and their implications for the euro area as a whole, once a year before the summer. Member States have to adopt complementary budgetary rules and institutions. "Ownership" of the SGP by national policy makers should be improved. Stability programmes valid for the legislature and involving the parliaments should be adopted. Reliable forecasts should be provided and statistical governance is to be improved. The implementation of fiscal discipline

---

[33] See *Mario Monti*, "Toughen up the reform agenda and make it count", *The Financial Times,* 22 March 2005: "...the fundamental principle of equality of treatment has been violated and the EU's credibility damaged."

and its credibility rely on the quality, reliability and timeliness of fiscal statistics at the national and European level. In a rather vague way, the report announces that "the Commission and the Council in the course of 2005 are dealing with the issue of improving the governance of the European statistical system."[34] On the other hand, "Member States and EU institutions should affirm their commitment to produce high quality statistics and to ensure mutual cooperation to achieve this goal. Imposing sanctions on a Member State should be considered when there is infringement of the obligation to duly report government data." No indication is given on the nature of these sanctions and their legal basis.

The second part bears on "*Preventive action*". It is here that the most specific reforms are listed. First, the definition of the "medium term objective" for the budgetary positions of the Member States will take into account the characteristics of the economy of each Member State and pursue a triple aim: to provide a safety margin with respect to the 3 % deficit limit, to ensure rapid progress towards sustainability and to allow room for budgetary manoeuvre, in particular taking into account the need for public investment. In other terms, the objective of "close to balance or in surplus" will no more been imposed on every Member State across the board, as it is now under Regulation N° 1466/97. The report specifies that "The range for the country-specific medium term objectives for euro area and ERM II Member States would thus be, in cyclically adjusted terms, net of one-off and temporary measures, between -1% of GDP for low debt/high growth countries and balance or surplus for high debt/low potential growth countries." The reform gives more attention than before on "debt and sustainability" but the Council renounced to impose a rhythm for the reduction of the debt. It must be reduced "at a satisfactory pace, taking into account macroeconomic conditions and debt dynamics." The Ecofin report expressly observed that "no change to the existing Regulations is required to that effect." There obviously was no enthusiasm on the part of some

---

[34] See the proposal of a Council regulation amending Regulation (EC) N° 3605/93 as regards the quality of statistical data in the context of the excessive deficit procedure, *COM* (2005) 0071 and the report of the European Parliament on this proposal, A6-0181/2005 of 7.06.2005.

Member States to provide for a strict monitoring of the evolution of public debt.[35]

The report also asks for "a more symmetrical approach to fiscal policy" which, in the jargon used by the specialists of the Pact, means an enhanced budgetary policy in periods of economic recovery in order to create the necessary room to accommodate economic downturns. The adjustment effort should be stronger in so-called "good times", which should be identified "as periods where output exceeds its potential level, taking into account tax elasticities", a definition that is only to be found in the report and not in the regulations. The Commission will issue "policy advice" to encourage Member States to stick to their adjustment path. These policy advices were to be replaced by "early warnings" under the Constitution. Structural major reforms which have direct long-term cost-saving effects will be taken into account when defining the adjustment path. A special attention should be paid to "pension reforms introducing a multi-pillar system that includes a mandatory, fully funded pillar."

The third and last part of the report relates to "*Improving the implementation of the excessive deficit procedure*". The Commission "will always" prepare a report under Article 104(3).[36] It shall examine in its report if the exceptions foreseen respectively in Article 104(2) (a) and (b) apply. Moreover, the Commission shall have to take into account, as provided by Article 104 (3), "whether the Member State's government deficit exceeds government investment expenditures (the so-called golden rule) and all other relevant factors, including the medium-term economic and budgetary position of the Member State". And the Council proposes both clarifications or revisions of the exceptions and illustrations of the concept of "other relevant factors."

---

[35] See the comment of the rapporteur, *Othmar Karas*, of the E. P. Committee on Economic and Monetary Affairs, in the Recommendation for second reading on the Council common position for adoption of a Council regulation amending Regulation (EC) N° 1466/97, A6-0204/2005, 20.06.2005, p. 10.

[36] Under the 1997 Resolution, the Commission "commits itself to prepare a report". Here the text states that the Commission "*will*" prepare (in French: "*élaborera*") a report, not "*shall* examine" (in French: "*examine*") as in the following sentence on the content of the report in the same paragraph.

The Council considers first the exceptions included in Article 104 (2). It takes the view that the current definition of "a severe economic downturn" in Article 2(2) of Regulation N° 1467/97 is too restrictive. This provision should be adapted "to consider as exceptional an excess over the reference value which results from a negative growth rate or from the accumulated loss of output during a protracted period of a very low growth relative to potential growth." In other words, a sluggish growth should be held as justifying an exceptional (and temporary) excess of the deficit over the reference value.

But it is on the concept of "all other relevant factors" in Article 104 (3) that the debates were the more vivid and the result presents all the features of a strongly disputed compromise. First, the report underlines the "overarching principle" to which taking into account of these factors is conditional: the excess over the reference value is temporary and the deficit remains close to the reference value. Second, the Council clarifies that the Commission's report should reflect developments in the medium-term economic position and in the medium-term budgetary position. And the Council adds in two sentences that must be reproduced in order to give an exact view of the result of the negotiations: "Furthermore, due consideration will be given to any other factors, which *in the view of the Member State concerned* (italics ours), are relevant in order to comprehensively assess in qualitative terms the excess over the reference value. In that context, special consideration will be given to budgetary efforts towards increasing or maintaining at a high level financial contribution to fostering international solidarity and to achieving European policy goals, notably the unification of Europe if it has a detrimental effect on the growth and fiscal burden of a Member State." The reference to the view of the Member State concerned was preferred to the establishment of an indicative list that would have included all the requests made by the Member States and would have had a disastrous effect on the credibility of the Pact. Is it better so? It is not sure because it leaves to the Member States and the institutions an extraordinary margin of discretion that all the commitments taken to apply the discipline seriously could not be able to counterbalance. The mention of the unification of Europe was made in order to have the agreement of the German Finance minister who strongly insisted to get the reference in the text to the costs of German unification. This pretension was finally accepted by its partners thanks to the generalisation of the formula to cover the costs of the "unification of Europe". The "other relevant factors" will be considered all along the procedure, except for the decision as to whether the Member State has corrected its excessive deficit. A paragraph is dedicated to the need for considering the net cost of pension reforms in a regressive way for a period of five years after the introduction of the reform. This last point clearly was an important concern for many Governments.

After a mention of the increasing focus on the debt to which we already alluded, the report foresees the extension of the deadlines for the adoption of the decisions under Article 104 and for the correction of the deficits. These adaptations take into account the practice followed by the institutions that were incapable to decide on time under the existing SGP, despite of the binding force of the deadlines, as recognised by the Court in its judgment of 13 July 2004 (point 33), already quoted.

The report, which indicates its preference for keeping changes to the existing regulations to a minimum, systematically mentions which of its proposals should be introduced in Regulations N° 1466/97 and N° 1467/97. It explains why there are few new elements in the regulations in comparison with the Ecofin report. As mentioned by the Commission in the memorandum of its proposals, "legislative changes were introduced only where strictly necessary to ensure full implementation of the agreement endorsed by the European Council." The proposals included "the four changes explicitly required by the Council report, in particular concerning the definition of a 'severe economic downturn', the definition and role of 'other relevant factors', the extension of the deadlines for taking action in the context of the EDP, and to allow the repetitions of steps in the procedure..." Some other amendments of a technical nature were also introduced. It is perhaps noteworthy that the "other relevant factors" under Article 104, paragraph 3, which were at the centre of the discussion within the Council, are listed both in the Preamble of Regulation N° 1056/2005 (recital 8), as the Commission proposed, but also, in the text of the Regulation (Article 1, paragraph 1). It is specified that these factors can be put forward to the Commission (for inclusion in its report, under Article 104, paragraph 3) but also to the Council, in the steps leading to the decision on the existence of an excessive deficit. This last point was indeed comprised in the Ecofin report. It may seem, at first glance, add to the Treaty but Article 104, paragraph 6, allows for the Member State concerned to make "such observations" it takes fit. As a curiosum, one will also notice the reference in the Preamble of Regulation N° 1056/2005, to "peer support and peer pressure" (recital 3), an element contained in the report but that the Commission did not believe necessary to include in its proposal. To be mentioned also is the fact that the European Parliament was unable to exert whatsoever influence on the texts of the respective regulations. The amendments recommended for second reading by the Economic and Monetary Affairs Committee in the cooperation procedure for the amendment of Regulation N° 1466/97[37] were rejected by the Plenary, on 23 June 2005, at a time where the examination of the proposals by the Council had in fact come to an end.

In the Preamble of its proposals, the Commission announced that it would draw up a Code of Conduct setting out how the changes not included in the amendments of the Regulations were to be implemented. It was referring, in particular, to the consideration to be given to the implementation of pension reforms in the budgetary assessments in the framework of the EDP. This element was introduced during the legislative process in Article 2, paragraph 7, of Regulation N° 1467/97, by Article 1, paragraph 1 of Regulation N° 1056/2005. At the time of reviewing this report, the Code was not yet published.

VI. Conclusion

For some, budgetary discipline is the substitute for the lack, in the hands of the Union, of important resources which could be used for the stabilisation of public finances. We are not qualified to judge if this affirmation is correct but everything leads us to think that we will have in the future, both insufficient resources and a flexible Pact. It is undeniable that the Treaty and the Stability and Growth Pact played an important role in the stabilising of the finances of many Member States but the lack of flexibility of the Pact has generated a lack of compliance especially by the bigger States. The credibility of the Pact was at stake but total automaticity was not a possible remedy. It is just not practicable and it was not allowed by the Treaty. The question is: does the reform not go too far in the direction of flexibility? The Ecofin report endorsed by the European Council repeatedly insists on the importance of increased peer support and peer pressure. But peer control has demonstrated

---

[37] See A6-0204/2005 final, 20-06-2005, rapporteur: *Mr Othmar Karas*.

its limits.[38] The report refers to the Luxembourg resolution on economic policy coordination and recalls the principle of subsidiarity and "respecting the prerogatives of national Governments in determining their structural and budgetary policies, while complying with the provisions of the Treaty and the Stability and Growth Pact." *Wolfgang Wessels* criticises in his report to the present conference the incongruity of intending to provide for budgetary discipline at a supranational level, because it goes again the basic principles of democracy, expressed in the power of national parliaments to vote the budget. This concern was, at least partially, present in the minds of the Ecofin ministers when they adopted the report, if one judges by the caution with which they allude to complementary national budgetary rules and institutions (point 1.3), and the involvement of National Parliaments (point 1.5) avoiding to provide any kind of legal obligations at this respect. But, if one wants to have an effective SGP, the Commission should have a more central role in order to limit the potential for "horse trading" within the Council and indeed accent was rightly put on prevention. Substantial improvements in economic policy coordination are difficult to provide under the terms of the present Treaty and the Constitution does not leave very much more leeway. The respective powers of the Commission and the Council were at the centre of the debate. The reform does not change the balance of power among the institutions, despite pressures in that direction. It also provides for a national counter face to coordination of fiscal policies involving national parliaments. The present sanctions will remain what they are in the Treaty and in the SGP. Many believe them to be either contra productive or not dissuasive. They should be replaced by political ones.[39] But that obviously exceeded the framework of the reform as undertaken on mandate of the European Council for a Pact which has proven its usefulness.[40]

The reform does not change the subtle relationship established under the original SGP between the Treaty, a (political) resolution of the European Council and Council Regulations. These latter texts

---

38 See *Smits* (2004a) p. 221 and p. 224. From the same author, see: (2004b) pp. 50-57.

39 See the suggestions included in the report of the *European League for Economic Cooperation* (2004) p. 25; *de Boissieu* (2004), quoted in: *Assemblée Nationale* (2005) pp. 37-38.

40 See Regulations N° 1055/2005 and N° 1056/2005, recital 1.

have been duly amended. It was not the case for the 1997 Resolution, which has now to be read in conjunction with the March 2005 Ecofin report, as endorsed by the European Council. It was indeed politically and technically difficult to formally modify the 1997 SGP charter, of which one officially only intended to strengthen and to clarify the implementation. It is precisely on the way it is implemented that the 2005 reform will be judged.

References

Assemblée Nationale (2005), Rapport d'information déposé par la délégation de l'A.N. pour l'Union européenne, sur Le renforcement de la gouvernance économique et la clarification de la mise en œuvre du pacte de stabilité et de croissance et présenté par *M. Daniel Garrigue*, N°2124, 2 Mars 2005, pp. 37-38.

Bandilla R., Ist der Stabilitäts- und Wachstumspakt rechtlich durchsetzbar? Anmerkungen zum Urteil des Gerichtshofes in der Rechtssache Kommission/Rat (C-37/04), in: *M. Zuleeg / C. Gaitanides / S. Kadelbach / G. C. Rodríguez Iglesias (eds.),* Festschrift für Manfred Zuleeg, Baden-Baden, Nomos, 2005, pp. 538-549.

Chaltiel F. (2004), Le Pacte de stabilité, entre exigences juridiques et pragmatisme politique, in: Revue du Marché Commun et de l'Union européenne, 2004, pp. 509-514.

de Boissieu Ch. (2004), What to do with the Stability and Growth Pact?, European Parliament Briefing Papers, February 2004.

de Witte B. (2001), Chameleonic Member States: Partial and Parallel Agreements, in: *B. De Witte / D. Hanf / E. Vos (eds.)*, The Many Faces of Differentiation, Antwerpen, Oxford, London, Intersentia, 2001, pp. 231-267.

European League for Economic Corporation (2004), European Economic Governance Revisited, Cahier Comte Boël n° 11, 2004.

Fitoussi J.P. / Le Cacheux J. (2005), L'état de l'Union européenne, Paris 2005, Fayard/Presses de Sciences Po.

Gros D. (1997), Towards a Credible Excessive Deficits Procedure, in: *M. Andenas / L. Gormley / Ch. Hadjiemmanuil,* European Economic and Monetary Union, Kluwer Law International, 1997/12, pp. 241-256.

Hahn H. J. (1998), The Stability Pact for European Monetary Union: Compliance with Deficit Limit as a Constant Legal Duty, in: CMLRev 1998, pp. 77-100.

Herdegen M. (1998), Price Stability and Budgetary Restraints in the Economic and Monetary Union: The Law as a Guardian of Economic Wisdom, in: CMLRev 35, 1998, pp. 9-32.

http://europa.eu.int/eur-lex/en/search/search_dpi.html (last visited May 2006).

http://europa.eu.int/eur-lex/lex/JOIndex.do? (last visited May 2006).

López Escudero M. (2005), El pacto de estabilidad ante el Tribunal de Justicia, in: Revista Española de Derecho Europeo Civitas, Thomson, N° 13, 2005, pp. 61-89.

Martenczuk B. (1998), Der Europäische Rat und die Wirtschafts- und Währungsunion, in: *EuR,* 1998, pp. 151-177.

Servais D. / Ruggeri R. (2005), The EU Constitution: its impact on Economic and Monetary Union and economic governance, in: ECB, Legal Aspects of the European System of Central Banks, in the *Liber Amicorum Paolo Zamboni Garavelli,* ECB, Frankfurt/Main 2005, pp. 43-71.

Smits R. (2004a), Het Europese Hof beslecht geschil over communautair toezicht op begrotingsdiscipline, in: Nederlandse Tijdschrift Europees Recht, 2004, pp. 221-227.

Smits R. (2004b), Het Stabiliteits- en Groeipact nagekeken, in: S.E.W., 2004, pp. 50-57.

Part 2:
Economic Problems with the SGP

Paul van den Noord*

Fiscal policies in EMU at the Crossroads

I. Introduction

The adoption of the euro represented a major step forward towards deeper economic integration. However, developments in the first six years of the single currency have been challenging. While monetary policy has done relatively well and established its credibility, fiscal policies have fared less well. Many euro area governments failed to take advantage of the 1999-2000 upturn to establish better budgetary positions. Fiscal policy was not made consistent with the longer-term requirements stemming from ageing populations, thus contributing to the uncertainty among households and removing the room for fiscal action. Meanwhile, calls by the major euro area countries to make the fiscal coordination framework more lenient in some respects have been endorsed by the European Council in March 2005. This will make compliance with the fiscal rules easier – as recurrent conflicts between the

* The views expressed in this paper are the author's and should not be attributed to the Organisation or its member countries.

member countries and the European Commission as the guardian of the fiscal rules would be less likely. But it also heightens the risk of fiscal profligacy, unless the underlying causes of deficit bias are addressed. This paper reviews the issues.

II. The Fiscal Framework in EMU

Fiscal policies in EMU have remained decentralised, but are subject to rules and co-ordination. This commits member countries to fiscal discipline while allowing them to respond, within certain bounds, flexibly and effectively to the cycle. The Treaty defines "excessive deficits": deficits that exceed 3 per cent of GDP or fail to ensure convergence towards gross public debt of 60 per cent of GDP. Its provisions are detailed in the Stability and Growth Pact (SGP). They contain a "preventive" and a "dissuasive" arm.

The preventive arm stipulates that governments achieve and maintain budgetary positions close to balance or in surplus over the medium term. Sticking to this rule allows the automatic stabilisers to play freely while respecting the 3 per cent of GDP deficit ceiling stipulated in the Treaty. The annual updates of the stability programmes submitted by the governments to the European Commission take stock as to how far they have progressed in moving towards close to balance or in surplus and provide a policy trajectory in the pursuit of this goal over the medium term.

The dissuasive arm details the "Excessive Deficit Procedure" embedded in the Treaty. It specifies when a waiver due to "exceptional circumstances" may be granted.[1] It also details the timetable countries should respect in the pursuit of ending the excessive deficit, and the sanctions to be imposed when a country fails to respect this timetable.[2]

---

1 The original Pact stipulated that as a rule a deficit above 3 per cent is not excessive if real GDP has fallen by 2 per cent or more. The Ecofin Council, could also grant a waiver if GDP has fallen by less than 2 per cent in view of the abruptness of the downturn or the accumulated loss of output relative to past trends, but member states have committed themselves not to invoke this possibility if the drop in GDP is less than 0.75 per cent. These provisions have been relaxed recently, see below.

2 The excessive deficit should be corrected in the year following its identification by Eurostat unless there are special circumstances. If, in the opinion of the Ecofin Council, a state fails to take sufficient measures to correct an excessive deficit, and after giving a further

The implementation of this framework has evolved over time. Concerning the preventive arm, one significant step has been the adoption of a clause stipulating that countries should include long-term scenarios in the Stability Programmes in order to allow the Commission, in its role as guardian of the fiscal rules, to assess the long-term sustainability of public finances. Another major step has been a decision by the Council in March 2003 to commit countries to meet the close to balance or surplus rule not only in nominal terms over the medium term but also in cyclically adjusted terms each year, with the cyclical adjustment underpinned by independent Commission estimates of potential output.[3] The dissuasive arm, in contrast, ended up in a stalemate in November 2003, when the Council decided to "hold the Excessive Deficit Procedure in abeyance for the time being" after Germany and France were found to renege on their earlier commitments to rein in their "excessive deficits" on time.[4]

From the outset this fiscal framework was seen as vital to underpin the single currency. It has been designed to address one key concern, namely that once exchange rates within the area had ceased to exist, financial markets would no longer act as a discipline on fiscal policy. Growing deficits in one country, rather than being reflected in wider yield spreads, would spill over into area wide interest rates and crowd out economic activity in other

---

notice it may impose measures, including the obligation of a deposit with the Commission. The SGP specifies that this deposit initially consists of a fixed amount equivalent to 0.2 per cent of GDP and a variable amount equal to one tenth of the difference between the actual deficit and the reference value, with an upper limit of 0.5 per cent of GDP. If the subsequent year shows again an excessive deficit, another deposit according to the same formula for the variable amount can be required. If after two years the excessive deficit is still found to exist, the deposit will "as a rule" be converted into a fine. The fine and the interest on the deposit will be distributed among the other member states according to their share in area wide gross national product (not GDP).

3 See *European Commission* (2002a, 2002b).

4 The Commission challenged these Council decisions before the European Court of Justice, which ruled that – while the Council was found to have made a procedural mistake – the Treaty entrusts the Council with the legal authority to exercise discretion on the Excessive Deficit Procedure.

member countries. Worse, moral hazard could heighten the risk of occasional financial crises, which could expose the ECB to pressure to bail out the country concerned, even though bailouts are prohibited by the Treaty. This line of argument has lost credibility for several reasons. First, as the ECB established its credibility, concerns over possible bail-outs look increasingly farfetched. Second, the sign of the cross-border spill-over effects of easy fiscal policy is ambiguous, since the interest rate channel may be offset by the trade channel. Third, the behaviour of sovereign risk premiums has hardly changed since the advent of the euro.[5]

Importantly, the arguments in favour of rules-based fiscal coordination have shifted towards longer-term issues. Several countries participating in the euro area required a "stick" to encourage fiscal consolidation, *i.e.* to "externalise the internality" of fiscal sustainability (as opposed to "internalising the externality" of crowding out). For example, the annual stability programmes were deemed to play a useful role, by providing an anchor for annual budget appropriations and obliging governments to recognise the implications of current budget decisions for government finances in the future. They also oblige governments to take account of changes in structural and demographic factors as well as the evolving cyclical situation. Over time, this consideration has gained prominence over the concerns regarding spill-over effects and fiscal stabilisation policy, and is now seen as the primary motivation for fiscal co-ordination in the euro area.

III. The experience to date

Having entered the seventh year of the single currency, it is possible to provide an assessment as to how the framework has worked. The record is mixed. While several smaller euro area countries continued fiscal consolidation, even moving into surplus, the three largest member countries – Germany, France and Italy – as well as Greece, the Netherlands and Portugal have breached or risk breaching the 3 per cent limit. Germany and France even posted an excessive deficit for several years in a row. Moreover, the reported fiscal balances have in some countries routinely been embellished by one-offs and creative accounting.[6] Notably the large economies are finding it hard to meet the fiscal objectives of the

---

5 See *Bernoth et al* (2004).

6 See *Koen/van den Noord* (2005).

SGP, while the rules are not binding for most of the smaller, dynamic, economies.

It is fair to assume that fiscal consolidation in the euro area would have progressed less well had there not been the SGP, given that it raised transparency, awareness of longer term fiscal issues and peer pressure. But recurrent disagreements between the European Commission and a qualified majority of the Council of Ministers over the appropriate measures to correct deficits in excess of the 3 per cent threshold have raised questions concerning the implementation of the Pact. Specifically, the implementation of the rules is found to suffer from incentive, surveillance and enforcement gaps, as elaborated below.

A. The incentive gap

A basic flaw of the fiscal framework is its asymmetric incentive structure. There are sanctions for breaching the 3% ceiling, but no rewards for staying below that ceiling or, indeed, complying with the "close-to-balance or in surplus" rule embedded in the SGP. Fiscal consolidation stalled as soon as the single currency was adopted, with the stability programme commitments having been akin to moving targets rather than anchoring fiscal policy in medium term goals (Figure 1, Panel A). Since 2001, automatic stabilisers have played a significant role as economic growth slowed down. But in several countries (notably the larger ones) there was not sufficient room for the full operation of automatic stabilisers without incurring excessive deficits, because these countries did not create enough leeway in the upturn. Indeed, it is as if the larger countries have targeted a deficit of 3 per cent of GDP over the cycle rather than close to balance or in surplus (Figure 1, Panel B). Why did fiscal behaviour change when the Pact came into force, and why has this affected larger countries more than smaller ones?

Figure 1: Fiscal consolidation: Moving targets+
General government balance in the euro area as a per cent of GDP++

A. Projections in the Stability Programmes

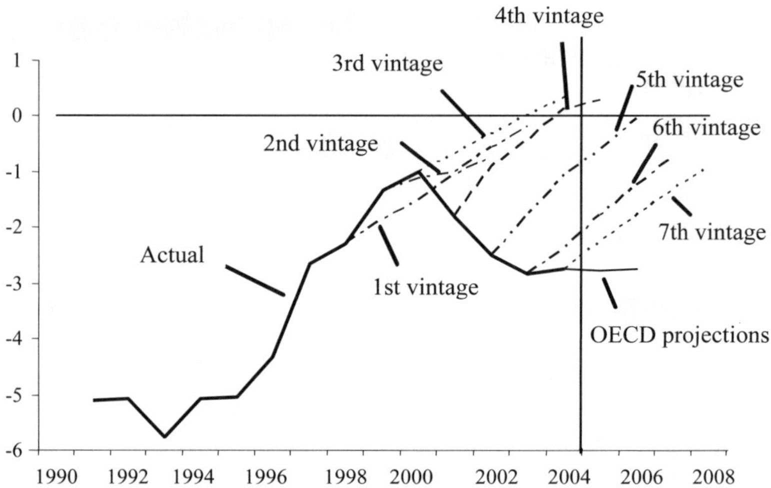

B. Developments by country

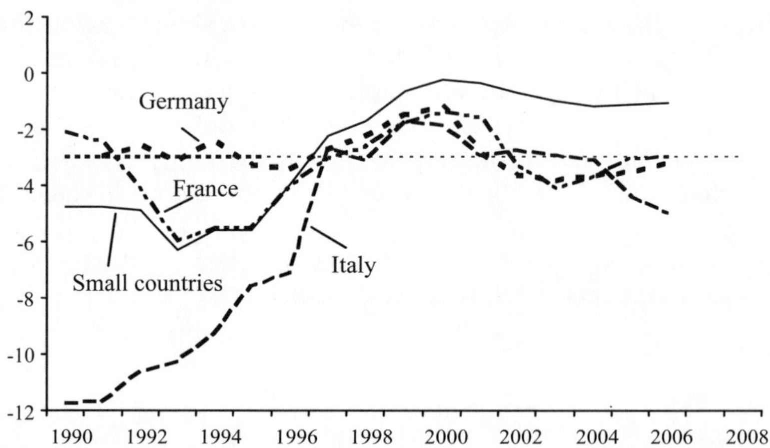

+ The various vintages of the Stability Programmes were released over the following periods: 1st 1998/99, 2nd 1999/2000, 3rd 2000/01, 4th 2001/02, 5th 2002/03, 6th 2003/04, 7th 2004/05.

++ Excluding UMTS licence proceeds.

Source: European Commission/Eurostat and OECD, Economic Outlook 77 database.

Concerning the first question, it is important to note that the SGP represented a profound regime switch. There are several dimensions to this regime switch.[7]

The Treaty set clear deadlines for moving to the final stage of EMU which together with the simplicity of the criteria facilitated the surveillance by the European Commission. Countries that were willing to join the euro area in the first wave had no choice but to make the required consolidation effort to meet the Maastricht convergence criteria in accordance with the timetable. The convergence criteria became the centrepiece of government strategies in most EU countries, with the 3 per cent of GDP deficit criterion providing a visible benchmark for success, especially in countries which entered the 1990s with high deficits and debt.

The incentive structure crucially changed with the move to the single currency. The only "stick" left to the EU authorities was the less tangible risk of uncertain and delayed pecuniary sanctions and loss of reputation. Since the SGP stipulated that fiscal positions have to be close to balance or in surplus "over the medium run", there was no clear timetable for compliance. As noted, the Council remedied this shortcoming by its decision in March 2003 to commit countries to meet the close-to-balance or surplus rule in cyclically-adjusted terms each year. However, the jury is still out as to whether this measure has actually changed fiscal behaviour.

At first sight it may be puzzling why the larger countries were more prone to this change in behaviour than most of the smaller ones. With hindsight this may be less surprising. A number of issues stand out.

First, the Maastricht convergence criteria were strongly supported by Germany and France. Germany regarded macroeconomic stability as an essential precondition to accept dilution of its monetary sovereignty. France was keen to satisfy the German demands, as it had *de facto* given up monetary sovereignty by pegging its currency to the Deutschemark and expected to recover some of this loss via its voice in the common monetary policy. With the advent of the euro the political ownership of the rules shifted towards the smaller countries whose fiscal positions were sound in most cases but had less weight in the surveillance process. The refusal by the Council to endorse an "early warning" recommendation to Germany and Portugal in early 2002 and the Council decision in

7 See *Buti/Giudice* (2002); *Buti/van den Noord* (2004).

November 2003 to hold the Excessive Deficit Procedure in abeyance confirmed that Germany and France had lost ownership of the rules.

Second, the timing of general elections has surely played a role. There is compelling evidence that the political business cycle is alive and well in the euro area: the fiscal rules did not curb this tendency.[8] Germany and France held general elections in 2002 and Italy in 2001 and in the run-up to these elections fiscal policy was considerably eased (Figure 2). The histories of two of the three smaller countries that have been in excessive deficit are quite different: the Netherlands and Portugal can rightly claim that their deficits have been largely of a cyclical nature. Greece is a special case. Its excessive deficit is largely structural, but it was hidden until recently due to, *inter alia,* a misclassification of military expenditure.

Third, there are several fundamental reasons why size matters for fiscal behaviour.[9] Fiscal multiplier effects are typically stronger in the larger (less open) economies; hence fiscal activism pays. Moreover, in larger countries it proves more difficult to conclude a "fiscal contract" then in smaller, more consensus-oriented, countries. In addition, fiscal consolidation is easier to pursue if the economy is growing fast than when it is not, as is reflected in an observed positive cross-country correlation between trend growth and the cyclically-adjusted fiscal balance (Figure 3, left panel). Trend growth in the larger economies is less than in the smaller ones: in the period 1999-2005 it was 1½ per cent per year on average in Germany, France and Italy against 3¼ per cent in the smaller countries. Importantly, strong growth in many smaller countries allowed them to maintain relatively robust growth in public expenditure, without running into fiscal deficits (Figure 3, right panel). The opposite applies to the larger countries, in particular Germany and Italy.

B. The surveillance gap

Deficit bias essentially results from co-ordination failure: weak budgetary institutions fail to internalise the externalities resulting from government spending which is commonly targeted at specific groups in society while financed from taxes to which all taxpayers

---

8 See *Buti/van den Noord* (2004b) pp. 737-756; *von Hagen* (2002).

9 See *Buti/Pench* (2004) pp. 1025-1032.

contribute. If governments are myopic and discount time more heavily than society does, they will be inclined to run down public assets (in the broadest possible sense, including the present value of future tax revenues) in order to finance the highest possible amount of present consumption. The imposition of numerical fiscal rules will fail to remove this incentive, and rather encourage countries to shift from overt to hidden forms of deficit bias.

One way to cope with a (potentially) binding deficit rule is for the government to forecast relatively robust GDP growth, which boosts projected receipts and helps contain some types of projected spending. The fiscal shortfalls are indeed impressive (Table 1, first two columns). In the period 2001-03 fiscal positions turned out on average each year more than 1 per cent of GDP worse than those projected in the stability programmes. Growth projections were undershot by as much as 1½ percentage points on average each year in this period (Table 1, third and fourth columns). This raises suspicion that the programmes were subject to forecasting inertia.

Admittedly, the downturn and the extent of its impact on fiscal outcomes contained a genuine element of surprise. Shortfalls associated with the turnaround in stock markets may have been particularly large, which suggests governments had misjudged the true structural fiscal position as revenues had been boosted by the stock market boom in the late 1990s.[10] However, as documented by *Milesi-ferretti*/*Moriyama* (2004) and in the 2004 *OECD* Economic Survey of the euro area, there is evidence that euro area governments burdened with large deficits have tended to put forth overly optimistic growth forecasts in their stability programmes. These recurrent shortfalls have compromised the process of fiscal surveillance.

---

[10] *See Jeager/Schuknecht* (2004); *Girouard/Price* (2004).

Table 1: Short-term forecasting errors in the stability programmes
Per cent, annual average over the period

	A. Fiscal balance[1]		B. Real GDP growth[2]		Ratio A/B	
	1999-00	2000- 03	1999- 00	2000- 03	1999- 00	2000- 03
Austria	-0.4	0.2	0.2	-0.9	-1.5	-0.2
Belgium	1.0	0.1	1.0	-1.3	1.0	-0.1
Finland	1.1	0.7	0.3	-1.4	3.7	-0.5
France	0.4	-1.3	0.9	-1.6	0.4	0.8
Germany	0.2	-1.4	0.2	-1.4	0.8	1.0
Greece	-0.2	-1.8	0.2	-0.3	-1.3	7.3
Ireland	1.9	-1.6	3.6	-0.4	0.5	3.5
Italy	-0.1	-1.7	0.1	-1.6	-0.5	1.0
Netherlands	2.1	-1.4	1.0	-1.7	2.1	0.8
Portugal	-1.3	-1.5	0.2	-1.9	-7.1	0.8
Spain	0.0	0.0	0.5	-0.6	0.1	0.1
Non-weighted average	0.4	-0.9	0.8	-1.2	0.6	0.7
Weighted average	0.3	-1.1	0.5	-1.4	0.6	0.8

[1] Difference between the realised and projected fiscal balance as a per cent of GDP. Projections as included in the stability programme issued at the start of the current year or the end of the previous year.

[2] Difference between the realised and projected real GDP growth rate. Projections as included in the stability programme issued at the start of the current year or the end of the previous year.

Source: European Commission; OECD.

Figure 2: Fiscal policy indicators
Per cent of actual/potential GDP[1]

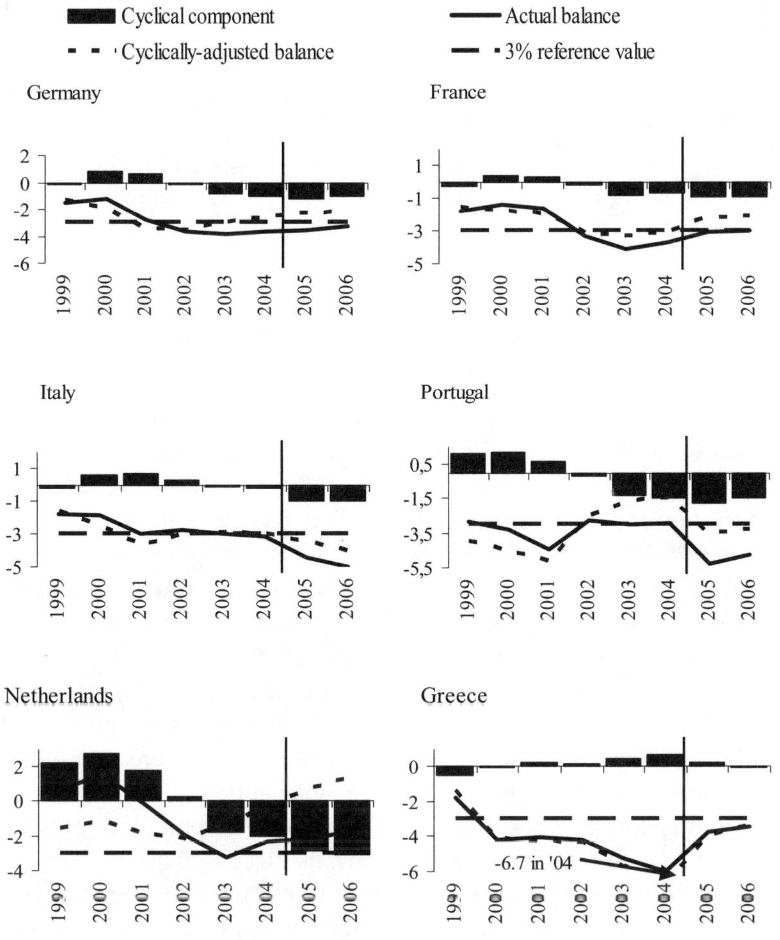

[1] Actual balance excludes UMTS licence proceeds and is in per cent of GDP, cyclically-adjusted balance is in per cent of potential GDP and the cyclical component is the difference between the two.

Source: OECD, Economic Outlook 77 database.

Figure 3: Trend growth and fiscal policy (Averages for 1999-2005)

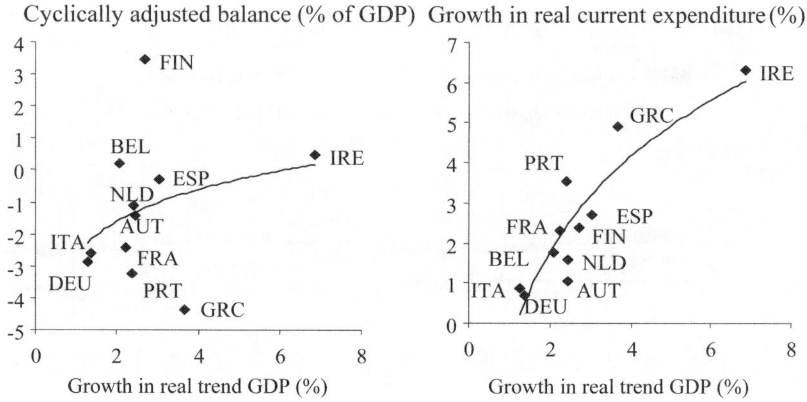

Source: OECD Economic Outlook 77 database.

A more sophisticated, and at times unintentional, form of hidden bias concerns cyclically adjusted flows rather than headline fiscal balances. It has involved the use of favourable methodologies and assumptions in the estimation of potential output. Specifically, Hodrick-Prescott filtering of real GDP coupled with optimistic "back to average growth" forecasting has provided euro area policy-makers with an overly rosy estimate of potential output growth and structural budget positions during the upswing of the late 1990s, hiding the extent of underlying fiscal fragility.[11] As a result, fiscal policy stances turn out easier (and structural deficits higher) than they looked when projections were made.[12] This phenomenon was one of the motivations for the European Commission to pursue its own estimates of potential growth and cyclically-adjusted budget balances, as discussed above.

A third way to formally meet, or to come closer to meeting, deficit rules is to embellish the reported fiscal position by one-offs and creative accounting, affecting headline as well as cyclically-adjusted fiscal balances, through:

- Privatisation, insofar as it is driven by a desire to replenish the treasury rather than the prospect of efficiency gains.
- Cuts in public investment projects that carry a high social return, which deprive taxpayers from prime investment opportunities and hence represent a net cost to society.

---

[11] See *Cotis et al* (2005).

[12] See *Larch/Salto* (2003); *Jonung/Larch* (2004).

- Cuts in operations and maintenance spending which, unless they seek to achieve efficiency gains, lead to faster wear and tear of public infrastructure.
- Shifting expenditures and revenues over time, typically by accelerating the collection of future tax liabilities or postponing the payment of subsidies or benefits.
- Eating into the net present value of contributions and benefits of an entitlement programme, such as public pensions, e.g. by forcing a public pension scheme to lend to the government at favourable rates.

In practice, several of the above elements may be combined. For example, the privatisation of a public agency may be motivated in part by the possibility to cut down expenditures in operations and maintenance, to bring revenues forward in time (by cashing the present value of future user fees) and to cut public investment. The list of one-offs and creative accounting operations – and the amounts that are involved is indeed impressive (Table 2). Interestingly, the incidence of these forms of gimmickry was even higher in the period 1994-98, when deficit convergence was required to qualify for the euro.

The shift from overt to hidden deficit bias does not argue against fiscal rules. Fiscal rules may foster genuine fiscal consolidation if the social cost attached to window-dressing is high and the probability of the true nature of these measures being discovered by taxpayers or the electorate is also high.[13] Indeed, improvements in the surveillance by the EU authorities could pay dividends. However, it is also important that the main source of deficit bias – *i.e.* the lack of internalisation in the budgetary process of the adverse externalities of fiscal profligacy – be addressed. This calls for stronger enforcement mechanisms, not only at the EU level, but also at the national level.

C. The enforcement gap

The fiscal consolidation that has been achieved since the Maastricht Treaty in 1992 has been impressive overall, suggesting that incentives to this effect have been forceful. Progress in consolidating budget balances has stalled since. Enforcement of the rules should have kicked in. It did not.

---

13 See *Milesi-ferretti* (2000).

Table 2: One-offs, "creative accounting" operations and reclassifications affecting the fiscal balance* (In % of GDP)

	´93	**´94**	**´95**	**´96**	**´97**	**´98**	**´99**	**´00**	**´01**	**´02**	**´03**
Austria	0.1	0.5	0.5		0.1			0.3			
Belgium	0.4	0.2		0.9					0.3	0.2	1.9
Finland		1.3		0.3	0.3			0.3			
France		0.2		0.3	0.5		0.1				
Germany					0.2						
Greece	3.7	0.5	1.7	1.3	2.8	1.9	1.8	3.4	2.6	3.4	2.8
Ireland	0.4			0.5	0.4			0.4	0.4	0.7	
Italy	0.9	0.6	0.7	0.4	1.4				0.7	0.9	1.7
Luxembourg									1.8		
Netherlands	1.1	1.1	0.9	0.4	0.1						
Portugal		0.7	1.0		0.5	0.2			0.6	1.7	2.3
Spain	1.3		0.4	0.4	0.4						0.3
Denmark			0.1		0.2						
Sweden	0.2	0.2	0.5		0.6	0.9					
United Kingdom					0.6	0.3					

* Abstracting from UMTS licence receipts and from operations amounting to less than 0.1 per cent of GDP.

Source: *Koen/van den Noord* (2005).

At the time of writing, five countries in the euro area were subject to an Excessive Deficit Procedure (EDP) consistent with the relevant provisions in the Maastricht Treaty. It is instructive to follow the various steps in the procedure:

- When in January 2003 the German 2002 budget deficit turned out to be above 3 per cent of GDP, the Council launched the EDP, recommending Germany to put an end to the excessive deficit by 2004 at the latest. The Council recommended Germany to adopt measures amounting to 1 percentage point of GDP by May 2003 at the latest. However, according to the Commission's 2003 autumn forecast the German fiscal deficit was expected to reach 3.6 per cent of GDP in 2003, and would remain above 3 per cent also in 2004. The Commission recommended the Council to establish that no effective action had been taken and to give notice to Germany. The Commission recommended that Germany cut its deficit to below 3 per cent of GDP by 2005 at the latest. On 25 November 2003, the Council rejected the Commission's recommendations and decided to "hold in abeyance" the EDP, but recommended that Germany cut its cyclically adjusted budget deficit by 0.6 and 0.5 per cent of GDP in 2004 and 2005, respectively, so as to ensure that the government deficit is brought down to below 3 per cent of GDP in 2005. However, it looks unlikely that Germany will comply.

- In January 2003 the Council issued an "Early Warning" against France as there were clear risks that the deficit would go above 3 per cent in 2003. Final budget numbers in March showed that the deficit had in fact already breached the 3 per cent of GDP mark in 2002, prompting the Commission to launch an EDP against France. This was followed in June by a Council recommendation to France to end the excessive deficit by 2004 at the latest. But the fiscal outlook deteriorated and the Commission's 2003 autumn forecast projected the French deficit at 4.2 per cent of GDP in 2003 and a deficit still above 3 per cent in 2004. The Commission accordingly recommended to the Council to establish that no effective action had been taken and to give notice to France. The Commission recommended that France take further measures in 2004 and 2005 in order to cut the deficit to below 3 per cent of GDP by 2005 at the latest, the deadline being extended in view of the economic circumstances. However, in its 25th November meeting, the Council also rejected these Commission recommendations and decided to "hold in abeyance" the EDP, while recommending that France cut its cyclically adjusted budget deficit by 0.8 and 0.6 per cent of GDP in 2004 and 2005, respectively, so as to ensure that the government deficit is brought down to below 3 per cent of GDP in 2005. But again this looks unlikely.
- In April 2004 the European Commission launched an EDP for the Netherlands after its budget deficit was found to have reached 3.2 per cent of GDP in 2003. The Council endorsed it in its June meeting, recommending the Netherlands to take measures so as to cut its deficit to below 3 per cent of GDP by 2005, which it did. In May 2004 the Commission also initiated an EDP for Greece after its budget deficit was found to have reached 3.2 per cent of GDP in 2003. On 5 July, the Council decided that an excessive deficit exists in Greece and recommended it to take action to put an end to the excessive deficit by 2005 at the latest. The Greek deficit has recently been revised up for the period 1998-2003; it appeared to have exceeded the 3 per cent mark all along.

One fundamental lesson from the recent episode is that the SGP needs to focus on the prevention of fiscal slippage in upturns while ensuring that fiscal policy remains anchored in medium and long term objectives. The excessive deficit provisions in the Treaty in principle offer the necessary "stick" to induce fiscal discipline, provided that these are credibly enforced in a pre-emptive fashion. This requires not only that the surveillance capacity of the competent authority is sufficiently strong, but also that enforcement is impartial. However compliance with the rules is assessed in the first instance by the Commission, which has competence but no legal power of enforcement, and in the final instance by the Ecofin Council which has such power but, being party and judge, is not impartial. As a result, the threat of fines is not credible and the only potentially effective instruments currently available are moral suasion, peer pressure and negative publicity.

IV. How to move forward?

A number of proposals have been around for some time and new ones popped up. They have in common their focus on longer-term issues.

A. Focus on long-term issues

Since long run sustainability of public finances is a growing concern of member countries, reflecting this concern in the Stability and Growth Pact would in principle enhance its legitimacy. A key question is to what extent the existing fiscal rules are already consistent with the requirement of long term sustainability of public finances in view of the increase in ageing related public spending. Analytical work reported in the 2004 *OECD Economic Survey of the euro area*, suggests that the fiscal policy rule prescribed in the SGP – i.e. balanced budgets or small surpluses of about ½ per cent of GDP – is the minimum needed during the transition period to the new demographic steady state until around 2020. In fact this rule may be far too lenient for some countries (Finland, Germany, the Netherlands and Portugal) and perhaps too tight for others (Italy). The upshot is that for the close to balance or in surplus rule to be consistent with the sustainability criterion for all countries, it will have to be converted into a set of country specific rules. This has prompted for example *Fatás et al* (2003) to propose to abolish the close to balance or in surplus rule altogether and to set up a EU "Sustainability Council" which monitors and advises national governments on ways to achieve fiscal sustainability.

Some observers have argued in favour of the "golden rule". Article 104(3) of the Maastricht Treaty stipulates that:

> "If a Member State does not fulfil the requirements under one or both of these [debt and deficit] criteria, the Commission shall prepare a report. The report of the Commission shall also take into account whether the government deficit exceeds government investment expenditure and take into account all other relevant factors, including the medium term economic and budgetary position of the Member State."

According to some interpretations,[14] this leaves open the possibility of adopting a golden rule.

The golden rule splits the government appropriation account into a general account and a capital account, and obliges the government to maintain at least a balanced general account, while allowing it to borrow for net investment. One rationale put forward is that such a rule would better fit the new EU member countries, who need to recover an infrastructure backlog and are also likely to grow fast – indeed grow faster if the infrastructure gap is filled. Another rationale for the golden rule is that it would be fair in an inter-generational sense – future generations pay for the infrastructure they inherit. However, a salient feature of the golden rule is that it will only result in sustainable public finances if simultaneously some prudent rule for the development of net debt is satisfied. This is how the golden rule is applied in the United Kingdom: the public sector is allowed to borrow for net investment provided that the ratio of net debt to GDP stays below 40 per cent. Most euro area countries would probably fail to satisfy the net debt criterion. Hence, if adopted as a general principle in the (enlarged) European Union, the golden rule would remain a dead letter in the euro area. In addition the golden rule may give rise to distortions and induce creative accounting.

Other (better founded) rationales for governments to be allowed to run temporary deficits – conditional on long term sustainability – have also been put forward:

- First, structural reform may yield long term economic gains but entail up front costs. The estimates of the benefits from structural reform are often uncertain whereas the immediate

---

14 Viz. *Blanchard/Giavazzi* (2003).

political and budgetary costs – such as compensation schemes to offset redistributive effects – are perceived with greater precision. This information asymmetry may hamper structural reforms, especially with regard to labour market reforms which entail the highest up front costs. Allowing governments to run temporary deficits to finance structural reform may therefore be welfare enhancing.[15]

- Second, a move (in itself commendable) towards privately funded pension schemes would lead to deficits in the public scheme but initial surpluses in the private schemes as contributors transfer to the private schemes. Pre funding public schemes is a more "SGP friendly" option as it would generate surpluses in the public scheme. However, such a pre funding strategy for public pensions has several disadvantages.[16] Most prominently, it does not directly address the adverse efficiency and distribution problems inherent in large sized public pension schemes and it also raises governance issues. The upshot is that the momentum for efficiency enhancing pension reforms is not necessarily helped by the close to balance or in surplus rule. More flexibility in interpreting this rule would yield a less distorted incentive structure.

Such arguments did not fall on deaf ears at the European Commission. In September 2004, the Commission put forward a proposal that encapsulates most of the ideas that have been around for some time.[17] It aimed to enhance the political ownership of the rules by the member countries, while strengthening the surveillance and enforcement by the Commission. Specifically:

- To raise the "ownership" of the rules, their implementation would have to become more tailor-made, giving greater weight to the debt criterion (as opposed to the deficit criterion) and long-term sustainability. Moreover, the budgetary upfront cost of countries' structural reform (including pension reform) would have to be taken into consideration when assessing the fiscal situation. The interpretation of the exceptional circumstances clause and the adjustment path towards compliance with the rules after a breach would both need to be adjusted.
- The Commission hoped to offset the asymmetric incentive

---

15 See for example *Beetsma/Debrun* (2005); *Von Hagen* (2003).

16 See *IMF* (2003).

17 See *European Commission* (2004).

balance by introducing a dissuasive mechanism in the hands of the Commission: it would issue an "early warning" also in good times, if a country fails to take out insurance against bad times. It also urged member countries to enhance the quality and transparency of their budgetary statistics – surely not a luxury given the embarrassing record of some countries recently.

According to the Commission's proposal, the interpretation and implementation of the SGP would thus increasingly move away from year by year compliance to focus on the longer term, which is welcome because it allows for more flexibility in the short run while taking better account of the government's inter-temporal budget constraint. The Commission resisted suggestions made by some (the largest) member countries to exclude certain expenditure items – such as defence, R&D, public investment or contributions to the EU budget – from the relevant deficit measure. The reform that was eventually adopted by the European Council in March 2005 went a long way towards adopting the Commission's proposal – except on the last point.[18]

Not surprisingly, it is this last aspect of the reform that attracted most attention. Under the heading "Improving the implementation of the excessive deficit procedure", the Council decided to grant a waiver under the Excessive Deficit Procedure to countries on the basis of "exceptional circumstances". According to the Treaty, aside from a "severe recession", "other relevant factors" might allow countries to temporarily exceed the 3% of GDP deficit mark under the exceptionality clause, but those "factors" were not specified. In its new incarnation, the Pact does specify these factors. Although phrased in coded language in the agreed text, these are well understood to include high levels of public expenditure for R&D, development aid, the cost of German unification and contributions to the EU budget. In addition, the definition of a "severe economic downturn" has become more lenient, redefining "a severe economic downturn" that may qualify countries for a waiver as "a negative growth rate" or a "protracted period of very low growth relative to potential growth", as opposed to "an annual fall of real GDP of at least 2%" as stipulated in the original provisions.

Aspects that have attracted less attention are the provisions to

---

18 Council of the European Union, *Presidency Conclusions*, 7619/04 CONCL 1, Brussels, 23 March 2005.

heighten the surveillance of the fiscal rules by the EU authorities ("improved governance") and to reinterpret the close to balance or in surplus rule so as to make it tailor made for individual countries ("strengthening the preventive arm"). Yet these are the elements that are best underpinned by economic rationale and therefore welcome. However, one fundamental lesson from the recent episode is that the fiscal rules need to focus on the prevention of fiscal slippage in upturns while ensuring that fiscal policy remains anchored in medium and long term objectives. The excessive deficit provisions in the Treaty in principle offer the necessary "stick" to induce fiscal discipline, provided that these are credibly enforced in a preemptive fashion. This requires not only that the surveillance capacity of the competent authority is sufficiently strong, but also that enforcement is impartial. However, as noted, this condition is not being met.

Inevitably, the burden of enforcement shifts from the European to the national level – except in extreme cases of fiscal misbehaviour. This requires stronger enforcement mechanisms at the national level. The obvious question then is whether euro area countries are ready to assume this responsibility. The observed progress in national budget institutions is encouraging, but it is not evident that all sources of fiscal profligacy have been removed.

B. Strengthening budgetary procedures

Some observers have suggested putting the surveillance process in the hands of a high level group of fiscal experts, nominated by the European Parliament to underpin their independence and legitimacy.[19] The experts group would have the right to make its judgment public and declare a member state in excessive deficit. National independent budget agencies could be set up to perform independent audits and to report to the experts group. However, such proposals are unlikely to be accepted and it is not obvious that creating a new institution side by side with the Commission would make a fundamental difference.

In stead, it would be advisable if the EU peer pressure process would be geared towards enhancing the institutional features of budgeting in the member countries. Countries that have been experiencing fiscal surpluses in the recent upswing are generally the same countries that have been the most active in reforming and

---

[19] See *Buiter* (2003); *de Haan et al* (2003); *Fatás et al* (2003).

modernising their budget processes.[20] These reforms went right at the heart of the fundamental flaw in budgeting: government expenditure is commonly targeted at specific groups in society but financed from general taxation which is spread over current tax payers or via a run up in debt which affects future generations of tax payers. Specifically, the following institutional features have been identified as crucial for effective expenditure control and sustainability:[21]

- Medium term budgetary frameworks. Budgets are enacted for one year and are notorious for their short term focus. Medium term budgetary frameworks serve to clearly state the government's targets – such as the level of revenue, expenditure and the balance for several years – beyond the fiscal year. These should result in hard budget constraints for individual ministries and programmes. Obviously changes could be made on the way, but it is imperative that such changes be clearly identified and explained.
- Prudent macroeconomic projections. Deviations of key macroeconomic variables underlying the budget from the projection pose a key fiscal risk. Great care must be taken in making these projections and disclosing them. The establishment of an independent body to do the economic projections to be used in the budget may be considered.
- Top-down budgeting. The traditional bottom-up principle of budgeting means that agencies and spending ministries submit requests for funding to the Finance Ministry which are negotiated until some common ground is found. This process has an inherent bias for increasing spending because new programmes or expansion of existing programmes are funded by new requests rather than by reallocation within the spending ministries. This manner of budgeting is being abandoned progressively and replaced with a top down approach, but it does involve considerable time to establish because the entrenched traditions work against it.

Other requirements for effective expenditure control include: i) to relax micro management at the top to encourage efficiency gains; ii) result based management to hold managers accountable and iii) enhanced budget transparency. According to the OECD's *Best*

---

[20] See *von Hagen et al* (2002).

[21] See *Blondal* (2003).

Practices for Budget Transparency governments should be encouraged to outline fiscal projections in a pre budget statement several months prior to the release of the government's budget proposal, provide explicit detail on contingent liabilities, and use the annual financial statements as a compliance report for accountability purposes to be certified by a national auditor. Governments can make progress in all these respects and the EU authorities should play an activating role in this regard.

V. Concluding remarks

Countries should avoid past fiscal mistakes by rooting their budgets in medium-term frameworks. More ambition in consolidating budgets is needed, independent of the fiscal rules enshrined in the Maastricht Treaty and the Stability and Growth Pact, which in many countries are the minimum required to underpin the sustainability of the public finances in the face of ageing populations. A strong mandate of the finance minister to set deficit, debt and expenditure targets is a way to internalise the externalities resulting from government spending which commonly benefit specific groups in society while financed from taxes to which all taxpayers contribute. Without such a strong mandate, the externalities prevail and deficit bias results. Moreover, the targets must be rooted in realistic and independent short- medium- and long-term projections of economic growth, public revenues and social benefit entitlements. The Stability Programmes could be based upon, if not become the centrepiece of, such multi-year budgeting.

References

Beetsma R. / Debrun X. (2005), Implementing the Stability and Growth Pact: Enforcement and Procedural Flexibility, IMF Working Papers, 2005, No. WP/05/59.

Bernoth K. / von Hagen J. / Schuknecht L. (2004), Sovereign Risk Premia in the European Government Bond Market, ECB Working Paper Series, No. 369, June 2004, Frankfurt.

Blanchard O. / Giavazzi F. (2003), Improving the SGP through a Proper Accounting of Public Investment, paper presented at seminars on the Stability and Growth Pact organised by the Bundesbank and DIW Berlin, revised version, February 2003.

Blondal J. R. (2003), Budget Reform in OECD Member Countries: Common Trends, in: OECD Journal on Budgeting, Vol. 2, No. 4, 2003, pp. 7-25.

Buiter W. H. (2003), Ten Commandments for a Fiscal Policy Rule in the EMU, in: Oxford Review of Economic Policy, Vol. 19, No. 1, 2003, pp. 84-99.

Buti M. / Giudice G. (2002), Maastricht Fiscal Rules at Ten: An Assessment, in: Journal of Common Market Studies, Vol. 40, 2002, pp. 823-848.

Buti M. / van den Noord P. (2004a), Fiscal Policy in EMU: Rules, Discretion and Political Incentives, in: Moneda y Crédito, No. 218, 2004, pp. 265-307.

Buti M. / van den Noord P. (2004b), Fiscal Discretion and Elections in the Early Years of EMU, in: Journal of Common Market Studies, Vol. 42, Nr. 4, 2004, pp. 737-756.

Buti M. / Pench L. (2004), Why Do Large Countries Flout the Stability Pact? And What Can Be Done About It?, in: Journal of Common Market Studies, Vol. 42, Nr. 5, 2004, pp. 1025-1032.

Cotis J. - P. / Elmeskov J. / Mourougane A. (2005), Estimates of potential output: benefits and pitfalls from a policy perspective, in: *Reichlin L.* (ed), The Euro Area Business Cycle: Stylized Facts and Measurement Issues, CEPR (forthcoming).

European Commission (2002a), Production Function Derived Output Gains, Information Note to the Members of EPC, ECFIN/528/02, Brussels 2002.

European Commission (2002b), Strengthening the Coordination of Budgetary Policies, Communication by the Commission, COM(2002)668, Brussels.

European Commission (2004), Strengthening Economic Governance and Clarifying the Implementation of the Stability and Growth Pact, Communication by the Commission, COM(2004)581, Brussels.

Fatás A. / von Hagen J. / Hughes Hallet A. / Strauch R.R. / Sibert A. (2003), Stability and Growth in Europe: Towards a Better Pact, CEPR Series on Monitoring European Integration, No. 13, Centre for Economic Policy Research, London 2003.

Girouard N. / Price R. (2004), Asset Price Cycles, "One-off" Factors and Structural Budget Balances, OECD Economics Department Working Papers, No. 391, 2004.

de Haan J. / Berger H. / Jansen D. J. (2003), The End of the Stability and Growth Pact?, CESifo Working Papers, No. 1093, Munich, December 2003.

IMF (2003), Ageing and the SGP, in: IMF Country Report, Euro Area Policies: Selected Issues, No. 03/298, September 2003, pp.75-93.

Jaeger A. / Schuknecht L. (2004), Boom-Bust Phases in Asset Prices and Fiscal Policy Behavior, IMF Working Papers, No. WP/2004/54.

Jonung L. / Larch M. (2004), Improving Fiscal Policy in the EU: the Case for Independent Forecasts, European Economy - Economic Papers, Nr. 210, 2004.

Koen V. / van den Noord P. (2005), Fiscal Gimmickry in Europe: One-Off Measures and Creative Accounting, Economics Department Working Papers, No. 417, Paris 2005.

Larch M. / Salto M. (2003), Fiscal Rules, Inertia and Discretionary Fiscal Policy, European Economy - Economic Papers, Nr. 194, 2003.

Milesi-ferretti G. M. (2000), Good, Bad or Ugly? On the Effects of Fiscal Rules with Creative Accounting, IMF Working Paper, No. 00/172, 2000.

Milesi-ferretti G. M. / Moriyama K. (2004), Fiscal Adjustment in EU Countries: a Balance Sheet Approach, IMF Working Paper, No. 04/143, 2004.

OECD (2004), Economic Survey of the Euro Area, Organisation for Economic Co-operation and Development, Paris 2004.

von Hagen J. (2002), More Growth for Stability – Reflections on Fiscal Policy in Euroland, ZEI Policy Paper, June 2002.

von Hagen J. / Hughes Hallett A. / Strauch R. (2002), Budgetary Institutions for Sustainable Public Finances, in: *Buti M. / von Hagen J. / Martinez Mongay C.* (eds.), The Behaviour of Fiscal Authorities – Stabilisation, Growth and Institutions, Palgrave 2002, Basingstoke, pp. 94-112.

von Hagen J. (2003), Fiscal Discipline and Growth in Euroland; Experiences with the SGP, ZEI Working Paper, No. B06 2003.

Andrew Hughes Hallett

Fiscal Policy Coordination with independent Monetary Policies - Is it possible?*

I. Introduction

The Stability Pact's 3% of GDP limit on fiscal deficits has now been breached by six out twelve members of the Eurozone, and the Pact (in its original form) set aside following a decision in the European Court of Justice. The less controversial and less often quoted debt limit (at 60% of GDP) was breached by nine of twelve members in 1999; and six of them still breach it in 2005, although there have been big improvements in many cases. This record has raised understandable concerns about the discipline and degree of

* The theoretical model used in section 3 is adapted from my work with *Diana Weymark* at Vanderbilt University. I am grateful for her help, but she is not responsible for my use of the results. I am also grateful to *Reinhard Neck* and *Ewald Nowotny* for very useful comments on the first version of the paper.

pre-commitment in fiscal policy, and the risks which that may pose in undermining the credibility and focus of monetary policy.[1]

There have been many suggestions for reforming the Stability Pact, most of them directed at loosening the deficit constraint to produce "soft" targets in place of the old "hard" targets without changing their substance. A few also suggest making the Pact debt sensitive. Fiscal restraints, however, have always been justified on the basis that we need to preserve sustainable public finances (a debt target), *and* to maintain the credibility of the policy mix (a deficit target). Concentrating on the deficit alone – to produce more flexibility by allowing a longer adjustment period, or wider deviations after a deficit limit is breached – is to return us to the short term "adjustment around the cycle" focus of the old Pact. It does not preserve the longer run (structural) goal of sustainability.

Equally, it is not clear why policy makers would keep to a soft target regime when they could not keep to the old hard target one. They would certainly find it easier to do so. But whether they would want, or be able to do so is quite another question – particularly if they find that the current framework lacks coordination, or that they need fiscal policy to counter spillovers and monetary policy effects that do not fit their specific circumstances. Are there alternative arrangements to give them the *incentive* to restrain their fiscal policies credibly?

The intention of the recent reforms, evidently, has been to produce a soft target version of the old regime without any change in the way that the ECB conducts monetary policy. In this paper I accept that premise, but add three important features. First, I introduce a debt rule in order to give fiscal policies a longer term focus – and the extra commitment or credibility which comes from that. Second, I recast the policy game in a form that allows coordination without the ECB having to surrender any of its ability to act independently. That frees fiscal policy from the need to react so strongly to spillovers or mismatched monetary policies. Third, I examine the incentive for keeping to a new Stability Pact regime, hard or soft. Given the poor compliance record under the old pact, it will

---

1 *Dixit/Lambertini* (2003) argue that monetary policies cannot be credibly pre-committed if fiscal policy is not also pre-committed in some way. Indeed to achieve credibility in fiscal policies, when policy makers face an electoral calendar, may have been the real motivation behind adopting fiscal restraints.

be crucial "to restore political ownership to member governments" in a new one. Indeed, I argue here that it is going to be more important to establish an economic basis for a new pact, in place of a legalistic, rule-based one.

Several authors have advocated replacing the deficit target with a debt rule,[2] and they show how debt would then fall at prevailing growth rates. But they do not show how well this would work in terms of overall performance, whether that rule should include hard or soft targets, or whether governments would have any more incentive to keep to a debt rule than to a deficit rule. In the model studied here, fiscal policy would be set to achieve certain longer term objectives: low debt, public services, social equality and economic efficiency. The income stabilising aspects are therefore left passive, to act through the automatic stabilisers inherent in any fiscal system. Monetary policy, meanwhile, is used to take care of any remaining output stabilisation around the cycle.

To draw a sharp distinction between actively managed long run policies, and short run stabilisation efforts restricted to the automatic stabilisers, is of course the strategic recommendation in *Taylor* (2000). Marrying that to an activist monetary policy directed at cyclical stabilisation, in order to exploit the credibility of an independent and conservative central bank to underpin the consistency of the short term policies, appears to be an innovation. It implies a leadership role for fiscal policy. That in turn allows fiscal and monetary policies to be better coordinated -- but without either losing their ability to act independently. In short, we arrive at a Stackelberg solution which lies somewhere between the discretionary (but Pareto superior) cooperative solution, and the fully independent (but non-cooperative) solution.

---

2 See *Pisani-Ferry* (2002); *Calmfors/Corsetti* (2003); *CESifo* (2003), *Saraceno/ Monperrus-Veroni* (2004) pp. 471-480.

Figure 1: fiscal and monetary policies coordination

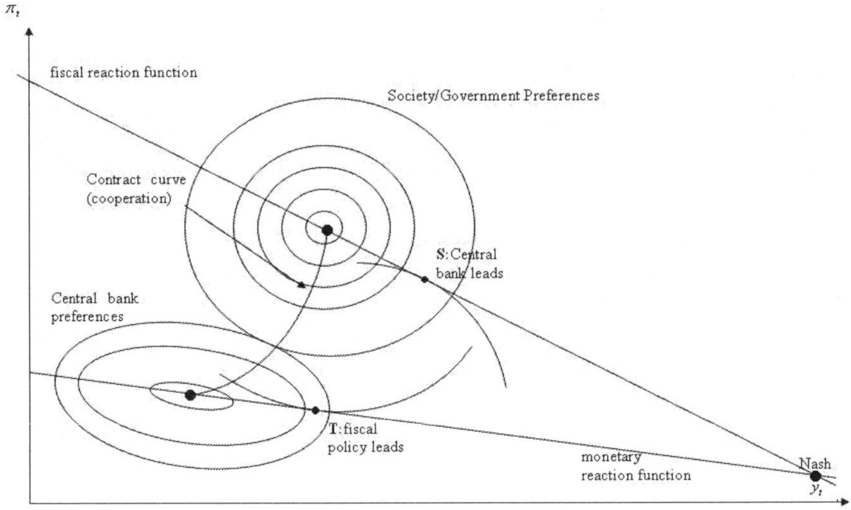

Figure 1 then applies. By shifting the focus onto long run objectives, at the expense of the short term, imposes a degree of fiscal pre-commitment (and potential for electoral punishment) because governments naturally wish to lead. That is why they stand for election. But the regime remains non-cooperative. So there is no incentive to renege on earlier plans in the absence of changes in information. The policies will be sustained by the government of the day.[3]

[3] Stackelberg games, with fiscal policy leading, produce fiscal commitment: that is, subgame perfection with either strong or weak time consistency; see *Basar* (1989) pp. 9-54; because the leader knows his opponent follows and would compensate (according to the follower's own preferences) if the leader were to deviate from his announced path. In that sense, we have rules rather than discretion. Hence commitment to the stabilization policies is assured by having an independent monetary authority; provided that the government does not try to relinquish fiscal leadership and they don't both try to lead at once. See *Brandsma/Hughes Hallett* (1984) pp. 13-32.

II. Fiscal Leadership with an Independent Central Bank

The argument of this paper is that fiscal policy lends itself naturally to longer term objectives, and that this provides an element of leadership which can be combined with independent monetary policies directed at shorter run (demand management) objectives to create an element of coordination which has been missing in Europe. In this case, leadership derives from the fact that fiscal policies typically have longer run targets (sustainability, low debt) and are not easily reversible (public services, social equality), and cannot easily be used for stabilisation if consistency is to be maintained over time.

However, there are automatic stabilisers in any fiscal policy framework, implying that monetary policy must condition itself on the longer term fiscal stance at each point. That puts monetary policy in a follower's role. This is helpful because it allows the economy to retain the benefits of an independent monetary policy. But it imposes a certain degree of coordination between the two sets of policy makers – active fiscal policies on one side, and active monetary policies on the other. That allows Pareto improvements over the conventional non-cooperative (full independence) solution, without reducing the central bank's ability to act independently on its short run objectives. However, retaining independent roles and a debt target for fiscal and monetary policies restricts us to a world of rule-based coordination. We stop short of the gains of full coordination which, being discretionary, would have been subject to time inconsistency and poor credibility.

The rest of this section develops a series of institutional comparisons that show how long term fiscal goals could be used, in practice, to introduce the kind of fiscal leadership and pre-commitment we need to generate the rule-based coordination results we derive from our theoretical model. The comparisons themselves are between the institutions for fiscal and monetary policy making in the Eurozone and the UK. However, the UK is just a benchmark here, to show what might be done to create the kind of performance gains and fiscal-monetary coordination we have in mind.[4]

---

[4] This is not to suggest that the UK example is one that has to be followed, or that the UK has followed the model we present –although there is some empirical evidence to suggest that she has; see *Hughes*

EMU, both in practice and in the underlying treaties, specifies very little about the intended relationship between fiscal and monetary policies. The main concern has always been the independence of monetary policy and the ECB. Article 107 of the Maastricht Treaty, and Article 7 of the ESCB statutes, guarantee the independence of the ECB and the decision making bodies responsible for monetary policy. Those articles also specify that the monetary authorities may not seek or take instructions from any government, government agency or European community organisation. Nor are those agencies allowed to influence the ECB's decisions; and Article 10.4 of the ESCB statutes requires that the proceedings of policy meetings at the ECB remain confidential. Finally, the fact that the ECB was given price stability as its "primary objective" (Article 2 of the ESCB statutes) without a formal definition, when other objectives can be entertained only "if they are without prejudice to price stability", means that the Bank has target independence – both in defining what price stability shall mean, and in giving price stability a "clear priority....as the basis for economic conditions that foster growth, employment and higher living standards", all of which are declared goals of the EU.[5] The ECB therefore has the freedom to set its own targets, but faces a mandate to pursue them with a close to lexographic ordering of price stability over the broader set of EU targets. This does not say the decisions will always be the same; but the targets and conservative priorities will not change with circumstances or the fiscal stance.

Since an independent ECB makes fiscal policy independent of the Bank, one would anticipate competitive (non-cooperative) policy making here with little coordination between the policies. Indeed there is very little room for even *implicit* coordination through information exchanges or some form of leadership. Any discussion that could be construed as taking instructions or attempted influence is ruled out, although the ECB president may attend ECOFIN meetings which could lead to a small information advantage. Monetary policy could still lead; but to go first would be difficult because an overriding price stability target means the ECB

Hallett (2005). The point is to show how longer run debt targets can be built into fiscal policy making in practice.

5 The quotes here are all taken from *Issing's* (1999) explanation of how ECB policy making actually works.

must stand ready to react to fiscal policies if need be. Any leadership advantage would therefore be limited. Similarly price stability is defined over a horizon of two years, which is no longer (and probably shorter) than that underlying most fiscal decisions. Moreover, additional targets can only be considered in so far as they "affect or pose risks to price stability", again a short term response to fiscal policy or wage bargains. So an independent ECB has no strategic advantage, and very little information or institutional advantage over other policy makers. Again the chances of implicit coordination are slight. Nevertheless, frequent statements from the ECB that it needs the "unequivocal support of sound fiscal policies and responsible wage bargains" suggest that fiscal policy had been intended to follow (the problem of compatibility with national priorities notwithstanding); and that the Stability Pact would have been a mechanism to force that. As things stand, the ECB's capacity to lead is small and made weaker by an ineffective Stability Pact. A model of competitive policy making is probably closer to the truth.

In the UK the demand management role of fiscal policy was phased out in the 1980s. That role passed to monetary policies – with limited success in the earlier phases of monetary targeting, but with more success when formalized as an inflation targeting regime with an independent Bank of England. In this period the role of fiscal policy was to provide "conditioning information" within which monetary management had to work. It was split into two parts. Short term stabilization of output/employment was left to the automatic stabilizers in the prevailing tax and expenditures regime. Discretionary adjustments would only be used in exceptional circumstances, if at all.[6] The rest of fiscal policy, being the larger part,

---

[6] This follows *Taylor* (2000). However, because of the inevitable trade-off between cyclical stability and budget stability; see *Fatas et al* (2003); it is likely to be successful only in markets with flexible wages and prices. The Treasury estimates that automatic stabilizers will stabilize about 30% of the UK cycle; the remaining 70% being left to monetary policy; see *HMT* (2003). The need for additional fiscal interventions is unlikely: first, because of the effectiveness of the forward looking, and activist inflation targeting mechanism adopted at the Bank of England; and, second, because the longer term expenditure (and tax) plans are deliberately constructed in nominal terms so that they add to the stabilizing power of the automatic stabilizers in more serious booms or slumps.

was then directed at longer term objectives: microeconomic flexibility that would reduce the need for stabilizing interventions (since relative wage and price adjustments would do the job better) and provide the conditions for employment creation and growth.[7] Given that, the longer run goals of low debt, better public services and social equity could be attained. Moreover, as market flexibility improves, it becomes possible to focus more directly on the longer run goals.

According to the Treasury's own assessment, UK fiscal policy now leads monetary policy in two senses. First, fiscal policy is decided in advance of monetary or other policies,[8] *and* with a longer time horizon.[9] Second, monetary policy is charged with controlling inflation and stabilizing output around the cycle – rather than steering the economy as such.[10] Fiscal policy therefore sets the conditions within which monetary policy has to respond and achieve its own objectives.[11] The short term fiscal interventions, now less than half the total and steadily declining,[12] are restricted to the automatic stabilizers - with effects that are known and predictable. The short run discretionary components have become negligible,[13] and the long run objectives of policy will always take precedence in cases of conflict.[14] Fiscal policy is therefore no longer used for fine tuning,[15] or for stabilization. That burden is carried by interest rates, given the existing fiscal stance and its forward plans.[16]

Third, given that consumers and firms may be credit constrained and that the impact of fiscal policy is often uncertain and subject to lags,[17] it makes sense for fiscal policy to be used consistently and in a way that is identified with the long term (not short run) objectives. The UK has determined these objectives to be:

---

7 The page and other references in this section are all taken from *HMT* (2003).

8 See *ibid.*, p. 5, p. 63, p. 64 and p. 74.

9 See *ibid.*, p. 5, p. 42, p. 48 and p. 61.

10 See *ibid.*, pp. 61-63.

11 See *ibid.*, p. 9, p. 15, pp. 67-68.

12 See *ibid.*, p. 48, box 5.3, section 6.

13 See *ibid.*, p. 59, table 5.5.

14 See *ibid.*, p. 61, pp. 63-68.

15 See *ibid.*, p. 11 and p. 63.

16 See *ibid.*, p. 1, p. 7, p. 11 and p. 37.

17 See *ibid.*, p. 19, p. 26 and p. 48; *Taylor* (2000).

- Sustainable public finances in the long term; that is, low debt (40% of GDP) stabilised symmetrically over the cycle.
- A sustainable but improving delivery of public services; improved supply side efficiency; social and inter-generational equity; the alleviation of poverty.
- Recognition that the achievement of these objectives is often contractual and cannot be reversed once committed. The long lead times needed to build up such programmes mean that the necessary commitments must be made well in advance, and that frequent changes cannot be made.
- The formulation of clear numerical objectives consistent with these goals implies a transparent set of institutional rules; and a separation of these goals from stabilization around the cycle to be achieved by a combination of automatic stabilizers and monetary policy.
- Public expenditures are planned with fixed three year expenditure limits which, when combined with decision and implementation lags of two years, means that the bulk of fiscal policy is planned with a horizon of up to five years – versus two years for inflation targeting at the Bank of England. In addition the Treasury smoothes taxes, having rejected the tax or expenditure regulators that could be used for short term stabilisation as being inconsistent with clarity, continuity and predictability. Fiscal policy remains focused on the medium to long term.

In short, it is the institutional structure which has delivered fiscal leadership in the UK. And, since the discretionary elements are smaller than the automatic stabilizers and declining, something else (monetary policy) must have taken up the burden of short run stabilization. This arrangement justifies our approach of setting up a Stackelberg game as the benchmark case, with endogenously chosen parameters for targets, independence, and priorities, for achieving a greater level of internal policy coordination.

III. A Model of Fiscal Leadership

A. The Economic Model and Policy Constraints

The key question now is: would governments actually want to pursue fiscal leadership? Do they have an incentive to do so; and would there be a clear advantage in terms of overall economic performance if they did? More importantly, would the "fiscal leadership with separation" model still be advantageous if fiscal policy was limited by a debt rule – either in the form of "hard" targets as in the original Stability Pact, or with "soft" targets?

To answer these questions, we extend a model used in to examine the problem of monetary policy design when there are interactions with fiscal policy.[18] For exposition purposes, we suppress the spillovers between countries and focus on the following three equations to represent the economic structure of any one country:[19]

$$\pi_t = \pi_t^e + \alpha y_t + u_t \quad (1)$$

$$y_t = \beta(m_t - \pi_t) + \gamma g_t + \varepsilon_t \quad (2)$$

$$g_t = m_t + s(by_t - \tau_t) \quad (3)$$

where π_t is inflation in period t, y_t is the growth in output (relative to trend output) in period t, and π_t^e represents the rate of inflation that rational agents expect will prevail in period t conditional on the information available at the time expectations are formed. Next, m_t, g_t, and τ_t represent the growth in the money supply, government expenditures, and tax revenues in period t; and u_t and ε_t are random disturbances which are distributed independently with zero mean and constant variance. All variables are defined as deviations from their long run equilibrium values, and we treat *trend* budget variables as pre-committed and balanced. Deviations from the trend budget are the only discretionary fiscal policy choices available therefore. The coefficients α, β, γ, *s,* and *b* are all positive by assumption. The assumption that γ is positive is sometimes controversial.[20] However, the short-run impact multipli-

---

[18] See *Hughes Hallett/Weymark* (2002; 2004a,b; 2005).

[19] Technically, we assume a blockwise orthogonalisation of the traditional multicountry model to produce independent semi-reduced forms for each country. The disturbance terms may therefore contain foreign variables, but they will have zero means so long as those countries remain on their long run (equilibrium) growth paths on average (all variables being defined as deviations from their equilibrium growth paths).

[20] *Barro* (1981) argues that government purchases have a contractionary impact on output. Our model, by contrast, treats fiscal policy as important because: (i) fiscal policy is widely used to achieve redistributive and public service objectives; (ii) governments cannot pre-commit monetary policy with any credibility if fiscal policy is not pre-committed; see *Dixit/Lambertini* (2003) pp. 1522-1542; and (iii) Central Banks, and the ECB in particular, worry intensely about the impact of

ers derived from *Taylor's* (1993) multi-country estimation provide empirical support for this assumption.[21]

According to (1), inflation is increasing in the rate of inflation predicted by private agents and in output growth. Equation (2) indicates that both monetary and fiscal policies have an impact on the output gap. The microfoundations of the aggregate supply equation (1), originally derived by *Lucas* (1972, 1973), are well-known. *McCallum* (1989) shows that aggregate demand equations like (2) can be derived from a standard, multi-period utility-maximisation problem.

Equation (3) describes the government's budget constraint. In my earlier papers, we allowed *discretionary* tax revenues to be used for redistributive purposes only, but permitted *discretionary* expenditures for enhancing output. We further assumed that there are two types of agents, rich and poor, and that only the rich use their savings to buy government bonds. On this view, b would be the proportion of pre-tax income (output) going to the rich and s the proportion of after-tax income that the rich allocate to saving. Tax revenues, τ_t can then be used by the government to redistribute income from rich to poor, either directly or via spending on public services. This fiscal structure therefore has output-enhancing expenditures g_t and discretionary transfers τ_t. Both are financed by aggregate tax revenues; that is, from discretionary and trend revenues. Expenditures above those revenues must be financed by the sale of bonds.

B. An alternative interpretation: debt management

We could, however, take a completely different interpretation of equation (3). It remains the government's budget constraint. But we could define b to be the current public debt to GDP ratio; τ_t to be the revenues that the government proposes to devote to paying down the existing stock of debt in period t; and s to be the proportion of any remaining increase in the debt stock (after transfers to pay it down) that the government expects to pay out in current expenditures this period. It is not immediately obvious that a government could ever spend anything out of an existing, and hence pre-

fiscal policy on inflation and financial stability. See *Dixit* (2001) pp. 589-613.

21 As does *HMT* (2003).

viously committed stock of debt. However, if b=B/Y where B is the absolute stock of debt and Y the level of national income, then

$$\dot{b} = [\dot{B} - b\dot{Y}]/Y \tag{4}$$

where $\dot{x}$ denotes the change in x per unit of time. But

$$b\dot{Y} = by_t \ , \tag{5}$$

since y_t is, by definition, the deviation of Y_t from its own steady state path. Hence by_t represents the amount of additional debt that could be created (and spent) without the debt to GDP ratio actually rising when national income rises or falls.[22] We now suppose governments spend only a proportion s of that new debt, after taking into account the revenues they plan to use to pay the debt stock down. This is a convenient formulation since it allows us to introduce a debt target into the government's objectives such that the value of τ_t is chosen to reduce the debt ratio from b to some other level, θ say. That can be done as a "soft" rule or a "hard" rule, as we show next. The implication however, is that $s(by_t - \tau_t)$ represents only that part of the increase in debt that the government plans to spend for short term stabilisation purposes. This follows from equations (2) and (3). The rest will be used for public expenditures, investment, structural reform, or other long term commitments. We might therefore regard s as the proportion of new fiscal policy expenditures going to automatic stabilisers (in the absence of discretionary stabilisation), and 1-s as the proportion going to longer term goals. We should therefore expect s to be about 0.5 for the Euro economy; or 0.33 for an economy like the UK.[23]

Given this interpretation, we can now solve for π_t^e, π_t and y_t from (1) and (2). That yields the following reduced forms:

$$\pi_t(g_t, m_t) = (1+\alpha\beta)^{-1}[\alpha\beta m_t + \alpha\gamma g_t + m_t^e + \frac{\gamma}{\beta} g_t^e + \alpha\varepsilon_t + u_t] \tag{6}$$

$$y_t(g_t, m_t) = (1+\alpha\beta)^{-1}[\beta m_t + \gamma g_t - \beta m_t^e - \gamma g_t^e + \varepsilon_t - \beta u_t]. \tag{7}$$

Solving for τ_t using (3) and (7), then yields

$$\tau_t(g_t, m_t) = [s(1+\alpha\beta)]^{-1}[(1+\alpha\beta + sb\beta)m_t - (1+\alpha\beta - sb\gamma)g_t$$

22 Governments may of course actually decide to create increases in debt which are larger or smaller than that, depending on whether they choose to make τ_t negative or positive.

23 See *op. cit.* (2003).

$$-sb\beta m_t^e - sb\gamma g_t^e + sb(\varepsilon_t - \beta u_t)]. \tag{8}$$

C. *Government and Central Bank Objectives*

In our formulation, we allow for the possibility that the government and an independent central bank may differ in their objectives in some significant way. In particular, we assume that the government cares about inflation stabilization, output growth, and the provision of public services or public debt; whereas the central bank, if left to itself, would be concerned only with the first two objectives directly,[24] and possibly only the first one. We also assume that the government has been elected by majority vote, so that the government's loss function reflects society's preferences to a significant extent.

Formally, the government's loss function is given by

$$L_t^g = \frac{1}{2}(\pi_t - \hat{\pi})^2 - \lambda_1^g y_t + \frac{\lambda_2^g}{2}[(b-\theta)y_t - \tau_t]^2 \tag{9}$$

where $\hat{\pi}$ is the government's inflation target, λ_1^g is the relative weight or importance that the government assigns to output growth,[25] and λ_2^g is the relative weight which it assigns to the debt rule. The parameter θ represents the target value for the debt to GDP ratio which the government would, ideally, like to reach: hence $(b-\theta)y_t$ becomes the target for its discretionary revenues τ_t. All other variables are as previously defined. We can regard large values of λ_2^g, $\lambda_2^g > \max[1, \lambda_1^g]$ say, as defining *a "hard" debt rule*; and smaller values, $\lambda_2^g < \min[1, \lambda_1^g]$, as representing *a "soft" debt rule.*

The objectives of the central bank, however, may be quite different from those of the government. We model them as follows:

---

24 Since the central bank has no instruments to control debt itself, it can only react to poor fiscal discipline indirectly: e.g. to the extent that its inflation objective is compromised, where it does have an instrument

25 See *Barro/Gordon* (1983) also adopt a linear output target. In the delegation literature, the output component in the government's loss function is usually represented as quadratic to reflect an output *stability* objective. In our model, the quadratic term in the debt term allows monetary and fiscal policy to play a stabilization role as well as pick a position on the economy's output-inflation trade-off.

$$L_t^{cb} = \frac{1}{2}(\pi - \hat{\pi})^2 - (1-\delta)\lambda^{cb} y_t - \delta\lambda_1^g y_t + \frac{\delta\lambda_2^g}{2}[(b-\theta)y_t - \tau_t]^2 \quad (10)$$

where $0 \leq \delta \leq 1$, and λ^{cb} is the weight which the central bank likes to assign to output growth. The parameter δ measures the degree to which the central bank is forced to take the government's objectives into account. The closer δ is to 0, the greater is the independence of the central bank in making its choices. And the lower λ^{cb}, the greater is the degree of conservatism in those choices.

In (9) we have defined the government's inflation target as $\hat{\pi}$. The fact that the same inflation target appears in the central bank's objective function would be correct for cases where the bank has instrument independence but not target independence. However, it is easy to relax that assumption and allow the central bank to choose its own (lower) inflation target as the ECB does. But, as we show in *Hughes Hallett/Weymark* (2004a), there is no advantage in doing so since the government would simply adjust its parameters to compensate. Hence, only if the bank is free to choose the value of λ^{cb} as well, do we get an extra advantage. Yet even that will not be enough to outweigh the advantages to be gained from fiscal leadership – for reasons noted formally in Section IV.

A second feature is that (9) and (10) specify *symmetric* inflation targets around $\hat{\pi}$. Symmetric inflation targets are particularly emphasized as being required of both monetary policy and the fiscal authorities.[26] We have therefore specified both to be features of the government and central bank objective functions here. However it is not clear that symmetry has actually been a feature of European policy making in practice; and the ECB has acquired a reputation for being more concerned to tighten monetary policy when $\pi > \hat{\pi}$, than loosen it when $\pi < \hat{\pi}$. Consequently, rather than symmetry in the output gap targets, we have asymmetric penalties (via the linear term in y_t) which tighten the debt rule in recessions, but weaken it in a boom (when the debt ratio will be falling anyway). That might not be ideal since it introduces an element of pro-cyclicality. But it does bring the rule closer to reality. And it captures the policy makers' revealed preference for an inequality constraint (even if it means saving for a rainy day becomes less likely).

---

26 See *HMT* (2003).

D. Institutional Design and Policy Choices

We characterize the strategic interaction between the government and the central bank as a two-stage non-cooperative game in which the structure of the model and the objective functions are common knowledge. In the first stage, the government chooses the institutional parameters δ and λ^{cb}. The second stage is a Stackelberg game in which fiscal policy takes on a leadership role. In this stage, the government and the monetary authority set their policy instruments, given the δ and λ^{cb} values determined at the previous stage. Private agents understand the game and form rational expectations for future prices in the second stage. Formally, the policy game runs thus:

Stage 1

The government solves the problem

$$\min_{\delta,\lambda^{cb}} EL^{g}(g_t,m_t,\delta,\lambda^{cb}) = E\left\{\tfrac{1}{2}[\pi_t(g_t,m_t)-\hat{\pi}]^2 - \lambda_1^2[y_t(g_t,m_t)]\right\}$$

$$+\frac{\lambda_2^g}{2}E[(b-\theta)y_t(g_t,m_t)-\tau_t(g_t,m_t)]^2 \qquad (11)$$

where $L^g(g_t,m_t,\delta,\lambda^{cb})$ is (9) evaluated at ($g_t,m_t,\delta,\lambda^{cb}$), and E denotes expectations.

Stage 2

- Private agents form rational expectations about future prices π_t^e before the shocks u_t and ε_t are realized.
- The shocks u_t and ε_t are realized and observed by the government and by the central bank.
- The government chooses g_t, before m_t is chosen by the central bank, to minimize $L^g(g_t,m_t,\bar{\delta},\bar{\lambda}^{cb})$ where $\bar{\delta}$ and $\bar{\lambda}^{cb}$ are at the values determined at stage 1.
- The central bank then chooses m_t, taking g_t as given, to minimize

$$L^{cb}(g_t,m_t,\bar{\delta},\bar{\lambda}^{cb}) = \frac{(1-\bar{\delta})}{2}[\pi_t(g_t,m_t)-\hat{\pi}]^2 - (1-\bar{\delta})\bar{\lambda}^{cb}[y_t(g_t,m_t)]$$

$$+\bar{\delta}L^g(g_t,m_t,\bar{\delta},\bar{\lambda}^{cb}). \qquad (12)$$

We solve this game by solving the second stage (for the policy choices) first; and then substituting the results back into (11) to determine the optimal operating parameters δ and λ^{cb}. From stage 2, we get

$$\pi_t(\delta,\lambda^{cb}) = \hat{\pi} + \frac{(1-\delta)\beta(\phi-\eta\Lambda)\lambda^{cb} + \delta(\beta\phi+\gamma\Lambda)\lambda_1^g}{\alpha[\beta(\phi-\eta\Lambda)+\delta\Lambda(\beta\eta+\gamma)]} \tag{13}$$

$$y_t(\delta,\lambda^{cb}) = -u_t/\alpha\ , \tag{14}$$

$$\tau_t(\delta,\lambda^{cb}) = \frac{(1-\delta)\beta s(\beta\eta+\gamma)(\lambda^{cb}-\lambda_1^g)}{[\beta(\phi-\eta\Lambda)+\delta\Lambda(\beta\eta+\gamma)]\lambda_2^9} - \frac{(b-\theta)u_t}{\alpha} \quad \text{where} \tag{15}$$

$$\eta = \frac{\partial m_t}{\partial g_t} = \frac{-\alpha^2\gamma\beta s^2 + \delta\phi\Lambda\lambda_2^g}{(\alpha\beta s)^2 + \delta\Lambda^2\lambda_2^g}, \tag{16}$$

$$\phi = 1+\alpha\beta-\gamma\theta s\ , \text{ and} \tag{17}$$

$$\Lambda = 1+\alpha\beta+\beta\theta s\ . \tag{18}$$

Evidently Λ is positive. We assume ϕ to be positive as well. One would certainly expect $\phi>0$ since, with $\theta<1$ and $s<1$, fiscal policy would otherwise have to have such a strong impact on national income that, together with a Phillips curve which is sufficiently flat and weak monetary transmissions, government expenditures can simultaneously boost output *and* be transferred to pay debt down without worsening the budget (or debt) at the same time: $\gamma>(1+\alpha\beta)/(\theta s)$. In practice, with $s \approx 0.5$ as noted above and debt limited to 50% of GDP, this would require fiscal multipliers in excess of 4 or 5. That is hardly plausible. In fact numerical estimates for ten of the larger OECD economies place ϕ very close to unity, rather than negative.[27] Nevertheless, the conflict that this reveals within fiscal policy is important. In order to get $\phi<0$, output has to be capable of growing fast enough to generate sufficient revenues to boost output when needed *and* to pay down the debt. If that is not possible, one will come at the expense of the other. That underlines the natural pro-cyclicality of any fiscal restraint under "normal" parameter values.[28]

---

27 See *Hughes Hallett* (2005) Table 4.

28 Formally $\partial\{(b-\theta)y_t-\tau_t]/\partial g_t = \phi/(1+\alpha\beta)$, which implies the gap between the debt adjustment needed, and the pay down allocated, will rise as more funds are used for stabilisation when $\phi>0$.

Substituting (13)-(15) back into (11), we can now get the stage 1 solution from:

$$\min_{\delta,\lambda^{cb}} EL^g(\delta,\lambda^{cb}) = \frac{1}{2}\left\{\frac{(1-\delta)\beta(\phi-\eta\Lambda)\lambda^{cb}+\delta(\beta\phi+\gamma\Lambda)\lambda_1^g}{\alpha[\beta(\phi-\eta\Lambda)+\delta\Lambda(\beta\eta+\gamma)]}\right\}^2$$

$$+\frac{\lambda_2^g}{2}\left\{\frac{(1-\delta)\beta s(\beta\eta+\gamma)(\lambda^{cb}-\lambda_1^g)}{[\beta(\phi-\eta\Lambda)+\delta\Lambda(\beta\eta+\gamma)]\lambda_2^g}\right\}^2 . \tag{19}$$

This part of the problem has first order conditions:

$$(1-\delta)(\phi-\eta\Lambda)\lambda_2^g\left\{(1-\delta)\beta(\phi-\eta\Lambda)\lambda^{cb}+\delta(\beta\phi+\gamma\Lambda)\lambda_1^g\right\}$$
$$-(1-\delta)^2(\beta\eta+\gamma)^2\alpha^2 s^2\beta(\lambda_1^g-\lambda^{cb})=0 \text{ and} \tag{20}$$

$$\left\{(1-\delta)\beta(\phi-\eta\Lambda)\lambda^{cb}+\delta(\beta\phi+\gamma\Lambda)\lambda_1^g\right\}(\lambda_1^g-\lambda^{cb})$$
$$\{\delta(1-\delta)\Lambda\Omega+(\phi-\eta\Lambda)\}\lambda_2^g-(1-\delta)(\beta\eta+\gamma)\alpha^2 s^2\beta$$
$$\{(\beta\eta+\gamma)-(1-\delta)\beta\Omega\}(\lambda_1^g-\lambda^{cb})^2=0 \tag{21}$$

where $\Omega=\partial\eta/\partial\delta$. There are two real-valued solutions which satisfy this pair of first-order conditions.[29] The first is when $\delta = 1$ and $\lambda^{cb}=\lambda_1^g$. That solution describes a fully dependent central bank, which is not appropriate in the Eurozone case. And it is inferior to the second solution: $\delta=\lambda^{cb}=0$. In this solution, the central bank is fully independent and exclusively concerned with the economy's inflation performance.

Out of these two possibilities, the solution which yields the lowest welfare loss, as measured by the government's (society's) loss function, can be identified by comparing (19) to the expected loss that would be suffered under the alternative institutional arrangements. Substituting $\delta = 1$ and $\lambda^{cb}=\lambda_1^g$ into (19) results in

$$EL^g=\frac{(\lambda_1^g)^2}{2\alpha^2} . \tag{22}$$

[29] Because η is a function of δ, (21) is quartic in δ. This polynomial has four distinct roots, of which only two are real-valued. The complete solution may be found in *Hughes Hallett/Weymark* (2002).

But substituting $\delta=\lambda^{cb}=0$ into the right-hand-side of (19) yields

$$EL^{g} = 0. \tag{23}$$

Consequently our results show that, when there is fiscal leadership, society's welfare loss (as measured by (19)) is minimized when the government appoints independent central bankers who are concerned only with the achievement of a mandated inflation target and completely disregard the impact their policies may have on output.

However, our results also indicate that fiscal leadership with an independent central bank will remain beneficial under more general conditions. When δ = 0, βη + γ = 0 and the externalities between policy makers are neutralised.[30] As a result, (19) will become

$$EL^{g} = \frac{1}{2}\left\{\frac{\lambda^{cb}}{\alpha}\right\}^{2}$$

for any value of λ^{cb}. Hence an independent central bank will always produce better results than a dependent one so long as it is more conservative than the government ($\lambda^{cb} < \lambda_1^g$), *irrespective* of the latter's commitment to the debt rule (λ_2^g). A conservative central bank will therefore be best, but any bank more conservative than the government will do if the debt rule is to be effective.

A more interesting question is whether fiscal leadership with an independent central bank also produces better outcomes, from society's perspective, than those obtained in a simultaneous move game without leadership – the model generally favoured in Europe. In the simultaneous move game, the solution to the stage 1 minimisation problem is

$$\delta = \frac{\beta\phi^{2}\lambda^{cb}\lambda_2^{g} + \alpha^{2}\gamma^{2}s^{2}\beta(\lambda^{cb} - \lambda_1^{g})}{\beta\phi^{2}\lambda^{cb}\lambda_2^{g} + \alpha^{2}\gamma^{2}\beta(\lambda^{cb} - \lambda_1^{g}) - \phi(\beta\phi + \gamma\Lambda)\lambda_1^{g}\lambda_2^{g}} \quad \text{and} \tag{25}$$

society's welfare loss will then be

---

[30] Because $\beta\eta + \gamma = (\partial y/\partial m)\partial m/\partial g + \partial y/\partial g$, and the central bank has already taken the impact of its decisions on the government's decisions (also zero in this case) into account.

$$EL^g = \frac{1}{2}\left\{\frac{\lambda_1^g}{\alpha}\right\}\left\{\frac{(\alpha\gamma s)^2}{(\alpha\gamma s)^2 + \phi^2\lambda_2^g}\right\}.^{31} \qquad (26)$$

That is always smaller than the loss incurred when fiscal leadership is combined with a *dependent* central bank. However, the optimal degree of conservatism for an *independent* central bank, in this case, is obtained by setting δ = 0 in (25) to yield:

$$\lambda^{cb*} = \frac{(\alpha\gamma s)^2\lambda_1^g}{(\alpha\gamma s)^2 + \phi^2\lambda_2^g}. \qquad (27)$$

It is now straightforward to show that (24) is always less than (26) as long as

$$\lambda^{cb} < [\lambda_1^g\lambda^{cb*}]^{1/2}. \qquad (28)$$

It is also evident that $\lambda^{cb*} < \lambda_1^g$ holds for *any* degree of commitment to a debt rule, $\lambda_2^g > 0$, however small. Consequently, fiscal leadership with *any* $\lambda^{cb} < \lambda^{cb*}$ will always produce better outcomes, from society's point of view, than any simultaneous move game between central bank and government. This is important because many inflation targeting regimes, such as those operated by the Bank of England, the Swedish Riksbank, and the Reserve Bank of New Zealand, operate with fiscal leadership; while several others, notably the European Central Bank and the US Federal Reserve System do not. They are better characterized as being engaged in a simultaneous move game with their governments.

IV. The Gains from Fiscal Leadership

A. Gains in Performance

Finally, where do these leadership gains come from? Substituting δ = 0 and $\lambda^{cb} = 0$ into (13)-(15) yields

$$\pi_t = \hat{\pi},\; y_t = -u_t/\alpha, \text{ and } \tau_t = -(b-\theta)u_t/\alpha \qquad (29)$$

as final outcomes. By contrast, the outcomes for the simultaneous move policy game are

[31] *Hughes Hallett/Weymark* (2002, 2004a) derive these results in more detail.

$$\pi_t^* = \hat{\pi} + \frac{\alpha(\gamma s)^2}{[(\alpha\gamma s)^2 + \phi^2\lambda_2^g]} = \hat{\pi} + \lambda^{cb*}/\alpha \tag{30}$$

$$y_t^* = -u_t/\alpha \tag{31}$$

$$\tau_t^* = \frac{\gamma s(\lambda^{cb*} - \lambda_1^g)}{\phi\lambda_2^g} - \frac{(b-\theta)u_t}{\alpha}. \tag{32}$$

Comparing the two sets of outcomes, we have five conclusions. These conclusions are the main results of this paper:

- Fiscal leadership eliminates the inflationary bias and results in lower inflation without any loss in output or output volatility. The proximate cause of this surprising result is that optimisation under fiscal leadership leads to higher taxes and larger debt repayments.[32]
- The deeper reason is that there is a self-limiting aspect to the long run design of fiscal policy. Unless the effect of fiscal policy on output is so large as to generate savings/taxes that could finance both fiscal expansions *and* debt repayments, each expansion designed to increase output would have to be accompanied by a greater burden of debt. Hence, in order to preserve the long run sustainability of its finances, the government is forced to raise taxes, and this takes some of the inflationary pressure off the central bank when fiscal expansions are called for. As a result the bank is less likely to tighten monetary policy and externalities are reduced on both sides. That is what generates the better coordination between the policy makers noted in sections III.D and IV.B below. But this can only happen if the government has a genuine commitment to long run goals (sustainable public finances, and a debt rule in this case) since only then will the leader take into account the predictable reactions (of the follower) to any short run deviations made by the leader. The follower then knows the leader is not likely to sacrifice his longer run goals by making such deviations (and anyway has the opportunity to clear up the mess, according to the follower's preferences, if the leader does so). If we lose this leadership aspect, both players will end up behaving like followers in the

---

32 Taxes are lower under simultaneous moves because $\lambda^{cb} < \lambda_1^g$. So $E\tau = 0$ in (29) vs. $E\tau_t^* \leq 0$ in (32).

sense that each will fail to account for the responses of the other to any deviation beyond the original optimal policy choices or reaction function. Thus, in the short run under simultaneous moves, each player fails to consider the predictable response, and costs, which the externalities he imposes on his rival would create. The ability to coordinate would be lost, and the outcomes worse for both.[33] Leadership accounts for those responses and extra costs by construction.

- These results hold independently of the commitment to the debt rule (λ_2^g) or its target value (θ); and independently of the government's preference to stabilise or spend (λ_1^g, s); and of the economy's transmission parameters (α,β,γ) or its initial state (b).
- Since $E\tau_t^* < 0$ in (32), but $E\tau_t = 0$ in (29), the simultaneous moves regime will always end up increasing debt levels. It will eventually exceed any limit set for the debt ratio therefore. Fiscal leadership will do neither of these things.
- The simultaneous moves regime will approach fiscal leadership as the debt rule becomes progressively "harder": $EL^g \to 0$, $\lambda^{cb*} \to 0$; $\pi_t^* \to \hat{\pi}$, and $E\tau_t^* \to 0$, as $\lambda_2^g \to \infty$.

B. The Coordination Effect

One of the central issues in the coordination literature is whether there are institutional arrangements that yield Pareto improvements over standard non-cooperative outcomes.[34] When such institutions exist, they may be viewed as a coordination device.

In our model, the central bank is independent. Without further institutional restraints, interactions between an independent central bank and the government would lead to non-cooperative outcomes. But if the government is committed to long term leadership in the manner we have described, the policy game will become an example of rule-based coordination in which both parties can gain without any reduction in the central bank's independence. However, that is not to say that both parties gain equally. If the inflation target is strengthened after fiscal policy is set, the leadership gains to the government will be less. This is an important point

33 We show this formally in *Hughes Hallett/Weymark* (2004a).

34 See *Currie et al* (1989) pp. 14- 47; *Currie/Levine* (1991) pp. 379- 417; *Hughes Hallett* (1992,1998); *Hughes Hallett/Viegi* (2002) pp. 341-362.

because it also means that granting leadership to a central bank whose inflation aversion is already greater than the government's, or whose commitment is greater, can produce no additional gains. In our model, as already explained, it is the impact of optimisation on debt repayments that produces the coordination gains associated with fiscal leadership. For that reason too, granting leadership to a central bank that cannot influence debt repayments directly, but puts a higher priority on inflation control, will bring smaller gains from society's point of view than the other way around (whatever it may do for the central bank).[35] Finally, given the structure of a Stackelberg game, there is no incentive to reoptimise for either party (Government or Central Bank) – so long as the government remains committed to long term leadership rather than short term demand management – unless both parties agree to reduce their independence through discretionary coordination.[36] That is a general result: it holds for any model where inflation and output both depend on both monetary and fiscal policy, and where inflation is targeted to some degree by both players.[37] Consequently, although coordination gains (Pareto improvements) do not always emerge for both parties in a Stackelberg game compared to a non-cooperative one, they will always do so in problems of the sort discussed here. Our results are therefore robust.

V. Summary and Conclusions

Fiscal leadership leads to improved outcomes because it implies a degree of coordination and reduced conflicts between institutions, without the central bank having to lose its ability to act independently. This places the outcomes somewhere between the superior (but discretionary) policies of complete cooperation; and the non-cooperative (but rule based) policies of complete independence.

---

35 These points are demonstrated formally in *Hughes Hallett* (2005).

36 This supplies the political economy of our results. We need no pre-commitment beyond leadership (the Stackelberg game supplies subgame perfection: see note 3) and no punishment beyond electoral results. The former will hold so long as governments have a natural commitment to sustainable public finances, or to public services (health, education, defence), or to a degree of social equity, all longer term "contractural" issues. The latter will then arise naturally from the political competition inherent in any democratic system.

37 See *Hughes Hallett/Viegi* (2002) pp. 341-362; *Demertzis et al* (2004) pp. 907-922.

The coordination gains come from the self-limiting action of fiscal policy when fiscal policy is given a long run focus in the form of a (possibly soft) debt rule. Leadership is the crucial element however; those gains do not appear in a competitive regime with the same debt rule.

Debt ratios increase in an optimal game without coordination, but do not do so under fiscal leadership.

Although it is hard to get definitive results from observation, the incentive to adopt fiscal leadership is clear from the theoretical results. Confirmation comes from the numerical evaluations in *Hughes Hallett* (2005), which show the fiscal leadership model predicts improvements in inflation and fiscal discipline worth 2%-4% of GDP in the OECD, without any losses in growth. In addition, leadership requires less precision in setting the strategic and institutional parameters than other strategies. It is easier to implement.

References

Barro R. J. (1981), Output Effects of Government Purchases, in: Journal of Political Economy 89, 1981, pp. 1086-1121.

Barro R. J. / Gordon D. B. (1983), Rules, Discretion, and Reputation in a Model of Monetary Policy, in: Journal of Monetary Economics 12, 1983, pp. 101-121.

Basar T. (1989), Time Consistency and Robustness of Equilibria in Non-Cooperative Dynamic Games, in: *van der Ploeg F. / de Zeeuw A.* (eds.), Dynamic Policy Games in Economics, North Holland, Amsterdam 1989, pp. 9-54.

Brandsma A. / Hughes Hallett A. (1984), Economic Conflict and the Solution of Dynamic Games, in: European Economic Review 26, 1984, pp. 13-32.

Calmfors L. / Corsetti G. (2003), How to Reform Europe's Fiscal Policy Framework, mimeo, University of Stockholm, 2003.

CESifo (2003), EEAG Report on the European Economy: 2003, Ifo Institute, Munich.

Currie D. A. / Holtham G. / Hughes Hallett A. (1989), The Theory and Practice of International Economic Policy Coordination: Does Coordination Pay?, in: *Bryant R. / Currie D. / Frenkel J. / Masson P. / Portes R.* (eds.), Macroeconomic Policies in an Interdependent World, International Monetary Fund, Washington DC, 1989, pp. 14- 47.

Currie D. / Levine P. (1991), The international Coordination of Monetary Policy: A Survey, in: *Green C. / Llewellyn D.* (eds.), Surveys in Monetary Economics, Vol I, Blackwell and Co, Oxford 1991, pp. 379- 417.

Demertzis M. / Hughes Hallett A. / Viegi N. (2004), An Independent Central Bank Faced with Elected Governments, in: European Journal of Political Economy 20, 2004, pp. 907-922.

Dixit A. (2001), Games of Monetary and Fiscal Interactions in the EMU, in: European Economic Review 45, 2001, pp. 589-613.

Dixit A.K. / Lambertini L. (2003), Interactions of Commitment and Discretion in Monetary and Fiscal Issues, in: American Economic Review 93, 2003, pp. 1522-1542.

Fatas A. / von Hagen J. / Hughes Hallett A. / Strauch R. / Sibert A. (2003), Stability and Growth in Europe, MEI-13,Centre for Economic Policy Research, London 2003.

HM Treasury (2003), Fiscal Stabilisation and EMU, HM Stationary Office, Cmnd 799373, Norwich 2003, also available from www.hm-treasury.gov.uk.

Hughes Hallett A. (1992), Target Zones and International Policy Coordination, in: European Economic Review 36, 1992, pp. 893-914.

Hughes Hallett A. (1998), When Do Target Zones Work?, in: Open Economies Review 9, 1998, pp. 115-138.

Hughes Hallett A. (2005), In Praise of Fiscal Restraints and Debt Rules: What the Eurozone Might Do, Discussion Paper 5043, Centre for Economic Policy Research, London 2005.

Hughes Hallett A. / Weymark D. (2002), Government Leadership and Central Bank Design, Discussion Paper 3395, Centre for Economic Research, London 2002.

Hughes Hallett A. / Viegi N. (2002), Inflation Targeting as a Coordination Device, in: Open Economies Review 13, 2002, pp. 341-362.

Hughes Hallett A. / Weymark D. (2004a), Policy Games and the Optimal Design of Central Banks, in: *Minford P.* (ed.), Money Matters, Edward Elgar, London 2004, pp. 251-279.

Hughes Hallett A. / Weymark D. (2004b), Independent Monetary Policies and Social Equity, in: Economics Letters 85, 2004, pp. 103-110.

Hughes Hallett A. / Weymark D. (2005), Independence before Conservatism: Transparency, Politics and Central Bank Design, in: German Economic Review 6, pp. 1-21.

Issing O. (1999), The Monetary Policy of the Eurosystem, in: Finance and Development, March 1999, pp. 18-21.

Lucas R. E. (1972), Expectations and the Neutrality of Money, in: Journal of Economic Theory 4, 1972, pp. 103-124.

Lucas R. E. (1973), Some International Evidence on Output-Inflation Trade-Offs, in: American Economic Review 63, 1973, pp. 326-334.

McCallum B. T. (1989), Monetary Economics: Theory and Policy, Macmillan, New York 1989.

Pisani-Ferry J. (2002), Fiscal Discipline and Policy Coordination in the Eurozone: Assessment and Proposals, mimeo, Universite Paris-Dauphine, Paris 2002.

Saraceno F. / Monperrus-Veroni P. (2004), A Simple Proposal for a Debt Sensitive Stability Pact, in: Quarterly Bulletin of Economic Research: DIW Berlin, 73, 2004, pp. 471-480.

Taylor J. B. (1993), Macroeconomic Policy in a World Economy: From Econometric Design to Practical Operation, W.W. Norton and Company, New York 1993.

Taylor J. B. (2000), Discretionary Fiscal Policies, in: Journal of Economic Perspectives 14, 2000, pp. 1-23.

André Sapir

Re-orientation of the Stability and Growth Pact[1]

I. Introduction

Few issues have stirred as much controversy since the launch of the euro as the Stability and Growth Pact (SGP).[2] To its supporters the pact is the cornerstone of the rules governing the single currency, which must be upheld to ensure monetary stability and economic growth. To its detractors the pact is "a nuisance", whose strict application is detrimental to short-term or even long-term economic performance.

II. Fiscal consolidation

Section II of the paper by *Paul van den Noord* gives a clue as to why the SGP generates so much controversy. It makes it plain that there is no consensus over the rationale for the pact by rightly pointing out that it was designed to address three main concerns "whose relative weight have, however, evolved over time".

The first concern is that fiscal profligacy in one country could spill over into the entire euro area through the common interest rate, thereby penalising other countries. The second is that with the loss of the monetary instrument, macroeconomic stabilisation might be insufficient unless fiscal policy regains counter cyclicality. The third concern is the need for fiscal consolidation at a time when demographic developments risk jeopardising the sustainability of public finances. *Van den Noord* concludes that: "Over time, this consideration has gained prominence over the concerns regarding spill-over effects and fiscal stabilisation policy, *and is now seen as*

---

1 Comment on the paper by *Paul van den Noord*.

2 A search with Google returned nearly 300,000 web pages containing the expression "stability and growth pact".

the primary motivation for fiscal co-ordination in the euro area" (italics added).

I concur with the statement that fiscal consolidation is badly needed in many euro area countries to ensure sustainable public finances in the face of population ageing. I also agree that fiscal and monetary authorities in the euro area *now* see this consideration as the primary motivation for the SGP. However I question whether the SGP is the right instrument to address this issue and above all whether the electorate's perception matches the view of their economic authorities. My disbelief stems from the fact that fiscal and monetary authorities have not sufficiently engaged in the kind of pedagogical activities required to convince the public that the SGP usefully contributes to the sustainability of public finances.

Take the issue of pensions, which is clearly a primary concern of most European voters. Most citizens seem to be aware that important reforms are needed to ensure the sustainability of their pension system. But I doubt whether many would see any link between the SGP and pension reform. And why should they anyway? After all the 1997 Stability and Growth Pact contains no reference to the notion of public finance sustainability leave alone to ageing or to pensions.[3]

In the mind of the public, the SGP basically means that government deficits must remain below the 3-percent limit, although this obligation was already contained in the Treaty of Maastricht. By contrast, the central tenet of the pact, namely the requirement to respect 'the medium term objective of budgetary positions of close to balance or in surplus', was never grasped by the public.

No wonder, therefore, that *van den Noord* finds that: "Fiscal consolidation stalled as soon as the single currency was adopted," despite the fact that the medium term objective of the pact was clearly not fulfilled at the launch of the euro. In 1997, the year before the Council took the decision about the initial membership of the euro area in May 1998, five of its eleven initial members had *actual* deficits of around 3 percent: France (3%), Germany (2.7%), Italy (2.7%), Portugal (3.4%) and Spain (3.2%). All these countries also had high *cyclically adjusted* deficits [France (2.2%), Germany

---

3 See *Council Resolution* 1466/97 on the strengthening of the surveillance of budgetary positions and the surveillance and coordination of economic policies, and *Council Resolution* 1467/97 on speeding up and clarifying the implementation of the excessive deficit procedure.

(2.1%), Italy (3%), Portugal (3.2%) and Spain (2.4%)], which clearly pointed to potential problems for respecting the 'close to balance or in surplus' requirement.[4]

A firm commitment to the SGP would have demanded serious fiscal consolidation in these five countries in 1998 and beyond. In reality, little or no progress was accomplished by the time the cycle peaked in 2000, the fourth year in a row of GDP growth above potential in all the countries concerned. In 2000, cyclically adjusted deficits were still far from the SGP requirement in those countries: France (2.5%), Germany (1.8%), Italy (2.9%), Portugal (4.4%) and Spain (2%).[5] Hence it was nearly inevitable that actual deficits would jump above the 3-percent limit when the downturn came. And indeed, between 2001 and 2004, actual government deficits were almost consistently above the limit in four of the five countries.[6] The only country that succeeded in staying well below the mark and in having a structural budgetary position 'close to balance or in surplus' is Spain, which adopted in 2001 a 'General Law on Budgetary Stability' mandating a balanced budget.

The situation of France, Germany, Greece (which joined the euro area in 2001), Italy and Portugal amply demonstrates that the SGP suffered from two mutually reinforcing problems. The first is the lack of clear rationale in the mind of the public, at least in those countries where political authorities failed either to embrace the fiscal consolidation argument or to communicate it to their electorate. The second, as *Paul van den Noord* states, is that: "Since the SGP stipulated that fiscal positions have to be close to balance or in surplus 'over the medium run', there was no clear timetable for compliance."

The combination of tough but ill grounded and weakly enforced rules that characterised the 1997 Stability and Growth Pact was

---

4 Among the other six countries, two had positive cyclically adjusted budget positions and the other four had deficits between 1 and 1.8 percent.

5 By contrast, the situation had significantly improved in the other six countries of the euro area, with the exception of Austria. By 2000, Belgium, Finland, Ireland, Luxembourg and Netherlands were clearly fulfilling the "close to balance or in surplus" requirement.

6 Greece, which joined the euro area in January 2001, has been in a similar situation, with actual budget deficits well above the 3-percent reference value and cyclically adjusted deficits far from being "close to balance or in surplus" throughout the period 2001-2004.

bound to break under the weight of repeated violation by five countries, which together account for more than 70 percent of the GDP of the euro area.

The question now is whether the 2005 Stability and Growth Pact adopted last year will fare better than its predecessor. The new SGP is definitely more flexible than the old one. So the question really is whether it offers a combination of more flexible but also better grounded and more strongly enforced rules than its ill-fated forerunner. I will not discuss the issue of flexibility here. Instead I will concentrate on the two main themes on this comment: the pact's rationale and its compliance.

As far as the rationale is concerned, the 2005 Stability and Growth Pact makes it explicit that its main concern now is fiscal consolidation. The new pact makes numerous references to the need to safeguard the "sustainability of public finances" in the long run and even to "pension reforms".[7]

What is crucial now is that the clear commitment to fiscal consolidation taken at the European level translates into action at the national level, especially in the five violating countries discussed above. It is obviously much too early to judge compliance with the new SGP since it was only adopted in the spring of 2005. However, the latest round of Stability programmes submitted by the members of the euro area and their assessment by the European Commission points towards continued problems with fiscal consolidation.[8]

These documents indicate that none of the five delinquent countries plans to achieve a fiscal position 'close to balance or in surplus' by 2007. Their programmes forecast cyclically adjusted deficits ranging between 1.8% (for Germany) and 2.8% (for Greece) in 2007. What is even more worrisome is that the Commission views that these forecasts are far too optimistic. Its own forecast is that cyclically adjusted deficits will actually range between 3% (for Germany) and 4.8% (for Greece), unless measures are taken. If the Commission's prediction turns out to be right, France, Germany, Italy and Portugal will be further away from 'the

7 See *Council Regulation* 1055/2005 amending *Council Regulation* 1466/97 on the strengthening of the surveillance of budgetary positions and the surveillance and coordination of economic policies, and Council Regulation amending *Council Regulation* 1467/97 on speeding up and clarifying the implementation of the excessive deficit procedure.

8 See http://europa.eu.int/comm/economy_finance/about/activities/sgp/year/year20052006_en.htm

medium term objective of budgetary positions of close to balance or in surplus' in 2007 than they were in 1997![9]

III. Conclusion

To conclude, I fully applaud the re-orientation of the Stability and Growth Pact towards the sustainability of public finances. If anything, I wish it had been even stronger. But in the end, the new pact, like the old one, will be judged on how well it is enforced. It can be argued that enforcement will be easier now that the pact has a stronger and clearer economic rationale. However, this is likely to be only part of the story. Effective enforcement also requires that national authorities share a sense of ownership towards the rules of the pact in general and towards fiscal sustainability in particular. The latest round of Stability programmes does not yet demonstrate that the five delinquent members of the euro area have taken sufficient ownership of the process to make it a success. A rapid turnaround on their part is needed if the new SGP is to avoid the fate of the old one.

---

9 The cyclically adjusted deficits for the respective countries are: France (3.1 in 2007 vs. 2.2% in 1997), Germany (3 vs. 2.1%), Italy (4 vs. 3%) and Portugal (3.6 vs. 3.2%). For Greece, there would be a slight improvement, although still with a huge deficit (4.8 vs. 5.6%).

Ewald Nowotny[1]

The debate on the SGP

I. Introduction

Starting point of *Prof. Hallett`s* paper is the view, that there is a need for reform of the SGP. Reform should bring more flexibility, but preserve sustainable public finances and credibility of the policy mix.

The debate on the SGP, as we know it, usually is about changes within the context of the SGP, e.g. referring to debt levels instead of deficits. *Hughes Hallett* takes a more fundamental and very interesting approach: He analyzes the problem as a policy game with two players – fiscal policy by governments and parliaments on the one hand and monetary policy, executed by the ECB. The interesting questions now are how to allow coordination without surrendering ECB independence and how to create an adequate incentive structure to conform with a new SGP.

II. The Stackelberg solution

I very much agree with his view that the aspect of incentive structures is more important than the question of hard or soft SGP criteria. The basic idea of the paper is that this game between fiscal and monetary policy should be solved in the way of a Stackelberg solution, i.e. one player takes leadership, and the other player reacts in an independent way, but this is reflected by the first player. So this Stackelberg solution is situated between a fully cooperative solution and a fully independent solution. The provocative twist (at least from a Frankfurt – ECB point of view) is his proposed divi-

---

1 Comment on the paper by *Prof. Andrew Hughes Hallett.*

sion of power between fiscal and monetary policy. Here his view is very innovative and is in fact worlds apart from the philosophy underlying the ECB – set-up, as represented e.g. in the writings of *Prof. Issing*, ECB-chief economist. I try to give a stylized overview of these two concepts, hoping to be fair to both of the two eminent economists.

Table 1: Two concepts of monetary and fiscal policy interaction

Hallett	**Issing**
• Inflation target set in cooperation, central bank has instrument independence	• Central bank has (specific) target independence and instrument independence
• Fiscal and monetary policy independent, but policy coordination	• Fiscal and monetary policy independent, coordination only via hard SGP criteria for fiscal policy
• Fiscal policy sticks to long-run policies, cyclical stabilization by activist monetary policy	• Neutrality of money, monetary policy oriented on long term price stability
• UK example (Treasury): automatic stabilizers stabilize about 30 % of the UK cycle, 70 % being left to monetary policy	• Stabilization only via automatic stabilizers and fully flexible markets
• In coordination leadership role for fiscal policy	• Leader trip role for monetary policy via direct and indirect sanctions

A first difference concerns targeting. Here the most important difference is not with regard to the policy goals as such, but between the notions of target independence and instrument independence of Central Banks. This then leads to the question whether there is a need of policy coordination between fiscal and monetary policies or whether there should be a strategy of separated policies and responsibilities. The latter is the view of the ECB, which sees policy coordination as a one-way approach, based on the criteria of the Stability Pact. This ECB-approach is also very different from the largely successful interplay of monetary and fiscal policy, which is an important structure of US economic governance.

A basic notion concerns the concept of “neutrality of monetary policy” – quasi a “litmus-test” between Keynesian and Monetarist views. The basic idea of the SGP, that markets are inherently stabile if they are only flexible enough and that economic stabilization policies, if need shod arise, should be restricted to automatic stabilizer – effects can be interpreted as a return to a pre-Keynesian world. This view is not supported by empirical evidence both in Europe and in the US and he also cites detailed studies that demonstrate both the need and the effectiveness of a more activist – non-neutral-monetary policy.

III. The results

Prof. Hallett in his paper now discusses the differences between his approach and the EMU-approach with regard to institutional, empirical, theoretical and policy aspects.

The main results of his very elaborate and convincing studies are:

- Fiscal leadership leads to improved outcomes.
- The crucial element is that fiscal policy has to be given a long run focus. This may be in the form of a soft debt rule, but the decisive element is fiscal policy leadership.
- For monetary policy instrument independence is decisive, whereas target independence could have the effect of undoing the complementarily between fiscal and monetary policies.

These results are very convincing and well founded. Two crucial questions, that are interconnected, however remain:

- Is the UK that forms the basis for institutional and empirical comparisons in this paper a specific case relative to the rest of Europe?
- What could be the policy recommendations to be derived from this paper?

Concerning the first question it seems to me that there are in fact many monetary aspects, where the UK is more comparable to the US than to the rest of Europe:

The main point is that we can expect a significantly higher interest rate-elasticity of investment and especially of consumption. This means that monetary policy is in a position to exert a much stronger and faster stabilization effect. The main channel is supposed to be via a higher degree of personal debt, mainly connected with home ownership. In the UK the percentage of private home-ownership is much higher than in most other Europe countries and this ownership is financed via private sector mortgage markets, whereas in most other European countries public financing plans a larger role.

Housing costs thus are much more interest sensitive in the UK and thus changes of interest levels directly affect the income available for other forms of consumption. In addition via home-ownership and via a stronger role of stock-markets asset price movements have a stronger impact on consumption and investment – these movements of asset prices being again very much sensitive to monetary policy. Thus altogether in the UK we can expect monetary policy to be able to deliver efficiently with regard to cyclical stabilization, whereas this may be significantly different in continental Europe. It has to be added however that continental Europe is moving in the Anglo-Saxon direction, so in future these differences may become smaller.

Concerning policy recommendation the recommendation for fiscal leadership seems to me to rest heavily on a specific institutional structure: *Prof. Hallett* stresses the long-term elements of fiscal policy, involving specific long-term objectives like long-term fiscal sustainability, long term planning both with regard to the expenditure and to the taxation side. This makes perfectly sense. The question however remains, whether this is also applicable for the EMU, where we do not have just one country but twelve countries, different electoral cycles, different policy goals, massive tax competition, etc. In such a context it seems difficult to imagine an efficient fiscal leadership, as it is difficult to see who would be the leader.

IV. Conclusion

Maybe I am to pessimistic, but I have the feeling, that his paper supports the views of those, who during the debate on EMU held the view that before entering EMU there should be substantial political unification in the field of fiscal policy (or at least substantial coordination).

Part 3:
The Theoretical Basis of the SGP

Wilhelm Kohler[1]

On the Theoretical Underpinning of the Stability and Growth Pact

I. Introduction

The Maastricht Treaty of 1992 has installed a special procedure to enforce fiscal discipline and convergence as a precondition for a country to participate in the Economic and Monetary Union (EMU). As regards government finance, the entry conditions, commonly referred to as the Maastricht criteria, specify a reference value for a country's general government net borrowing equal to 3 percent of its GDP, and for gross government debt equal to 60 percent of GDP. The Treaty of Amsterdam, signed in 1997, has enshrined such reference values in the so-called Stability and Growth Pact (SGP), which is intended an integral part of the practical operation of EMU.[2] While the reference value for debt still con-

---

1 I am grateful to *Helen Lückge* for valuable research assistance. Thanks go to *Gabriel Felbermayr* for helpful comments on an earlier version of this paper. Special thanks are due to *Waltraud Schelkle* for very detailed and constructive comments on the paper delivered at the conference. I am also grateful to *Heiiki Oksanen* and *Werner Roeger* for comments on a presentation at the DG EcfinI of the European Commission.

2 Indeed, the Maastricht criteria are both an entry ticket and an entry

stitutes a requirement for future entry of new members, it loses relevance once a country becomes a member. On the other hand, in addition to the 3 percent reference value for *actual* net government borrowing, the Pact also requires each member country government to aim for a *medium term* budgetary position which is "close to balance or in surplus." A surveillance procedure is meant to ensure consistency of each government's fiscal policy with this requirement, and with a proper functioning of EMU more generally. More importantly, if a country exceeds the 3 percent reference value, a so-called Excessive Deficit Procedure (EDP) is set in operation which involves corrective action, and even fines in case of lasting violation. The SGP thus includes an enforcement mechanism which is unusually tough for agreements between sovereign nations.[3]

At the time of the Amsterdam Treaty, *Eichengreen / Wyplosz* have argued that the SGP might be no more than a minor nuisance "if European countries succeed in moving their budgets into balance or, better, into surplus, making room for their automatic stabilizers to work. But if their deficits remain right up against their 3% reference values when EMU begins, the pact becomes more of a problem."[4] While early EMU experience has been reassuring, recent developments have been more sobering and it now seems that the SGP has become more than just a minor nuisance. Its application is causing headache and debate in several member countries, as well as in Brussels. The crucial question is: Has it become a nuisance in a purposeful way, i.e., an intended disciplinary nuisance to governments who have ignored important economic principles, thus endangering stability, not only in their own countries, but also in the EMU as a whole? Or is it a counterproductive nuisance, not serving any useful purpose, perhaps even forming an obstacle for well-balanced macroeconomic policies and a distraction of political reform capacity from more important policy areas, like labor market and commodity market deregulation.[5]

There is no way of denying that, from the start, economists have

---

obligation, unless there is an "opting out clause", as for the UK and Denmark.

3 See *Buiter/Grafe* (2003) for a concise description of the SGP.

4 See *Eichengreen/Wyplosz* (1998) p. 104.

5 Well-balanced macroeconomic policies play an important role, not only with respect to short-run macroeconomic performance over the business cycle, but also with respect to long-run evolution of productivity; see *Baily/Kirkegaard* (2004).

been less than fully convinced about the rationale behind the fiscal criteria for Euro-eligibility laid down in the Maastricht Treaty.[6] The same holds true for the SGP as a governing principle for operating the EMU.[7] Indeed, as I shall try to show in this paper, from an economic theory point of view the SGP is difficult to justify. Yet, questioning the economic rationale of the specific rules of SGP, or – more fundamentally – the principal need of a supra-national fiscal constraint, is often regarded as advocating irresponsible fiscal policies. This is unfortunate. It is almost trivial that the SGP is conducive to fiscal discipline. But not everything that does so is necessarily good, or worth having. There are always side effects to be considered, and the economist's approach in such cases is to identify first-best solutions and avoid arrangements that are second- or third-best. It is probably true that fiscal prudence is hard to attain without fiscal rules. However, trying to enforce rules that lack a convincing theoretical rationale and have unintended and unwelcome effects, even if exerting some disciplinary effect, is not necessarily an improvement. The problem is aggravated by the fact that the SGP departs in a rather fundamental way from conventional fiscal rules in that it is supra-national in nature, including cross-country coercive elements. These are hard to swallow, and they need appropriate justification in an environment like the EU where fiscal policies have deliberately *not* been centralized. A key question is whether something of this sort is necessary for, or at least strongly conducive to, a stable macroeconomic environment, if monetary policy *is* centralized, as in the EMU.

Political pressure, as well as a recent ruling of the European Court of Justice on the ECOFIN decision to suspend the Commission recommendation to initiate an EDP against France and Germany, has prompted the European Commission to issue a Communication on reforming the SGP.[8] The Commission does not question the necessity of the Pact as such, but it proposes to remove what may be called "excessive uniformity" in the deficit procedure, coupled with an increase in transparency in order to avoid abuse of

6 See in particular *Buiter et al.* (1993).

7 See *Eichengreen/Wyplosz* (1998).

8 See "Strengthening economic governance and clarifying the implementation of the Growth and Stability Pact", Communication from the Commission to the Council and the European Parliament, 3 September 2004.

procedural flexibility. Not surprisingly, the proposal has met harsh criticism from staunch supporters of the SGP who argue that such flexibility is fundamentally at odds with the principal orientation and very purpose of the SGP.

In this paper, I do not intend to evaluate the Commission proposal, but the issues of uniformity and flexibility will come up at certain stages of my analysis.[9] What I want to do instead is to explore, on a fundamental level, the possible theoretical underpinnings for an SGP-like institution as a necessary, or at least useful, part of the European Monetary Union. By SGP-like institution, I mean a fiscal constraint imposed on independent countries that form a monetary union which is characterized by an almost complete absence of fiscal centralization. Moreover, I mean a constraint that is focused on "single-number" deficit and debt ceilings, and is applied uniformly to all countries. The SGP-like rule is meant to draw its justification entirely from monetary union, although pre-existing imperfections of fiscal systems in constituent countries may play a role. And finally, it is a rule that is self-imposed ex ante, jointly by all members of the monetary union, and enforced ex post by these same countries. For a large part of my analysis, this rather "soft" and general description of an "SGP-like institution" will do, since I shall focus on principle lines of argument. Reference to more detailed rules of the SGP will be made where appropriate as I go along.

The purpose of the paper is a structured synthesis of various strands of theoretical reasoning that may be invoked as a theoretical underpinning of an SGP-like arrangement. The vastly different orientations of reasoning involved are almost impossible to incorporate into a single theoretical model. I shall thus largely abstain from explicit modeling. Although the paper is not intended as a direct contribution to the ongoing reform discussion, the insights gained should be helpful to avoid certain pitfalls on the road to a better way of dealing with independent fiscal policies in the European Monetary Union.

The paper is structured as follows. Section II presents some empirical evidence on how close European economies have been, throughout the past 15 years, to the reference values of the SGP. Section III then briefly investigates how far conventional theory of

---

[9] The Commission proposal finds detailed scrutiny in *Eijffinger* (2005), *Gros* (2005) and *Hefeker* (2005).

optimum currency areas can take us in underpinning the Pact, including some suggestive empirical evidence from other monetary unions. In section IV, I shall address the issue from a policy coordination perspective, to see if a rationale can be found from coordination failure, i.e., inefficiency of non-cooperative fiscal policies in a monetary union. Section V then moves on to the standard argument that the SGP is needed to compensate for the notorious European tendency to run excessive public deficits. I define an excessive deficit path as arising from policy and/or market failures, but not necessarily a path leading to government insolvency. Finally, in section VI I turn to the potential role that the pact may play for avoiding government insolvency, and the international spill-overs within a monetary union that may arise from such insolvency. Section VII will briefly look at the "numerology" of the pact, and section VIII concludes the paper.

II. Some empirics of the SGP

This section substantiates the point mentioned above that of the two scenarios envisaged by *Eichengreen/Wyplosz* (1998), the less optimistic one appears to have materialized. For instance, the Commission and Council actions under the excessive deficit procedure (EDP) have no doubt been more numerous, particularly in 2003 and 2004, than expected under a "smooth-operation-scenario".[10] A more comprehensive and telling view on how successful the Pact was in terms of enforcing its own criteria of fiscal prudence is presented in table 1, which covers the 1990's-period leading up to EMU, as well as the first years of EMU-practice under the SGP, including forecasts where available. Since the criteria are addressed to all EU members, the table covers all EU-15 countries, but leaves out the new members from Eastern Europe.

As a first measure, table 1 looks at the number of countries with net-lending-positions below –3, –2, –1, and 0 percent of GDP, or with a surplus, during the period in question. The next four columns measure the share of EU-15 GDP "at risk" in the sense of the SGP deficit criterion of 3 percent, fist taking all countries with excessive

[10] I abstain from a detailed recount of the EDP-history. Details on these actions may be found on http://europa.eu.int/comm/economy_finance/about/activities/sgp/procedures_en.htm.

deficits,[11] and then isolating those few cases where the deficit-country is hit during the same year by an "exceptionally severe recession" (real growth lower than –2 percent), by a "severe recession" (real growth between –2 and –0.75 percent), or by a "plain recession" (negative growth). It becomes clear very quickly that the justification of excessive deficits by recessions plays a minor role. The table then gives the same measure for countries with deficits between 2 and 3 percent, and correspondingly for lower intervals, followed by those with a surplus, and reiterating the exercise focusing on overall government expenditure "at risk", instead of GDP.[12] The picture is roughly the same for both measures. The next columns give weighted averages of annual deficits and cyclically adjusted deficits, first using GDPs, and then using government expenditure as weights. The table also includes a column with net-lending adjusted for public gross fixed capital formation (investment) in percent of GDP.[13] And finally, table 1 reports the stock of EU-15-wide gross government debt.

[11] The measure is defined as $\sum_{i=1}^{15} d_{it} Y_{it} / Y_{Et}$, where Y_{it} and Y_{Et}, respectively, are country i's and EU-15 GDP in year t, and d_{it} is a dummy with value 1 if country i's deficit was excessive (>3% of GDP), and 0 otherwise. For the expenditure-related measure we simply replace Y_{it} by overall government expenditure.

[12] See the previous footnote.

[13] The numbers are net lending ratios (negative for deficit countries) plus investment ratios.

Table 1: Net-lending by general government in EU-15 countries (to be continued)

	# of countries with net lending < x percent of GDP					GDP-share of countries with net lending below x percent of GDP							
Year	<-3%	<-2%	<-1%	<0%	Surplus	< -3%				[-3, -2]	[-2, -1]	[-1, 0]	Surplus
						all	exc. rec.	sev. rec.	rec.				
1992	9	11	12	12	3	0,5971	0,0139	0,0000	0,0000	0,2658	0,0249	0,0000	0,1122
1993	11	13	13	13	2	0,8749	0,0000	0,6925	0,0000	0,0528	0,0000	0,0000	0,0723
1994	11	12	13	13	2	0,6457	0,0000	0,0000	0,0000	0,2780	0,0073	0,0000	0,0690
1995	13	14	14	14	1	0,9902	0,0000	0,0000	0,0000	0,0077	0,0000	0,0000	0,0021
1996	9	11	13	14	1	0,8768	0,0000	0,0000	0,0000	0,0453	0,0676	0,0083	0,0021
1997	3	7	11	13	2	0,0955	0,0000	0,0000	0,0000	0,7271	0,1153	0,0504	0,0118
1998	1	7	7	9	6	0,0131	0,0000	0,0000	0,0000	0,6687	0,0000	0,0753	0,2428
1999	0	2	7	8	7	0,0000	0,0000	0,0000	0,0000	0,0383	0,6374	0,0293	0,2950
2000	1	2	4	6	9	0,0144	0,0000	0,0000	0,0000	0,0135	0,1902	0,2073	0,5746
2001	2	4	5	7	8	0,0286	0,0000	0,0000	0,0000	0,3712	0,1664	0,1221	0,3117
2002	3	5	7	10	5	0,4112	0,0000	0,0000	0,0000	0,1513	0,2293	0,1141	0,0941
2003	5	7	8	8	7	0,6318	0,0000	0,0488	0,2285	0,1537	0,0243	0,0000	0,1902
2004*	3	7	8	12	3	0,4078	0,0000	0,0000	0,0000	0,3772	0,0239	0,1281	0,0641
2005*	3	7	9	12	3	0,2516	0,0000	0,0000	0,0000	0,5263	0,0265	0,1277	0,0649
2006*	3	7	9	11	4	0,3191	0,0000	0,0000	0,0000	0,4557	0,0264	0,0451	0,1497

	Public expenditure share of countries with net lending below x percent of GDP					expenditure share of countries with net lending below x percent of GDP				
Year	< -3%	[- 3, -2]	[- 2, -1]	[-1, 0]	surplus	< -3%	[-3, -2]	[- 2,-1]	[-1, 0]	surplus
1992	0,6898	0,2792	0,0292	0,0000	0,0017	0,6898	0,2792	0,0292	0,0000	0,0017
1993	0,9399	0,0583	0,0000	0,0000	0,0018	0,9399	0,0583	0,0000	0,0000	0,0018
1994	0,7110	0,2805	0,0067	0,0000	0,0019	0,7110	0,2805	0,0067	0,0000	0,0019
1995	0,9919	0,0062	0,0000	0,0000	0,0019	0,9919	0,0062	0,0000	0,0000	0,0019
1996	0,8655	0,0564	0,0698	0,0065	0,0018	0,8655	0,0564	0,0698	0,0065	0,0018
1997	0,0836	0,7256	0,1196	0,0620	0,0092	0,0836	0,7256	0,1196	0,0620	0,0092
1998	0,0120	0,6878	0,0000	0,0758	0,2243	0,0120	0,6878	0,0000	0,0758	0,2243
1999	0,0000	0,0404	0,6547	0,0308	0,2741	0,0000	0,0404	0,6547	0,0308	0,2741
2000	0,0163	0,0133	0,2176	0,2016	0,5512	0,0163	0,0133	0,2176	0,2016	0,5512
2001	0,0293	0,3807	0,1849	0,1094	0,2958	0,0293	0,3807	0,1849	0,1094	0,2958
2002	0,4371	0,1515	0,2069	0,0991	0,1054	0,4371	0,1515	0,2069	0,0991	0,1054
2003	0,6377	0,1548	0,0254	0,0000	0,1821	0,6377	0,1548	0,0254	0,0000	0,1821
2004*	0,4274	0,3615	0,0252	0,1126	0,0734	0,4274	0,3615	0,0252	0,1126	0,0734
2005*	0,2482	0,5374	0,0275	0,1126	0,0743	0,2482	0,5374	0,0275	0,1126	0,0743
2006*	0,3470	0,4369	0,0270	0,0428	0,1463	0,3470	0,4369	0,0270	0,0428	0,1463

Table 1(continued): Net-lending by general government in EU-15 countries

Year	average net lending					aggreg. gross debt-ratio
	GDP-weighted			expend.-weighted		
	current	cycl. adj.	net of inv.	current	cycl. adj.	
1992	-4,8078	-5,0274	-1,2060	-5,5192	-5,7383	58,9469
1993	-5,6926	-4,9594	-1,0577	-6,2518	-5,3967	64,6169
1994	-4,9438	-4,6041	-0,9040	-5,3848	-4,9817	66,9349
1995	-5,1499	-4,8954	-0,6945	-5,1766	-4,9059	70,3117
1996	-4,1812	-3,7562	-0,1534	-4,1778	-3,7382	72,1442
1997	-2,4502	-2,2659	1,0257	-2,4462	-2,2432	71,0407
1998	-1,6699	-1,7987	1,5880	-1,7069	-1,8234	68,9343
1999	-0,7264	-1,1067	2,3935	-0,7758	-1,1617	67,4208
2000	0,9614	-1,1820	0,9522	0,8290	-1,2484	64,3414
2001	-1,0341	-1,6899	1,8377	-1,0808	-1,7413	63,0871
2002	-2,1171	-2,1776	1,2624	-2,1582	-2,2281	62,8767
2003	-2,6535	-2,1965	1,3976	-2,6957	-2,2312	64,3596
2004*	-2,6898	-2,1514	1,4060	-2,7041	-2,1781	64,6269
2005*	-2,3426	-2,0831	1,3958	-2,3590	-2,1254	64,4042
2006*	-2,2775	0,0000	:	-2,3121	0,0000	64,1667

Source: Government data from European Commission, ECOFIN, Economic data bases and statistical co-ordination, General government data (Autumn 2004) and Cyclical adjustment of budget balances (Autumn 2004). GDP-data from Eurostat, GDP and main components at current prices. *: Forecasts by the Commission Services (ECOFIN).

The basic message, further illustrated by figures 1 and 2, is easy to discern. During the 90's, running up to the start of EMU in 1999, all countries have significantly improved their deficit positions, but subsequent to the start of EMU there has been a significant worsening again. Indeed, there is but one year where no country had an excessive deficit by the SGP criterion (higher then 3 percent of GDP), and this is 1999, year one of EMU (see figure 2). Although growth has been worsening in the early years of this decade, it is difficult to justify the recent worsening of net-lending positions by recessions. Instead, the picture seems to indicate a certain degree of reform fatigue. Figure 1 highlights this by depicting the GDP-share of countries with deficit-ratios that fall into separate intervals. Thus, by 1995 almost the entire GDP of the EU-15 was "at risk" in the sense of the SGP excessive deficit criterion. This share has fallen to zero in 1999 when EMU has started, but by 2003 it has risen again to more than 60 percent, with excessive deficits in four countries: Germany, Greece, France, and the Netherlands. A mirror-image pattern is observed for surplus countries, and for countries with deficit-ratios in the interval between 3 and 2 percent of GDP.

Figure 2 gives a more continuous measure of the fiscal stance of EU-15 by looking at the GDP-weighted average of national deficit ratios. There is but one period with an overall surplus, year 2001, which forms a peak followed by marked deterioration. Moreover, the cyclically adjusted deficit follows roughly the same pattern. The EU-15 as a whole is thus still quite far from the medium-run target of "close to balance" public finances.

Figure 1: GDP-shares of EU15 countries in different ranges of net lending in percent of GDP

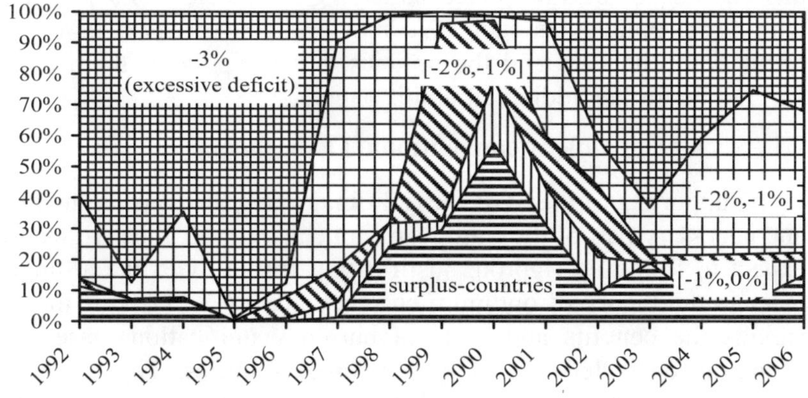

Source: See table 1.

Figure 2: General government net lending in percent of GDP (GDP-weighted average of EU15 countries)

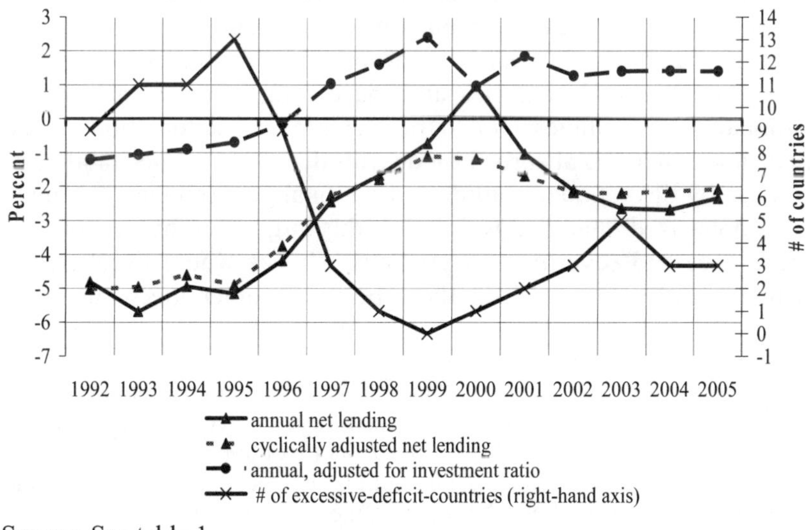

Source: See table 1.

It is difficult to avoid the conclusion from this brief empirical view that the SGP has not been a self-enforcing contract. Taking into account the severe difficulties of invoking its own enforcement mechanism in the case of France and Germany,[14] the situation is certainly one where the SGP is more than just a minor nuisance. The question, then, is whether we should worry about fiscal policy as such, or about the Pact. The subsequent sections of the paper enquire into possible theoretical justifications of the Pact, and I shall argue that these are somewhat difficult to come by. However, this should not be interpreted as saying that there is no problem with fiscal policies as such. We may well have reason to worry about both, the Pact and the policies, but the policies themselves will not be further addressed in this paper.

III. A brief look at conventional OCA-theory

If supporters of the SGP are right in arguing that it is an integral and necessary part of the European Monetary Union, then we would expect to find duly rigorous justification for an SGP-like arrangement in the theory of optimum currency areas (OCA). This theory weighs the benefits and costs of currency unification, based on economic characteristics of participating countries. Thus, considering the specific characteristics of EMU member countries, can the SGP be seen as a useful device to minimize the cost of having a common currency?

Traditional OCA theory suggests that currency areas should either have a significant amount of fiscal centralization, so that asymmetric shocks can partly be absorbed by asymmetric transfers between individual countries and the central government, or else national fiscal policies should be flexible and autonomous, such that shocks may be absorbed by decentralized automatic stabilizers, or even by discretionary policies of national governments.[15] It must be emphasized that the weight of this argument hinges on the prevalence and severity of asymmetric shocks where fiscal policy makes a difference, and on there being no other mechanisms of

---

14 In November 2003, Ecofin Council has suspended a Commission recommendation to start sanctions against these two countries. The Court of Justice has, in turn, ruled in July 2004 that there is no obligation for the Council to take any decision, but that its declaration on France and Germany was illegal, thus abrogating the council decision.

15 See *De Grauwe* (2003a) ch. 9.

shock absorption, like international factor mobility within the union, or flexibility of nominal prices.[16] In the European context, the argument clearly has some validity. Oddly enough, however, it is largely ignored by SGP, which puts national fiscal policies under a strict rule which may become a binding constraint for efficient decentralized stabilization, despite there being no apparent willingness of the EU to generate even moderate fiscal centralization.[17] To be fair, it needs to be emphasized here that the SGP does allow for considerable flexibility for countries to absorb fiscal implications of business cycles. Indeed, the specific "numerology" of the Pact may be "read in reverse", inferring an implicit underlying view of the fiscal consequences of the business cycle for a typical European economy.[18] But if the future course of economic development in Euroland defies the underlying numerical assumptions of the SGP,[19] then there are ample possibilities for the Pact to become a severely binding constraint for optimizing national fiscal policies along the lines of the "asymmetric shocks paradigm" of OCA. The conclusion at this stage thus is that the SGP is grossly at odds with OCA theory.

However, supporters of the SGP will probably regard this as a strawman-type argument. More specifically, the theory of OCA seems like an ill-guided paradigm for evaluating the SGP, since it relies on questionable assumptions: nominal rigidities coupled with money illusion, relevance of fiscal policy for asymmetric shocks. Perhaps most importantly, it relies on the notion that benevolent and well-informed governments use fiscal policy to correct market failures leading to excessive costs from asymmetric shocks. Any

---

16 These are standard caveats of OCA theory that I do not elaborate in this paper. It should also be pointed out here that countries participating in a currency union forgo a useful adjustment mechanism only if the adjustment problem is not caused by real price rigidity, and to the extent that there is money illusion.

17 Proposals towards some fiscal centralization within the EU have on occasions been made, such as for instance in the so-called MacDougall report, but they were never favorably received; see *Masson* (1996).

18 There are, however, several ways of inferring key numerical assumptions that may have played a role in designing the SGP numerology, and no "official" reasoning has ever been given for the specific numbers chosen; see *Buiter/Grafe* (2003). I shall return to the "numerology" in section VII below.

19 See *Canzoneri/Diba* (2001).

one of these premises seems questioned by modern macroeconomics, which focuses on government failures, particularly regarding fiscal policy incentives, and on coordination failures due to cross-country spill-over effects of macroeconomic policies. This certainly seems a more promising theoretical paradigm to justify the SGP. Indeed, the concern that has lead to the Pact is that decentralized and unconstrained fiscal policies, combined with complete centralization of monetary policy, may generate free-rider-type incentives for over-borrowing which need to be corrected by some form of union-wide constraint. In addition, there was the concern that institutional failures in almost all EMU member countries install a tendency to run excessive deficits, and that this would be aggravated by installing a common currency and unified monetary policy. It is obvious that these concerns cannot properly be addressed with conventional OCA theory. As a bridge to a more detailed investigation of the theoretical underpinning that one may draw from this modern view of macroeconomic policy, I now turn to some empirical questions suggested by an "incentives-augmented" theory of OCA.

The first is whether or not we can find systematic empirical evidence that currency unions with a high degree of fiscal *de*centralization tend to impose fiscal restraints on sub-central governments. *Von Hagen/Eichengreen* (1996) have looked at a cross-section of alternative fiscal structures in different monetary unions, including unitary states and federal states. Measuring fiscal decentralization by the share of a government's expenditure financed by *own* taxes, they find a significant *negative* relationship between the degree of fiscal *de*centralization and the prevalence of SGP-like borrowing restrictions on sub-central governments. They explain this by a bail-out argument: With a significant own tax base to resort to on the sub-central level, the central government (central bank) may feel *lower* pressure to bail-out.[20] This finding and explanation clearly does not lend support to the view that the EMU, which features complete fiscal *de*centralization, needs something like a SGP to offset an over-borrowing-incentive on the national level. Conversely, *von Hagen/Eichengreen* do find empirical sup-

[20] In the European context this argument seems questionable on the grounds that national right of taxation may have only limited leverage if a significant part of the tax base is highly mobile internationally; see *McKinnon* (1997).

port for the traditional OCA-hypothesis that monetary centralization, if coupled with severe fiscal constraints on the sub-central level, creates a tendency to shift responsibility for "automatic stabilization" onto the central level. In their sample, there is a positive relationship between debt exposure of the central government and the prevalence of binding rules imposed on sub-central governments. Again, this hardly justifies the SGP. A possible interpretation, of course, is that SGP-type rules may eventually cause political pressure towards some fiscal centralization also within the EMU. But this is hardly an outcome that advocates of the SGP, or the signatories of the Maastricht and Amsterdam Treaties, have intended.[21]

A second question is whether monetary unions with different degrees of fiscal centralization do react differently over time to various exogenous shocks. OCA-theory would suggest that there is a "softer apparent budget constraint" in more centralized fiscal structures, where a larger part of public finance has access to monetary financing. This is, indeed, what *Moesen/van Rompuy* (1990) have found in their analysis of industrial countries' fiscal policies during 1973-1986: Increases in public deficits have been *positively* correlated to the degree of fiscal centralization.[22] This questions the view that fiscal decentralization with centralization of monetary policy creates incentives for less responsible fiscal policies. Given the almost complete absence of fiscal centralization in the EMU, it therefore also casts doubt on the necessity of the SGP.

This is but a brief look at some empirical evidence. It is by no means exhaustive and does not warrant sweeping conclusions. But it should give rise to caution. Ad hoc views on government behavior that follow from an "incentives-augmented" OCA-theory do not receive straight and obvious empirical support. On the other hand, there is unquestionable evidence that EU member countries' fiscal positions have improved significantly along the Maastricht way towards EMU.[23] Moreover, the first two years of EMU have also

---

21 *Von Hagen/Eichengreen* even conclude that the EU may, as a result of EMU plus SGP, be willing to give way to such pressure and move towards fiscal centralization.

22 The above summary of the findings by *Moesen/van Rompuy* is based on *De Grauwe* (2003a).

23 See, for instance, *Buti/Sapir* (1998) ch. 2.

been very promising to supporters of the SGP. Hence, the "Maastricht-Amsterdam orthodoxy" may have been effective under specific European conditions in a way that escapes the aforementioned empirical studies. But it is also true that since 2002 the picture of Euroland public finance has increasingly turned less bright on average, and more diverse across countries.[24] This may indicate no more than a temporary reform fatigue, but it may also indicate more fundamental problems with the underlying rationale for the SGP.

Turning back to theory, what we need is a clear identification of the problem that the Pact is intended to solve, duly taking into account government incentives and government failure, and a convincing argument that it is solved in an efficient, i.e., first-best way. Moreover, it needs to address specific conditions that characterize the EMU. For the purpose of this paper, the arguments that have been advanced in the literature and policy debate on the SGP can be grouped according to three types of concerns. The first is that, given unified monetary policy via EMU, if all Euroland countries pursue uncoordinated fiscal policies the outcome is likely to be an inefficient policy equilibrium. In other words, the Pact may serve a useful purpose towards mutually beneficial short- to medium-run *international policy coordination*. The second is that something like the SGP is needed to guard European monetary policy against unsustainable fiscal positions that violate *long-run solvency constraints*. Insolvent financial positions, if sufficiently large in magnitude, tend to build up inflationary pressure which even hardline and credible monetary authorities may at some stage not be able to resist.[25] This may impair their credibility and put their economies on paths of undesirably high inflation. And finally, the Pact may be a useful instrument for curbing European governments' inclination, based on certain institutional failures, to run *excessive public deficits*. Singling out this last point, of course, suggests that a deficit may be excessive even if it is sustainable against the long-run solvency condition. I shall address all three is-

[24] See the yearly publications by the European Commission, "Public Finances in the EMU", No. 3 of *The European Economy,* as well as section II of this paper.

[25] It is perhaps worth pointing out at this stage that this problem is not at all specific to the public sector. Witness the recurring debates about the appropriate central bank policy with respect to asset price bubbles.

sues in turn below. There are common themes that run through all of these concerns, viz. cross-country spill-overs and free-riding, and the idea that monetary policy is not completely insulated from fiscal policy. But as will become evident, the themes appear in different forms, with different implications. Moreover, it seems useful to make a distinction between *general arguments* that may in principle support an SGP-type fiscal rule, and the *specific "numerology"* involved. I will first address principal issues and turn to the numerology in the last section of the paper. Specific issues of enforcement that appear quite important from a practical perspective will not be dealt with.

IV. Policy coordination

Even if countries do not violate long-run solvency conditions, and even if there is no institutional failure leading to excessive deficits, they may gain from fiscal policy coordination. And they may do so in a particular way if they share a common currency and, therefore, a common monetary policy. As a general statement this may sound utterly plausible, but on closer inspection it appears like a rather odd argument to invoke for a justification of the SGP. A serious attempt to mutually internalize cross-country spill-overs from fiscal policies would most likely involve more flexibility and fine-tuning than the SGP permits, both in letter and in spirit. Indeed, if issues of time-consistency come into play, as many supporters of the SGP would argue (see below), then flexibility is almost anathema to the intention of the Pact, at least insofar as the deficit ceilings are concerned. In any case, a coordination attempt would probably go beyond imposing deficit and debt ceilings. Conversely, it seems open to what extent such ceilings, once in place, are binding constraints for policy coordination proper, and if the constraint aggravates or alleviates the coordination problem.

It is also important to recognize that the mere presence of cross-country effects of fiscal policy as such is not enough for a coordination issue to arise. It arises if a non-cooperative policy equilibrium is inefficient in that a certain coordinated policy change would simultaneously allow all countries to achieve their policy objectives to a greater extent. The issue thus relies on a clear notion of the relevant policy goals pursued by different countries, in addition to the policy goal pursued by the European Central Bank (ECB). A key observation which is often ignored in this context is that pecuniary spill-overs do not give rise to inefficiency. They affect distribution, but have no adverse impact on efficiency. Therefore, they do not establish a case for coordination in the above sense. A case in point is the oft-quoted interest rate spill-over. Suppose the supply of funds in a monetary union is imperfectly elastic with respect to the interest rate. Then, if a single government places additional debt on the capital market, this will raise the interest rate for all debtors in the union (assuming perfect capital mobility within the union). Like all relative price changes, this has a redistributive effect. It redistributes from borrowers to lenders, and depending on international wealth portfolios it may also redistribute between countries. But unless there are price rigidities or other types of distortion, non-cooperative policies do not entail inefficiency, as noted by *Eichengreen/Wyplosz* (1998).[26] Any one country's gain comes at the expense of some other country's loss.

If such rigidities are present, as in Euroland they surely are, a coordination issue may arise with respect to short-run macroeconomic policy objectives like employment and inflation. Although, as I have already pointed out, the Pact's primary orientation is not coordination of macroeconomic policies, it may still be helpful in an indirect way. However, to make sense as an indirect solution to the coordination problem, the non-cooperative short-run policy equilibrium would need to involve fiscal policies that are not restrictive enough against the aforementioned efficiency criterion. And it would help only in cases where the rule becomes a binding constraint. However, the non-cooperative equilibrium may just as well involve overly restrictive policies.[27] The reason is that, in addition to the interest rate spill-over, fiscal policies also have direct demand spill-overs which work in the opposite direction. Within a monetary union, country-specific demand shocks are not bottled up domestically, as with a flexible exchange rate, hence this second spill-over might be quite significant. Of course, the specific way in which the inefficiency arises would also depend, not only on the

---

[26] This argument also applies to government bond yields. If investors for whatever reason regard different government bonds as perfect substitutes, but imperfect substitutes for other assets, then additional debt placed by any one government raises the cost of debt for all others, while potentially leaving the general interest rate unchanged. But this is no more than a pecuniary externality that any individual increasing its demand for a certain product inflicts on other consumers. See also *Buiter/Grafe* (2003).

[27] See *Eichengreen/Wyplosz* (1998) and *Buiter/Grafe* (2003).

fiscal policies, but also on other asymmetric shocks affecting the member countries at the same time. A general conclusion seems hard to come by.[28]

A different form of coordination problem which is less dependent on the incidence of short-run shocks relates to the optimal tax structure. If we accept that the size of the public sector should be left to a domestic political decision, and if preferences are different so that Euroland ends up with different general levels of taxation in different countries, then the theory of optimal taxation would require that the inflation tax should also be different. However, barring non-tradable goods, a monetary union implies a uniform inflation tax.[29] Obviously, there may then be room to reduce the efficiency losses from taxation, not just by an appropriate choice of the union inflation rate, but also by adjusting national tax rates, and deficit financing of national expenditures. Notice that the issue is quite complicated, since it involves two levels of coordination: the ECB vis á vis national governments, and coordination between governments. One may construct scenarios with opposite conclusions regarding the role of SGP-like constraints on national governments. According to one view, expressed for instance in *Eichengreen* (1998), the Pact, by restricting present deficits, avoids the necessity of high *future* taxes and, thus, a justification of high *future* inflation on account of optimal taxation. The underlying assumption here is that present expenditure is adjusting endogenously in order to ensure compliance with a deficit ceiling. However, if present expenditure is exogenous, say determined by political considerations, then the SGP plays a much different role. Assuming the deficit rule

---

28 There is a further line of reasoning that one may pursue, starting with the question of whether a principal case can be made for coordinating monetary policy and fiscal policy, first assuming that there is considerable amount of fiscal centralization (see the paper by *Hughes-Hallett* in this volume). If so, and if the desired coordination implies a simple rule, then a need to coordinate national fiscal policies may follow from the fact that in the EU fiscal policy is completely *de*centralized. And this coordination may similarly be achieved by a simple rule. But, again, it is difficult to see that this rule would take the form of the SGP.

29 Notice the difference between the inflation tax and seigniorage, which may arise even with a zero inflation rate, and which may be distributed across Euroland countries according to any rule that may seem desirable.

is binding, the outcome would be higher *present* taxes, and optimal taxation would then also suggest higher *present* inflation. In either scenario, the common inflation rate acts as a leverage for cross-country spill-overs from one country's fiscal policy to the rest. As these scenarios make clear, whether the SGP serves a useful purpose in solving the coordination problem depends on what is exogenous, and what is endogenous in national fiscal policy. It also depends on whether the ECB acts as a leader or follower in this game. The above argument assumes it is a follower, in which case governments as the leaders need to be put under a constraint, assuming that they are willing to reduce expenditure, rather than increase taxes to meet the deficit ceiling. However, one may just as well envisage a game where the ECB acts as a leader, which further limits the justification for an SGP-like institution that may be found along these lines.

One may also argue, as in *Buti et al.* (2003), that what truly matters for monetary stability of a monetary union is not necessarily the fiscal balance in each of its constituent countries, but the aggregate position of the public sector in the union as a whole. If this is true, then there is a clear efficiency case for trading off one country's additional deficit (or debt) against a lower deficit (or debt) of some other country. Obviously, the size of efficiency gains facilitated in this way would depend on differences in political preferences, and on the incidence of asymmetric shocks in different countries. But the SGP forgoes any such gains, since it imposes a priori uniform ceilings on each individual member country. What are the alternatives? Efficient *administered* allocation of restrictions that vary across countries, consistently with a pre-determined overall macroeconomic policy mix of the union, seems all but ruled out by prohibitive information requirements. One might also add here that administered allocation of country-specific restrictions would seem to come quite close to mechanisms of international redistribution that attempt to mimic international risk sharing with respect to asymmetric shocks, as opposed to intertemporal smoothing in the case of national fiscal policies. Such proposals have been made in the EMU context, but they obviously suffer from severe moral hazard problems.[30] Hence, the uniform approach of the SGP may not be all that bad, assuming for the time being that some binding fiscal rule for the union as a whole is necessary. However, one might also

[30] See *Masson* (1996) and *Onenga/Winkler* (2001).

rely on decentralized exchange of deficit permits, as suggested in *Casella* (2000). Under ideal conditions, this would indeed imply that a certain aggregate fiscal stance of the union is achieved in an efficient way, irrespective of the initial allocation of deficit permits. But the allocation has important distributional implications and would, therefore, likely be subject to hot political debate.

The conclusion to be drawn from this seems fairly straightforward. National fiscal policies within a monetary union like EMU are likely to suffer from inefficiencies if pursued in an uncoordinated, non-cooperative way. But the SGP has never been intended to solve these inefficiencies. Nor does it seem likely to contribute in an indirect way to a fine-tuned effort of policy coordination, if adhered to in a strict and rigorous way. Indeed, in its operation the SGP follows the principle of *non-coordination*: the excessive deficit procedure is always applied on a strict on-for-one-basis, always looking at one country in isolation. And the surveillance procedure is similarly geared towards meeting the ceilings separately, and independently. One may add that any notion of serious fiscal policy coordination is conspicuously absent in the EU.[31]

V. Excessive Deficits

The Maastricht and Amsterdam Treaties reflect an a-priori view that European economies are liable to run excessive public deficits. Both treaties were negotiated and agreed upon against the backdrop of prolonged periods of high-level deficit spending during the 1970s and 1980s. Further prolongation of these trends was regarded as undesirable, given demographic trends and underlying economic constraints, and given the EU's ambition towards currency unification. The Maastricht and Amsterdam treaty reflect this notion of excessive deficits, and they include a specific "excessive deficit procedure" to deal with them. The treaties thus reflect a significant shift that had taken place in economic science in the 70s and 80s, away from focusing on the "market-failure-role" for fiscal policy, towards emphasizing "government-failure-characteristics" of such policy.[32]

However, the shift in terms of policies pursued seems halfhearted, at least insofar as the SGP is concerned. The solution to alleged government failure is again sought in government policy.

---

[31] See *Buiter/Grafe* (2003).

[32] See the preceding section, and *Onenga/Winkler* (2001).

After all, the SGP is a policy determined restriction on policies, and its practical application is subject to policy influence. The principal alternative would have been to entrust the question of whether or not certain government deficits and levels of public debt are excessive to private capital markets. EMU does away with country-specific exchange rate risk, and it shuts the way to national monetization of government deficits. Hence, given credibility of the ECB, capital markets must deal only with pure default risk, as with private borrowers. Their verdict on the soundness of a specific government's debt path would be delivered in the form of yield spreads on government bonds.

What does the verdict look like? I cannot go into any detailed analysis here, but a few things are worth pointing out. Figure 3 depicts the average level of long-term government bond yield in EU-15 countries on monthly observations from 1992 up to 2005, as well as the mean absolute deviation of country-specific deviations from the EU-11/12-average, and the cross-country variance in monthly changes. What is striking here is not so much that the average bond yield has become lower after formation of the EMU, but that the country-specific spreads have virtually disappeared, and the monthly changes exhibit almost no cross-country variance in the EMU-era.

Figure 3: Government bond yields in EU15 (levels, spreads and cross-country variance of monthly changes)

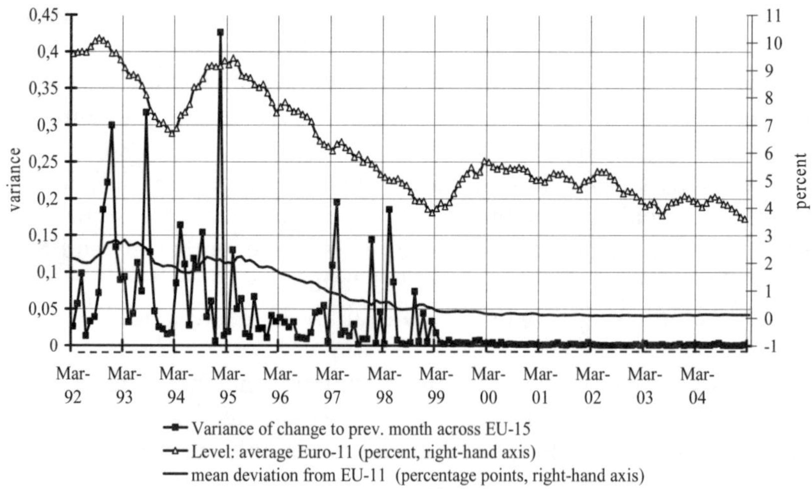

Source: EUROSTAT online, Euro-Indicators, Key short term indicators, Monetary and financial indicators, Long term government bond yields (monthly averages, not seasonally adjusted).

Table 2 makes this same point for all EU-15 countries individually by comparing the correlation of monthly and quarterly changes, respectively, with the contemporaneous changes for the EU-11/12 as a whole. While the correlation coefficient was positive and quite high even prior to EMU, it has increased further after the start of EMU for all countries.

Table 2: Correlation of changes in government bond yields (correlation coefficient: country changes vs. changes for EU11/12)

	monthly changes		**quarterly changes**	
	1992-1998	**1999-2005**	**1992-1998**	**1999-2005**
Belgium	0,7437	0,9869	0,8261	0,9973
Denmark	0,8467	0,9700	0,9227	0,9777
Germany	0,8035	0,9907	0,8411	0,9967
Greece	-0,0465	0,7932	0,0060	0,6572
Spain	0,8766	0,9871	0,9200	0,9959
France	0,8984	0,9940	0,9414	0,9981
Ireland	0,7494	0,9837	0,7753	0,9943
Italy	0,8571	0,9858	0,9059	0,9949
Luxembourg	0,4463	0,9010	0,7558	0,9581
Netherlands	0,8223	0,9880	0,8436	0,9943
Austria	0,7917	0,9749	0,8614	0,9951
Portugal	0,5486	0,9869	0,8049	0,9920
Finland	0,6071	0,9837	0,8731	0,9921
Sweden	0,6636	0,9422	0,8781	0,9433
United Kingdom	0,7217	0,9005	0,7734	0,9034

Source: EUROSTAT online, Euro-Indicators, Key short term indicators, Monetary and financial indicators, Long term government bond yields (monthly averages, not seasonally adjusted).

Hence, markets apparently no longer perceive any government-specific (or default) risk, despite grossly different positions, both absolutely and relative to the SGP benchmark.[33] One interpretation of this finding is that markets simply do not bother about government-specific risk *because* of the Stability Pact. If they view the Pact as a fully credible and entirely sensible way to avoid any country-specific risk associated with government debt, then they see no further need to worry. According to this line of reasoning,

[33] See also *Boonstra* (2005). A similar story is found in *De Grauwe* (2003a).

one would not even expect markets to react when a government meets the ceiling and faces an excessive deficit procedure, since the EDP is no mere warning signal, but a procedure that involves corrective action. However, an alternative – and perhaps more worrying – interpretation is that capital markets anticipate a bail-out, should any country run into debt-servicing problems. In this case, the absence of yield spreads reflects lacking credibility of the no-bail-out commitment, rather than trust in a well designed and credible Stability Pact. The principle commitment to rely on government policy instead of capital markets would be consistent with this latter interpretation. Pursuing an empirical discrimination between these two rivalling interpretations is beyond the cope of this paper, but a possible strategy might run as follows. If the malign interpretation is correct, then one should observe co-movement of all government bond yields and interest rates in Euroland, both jointly driven by Euroland countries' excessive public debt accumulation. The reason is that interest rates as a whole would need to reflect likely devaluation of the Euro that comes along with inflationary bail-out. If the benign interpretation is true, then there is less co-movement between government bond yields and interest rates, and a lower sensitivity of both with respect to public debt accumulation. This holds true at least if governments borrow on world capital markets with a relatively flat supply of funds.

However, even the benign interpretation hardly reflects an intended and welcome side effect of the SGP. Surely, the SGP was not intended to lull capital markets into a state of low alertness with respect to country-specific risks associated with government debt, and thus to soften the disciplinary pressure that governments feel from financial markets. The narrowing of yield spreads since 1999 as such does not, of course, warrant a firm conclusion that such an effect is present, but it nevertheless is a somewhat worrying signal.

Exposing governments to the full disciplinary force of capital markets may, however, not be enough, if there are genuine government failures that lead to excessive deficits. It is useful at this point to make a distinction between alternative ways to define excessive government deficits. One is to invoke long-run sustainability, meaning a close to zero probability of even partial debt repudiation, whether for blunt violation of a long-run solvency constraint, or for a dominating default incentive. I shall take this up in the subsequent section of the paper. In this section, I stick to a somewhat broader notion of an excessive government deficit and public debt, which may emerge even without the risk of default or insolvency. The difference has also been stressed by *Buiter/Grafe* (2002). By this definition, a deficit is excessive if the resulting debt accumulation imposes a cost on the society which exceeds its benefit.

This may arise due to institutional failures in government decision making and incentives. We may call this a *"political debt bias"*. It may, however, also be due to imperfections and distortions in the financial sector that the government relies upon for debt financing. This is the case, for instance, if capital markets fail to correctly evaluate the risk associated with government debt, say because of informational problems, or because they misread the SGP as a perfect insurance. A *"market-induced debt bias"* then emerges if financial markets are willing to finance government deficits under conditions that understate the true opportunity cost of the funds used. Obviously, either type of failure may, but need not, eventually lead to insolvency and default.

The issue here is not whether or not such inefficiencies exist (which in any case seems difficult to deny), but their interrelationship with monetary policy, and whether monetary unification provides a rationale for institutional provisions like the SGP. Moreover, the issue has nothing to do with the size of the public sector as such, but the fiscal deficit or debt. Arguably, the underlying failures should be dealt with as directly as possible, and relying on SGP-like rules is certainly not a first-best policy strategy. The relevant questions to ask are the following. First, does the move to EMU aggravate or alleviate the efficiency cost of the pre-existing distortions? Does it introduce new distortions? And, assuming that the institutional failures for some reason are difficult to deal with directly, is the SGP a promising second- or third-best policy to pursue?

It is important to realize that a distortion-free, first-best world does not imply optimal steady-state levels of government debt that are equal to zero. To the extent that governments accumulate a capital stock, we should expect them to incur debt up to the point where the steady-state opportunity cost of a debt-financed public capital stock is equal to its value to society.[34] Determining this

[34] For a private capital stock accumulated by profit maximizing firms under competitive conditions, the condition for the optimal capital stock $\widetilde{K}$ is $\delta + i = F_K(\widetilde{K})p_K$, where δ is the rate of physical decay,

value is, of course, a difficult task since there will often be no market prices reflecting the value of the relevant (public) services, but this does not affect the principal point that the efficient level of public debt is generally larger than zero.[35] As a corollary to this, we must also conclude that different societies may have different optimal levels of long-run public debt, depending on their preferences. I shall return to this in section VII below.

All of this is not to say, of course, that the notion of excessive public debt in Europe is wrongheaded. High public debt is a real problem, not only in Europe. Somewhat paradoxically, however, the European history of excessive public debt build-up, in and of itself, may even give some reason for comfort. The point is that the build-up did not start before the break down of the Bretton Woods system. A reasonable interpretation is that the monetary discipline associated with a fixed exchange rate system, even absent SGP-like rules, has prevented the process to start earlier,[36] although factors not related to the exchange rate system have certainly played a role as well. If this interpretation is valid, then EMU should, in the long-run at least, re-install some of the constraints that had been effective during the Bretton Woods system. However, as emphasized by *McKinnon* (1997), the short run may involve considerable risk, since many countries enter EMU with huge public debt inherited from the past. Barring access to inflationary devaluation of their debt, countries may feel a stronger incentive to default. This gives rise to a short-run rationale for the SGP, according to which it is needed in order to ensure a quick reduction of such excessive debt positions inherited from the past. In the long run, however, the monetary discipline that comes from a loss of access to monetary finance and inflationary devaluation of debt may again be strong enough, rendering SGP-like rules unnecessary, or at least less compelling.

Monetary unification affects the incentive structure for governments to incur public debt in various ways, and it is not at all clear, a priori, that the net result should be to aggravate a pre-existing debt bias of fiscal policy, as it is sometimes argued. As I have mentioned

---

i is the real interest rate, and F_K is the marginal productivity of the capital stock. p_K is the price of the good produced with this capital, relative to the capital good.

35 See also *De Grauwe* (2003b).

36 See *McKinnon* (1997).

before, the debt bias may be of a political nature, due to the time-inconsistency of an efficient debt path, or to more general inefficiencies of the decision making process, such as inherent myopia or free-rider problems associated with multiple layers of government. Or it may be due to financial market imperfections. In both cases, of course, the first-best policy would be to tackle the imperfections directly.[37] As long as such imperfections persist, however, any change in the incentive structure brought by monetary unification that leads to lower deficits amounts to a second-best-type improvement. If there is a change in the opposite direction, then an SGP-like rule may be justified.

It can be argued that the move to EMU aggravates the political debt bias, since it removes *country-specific* exchange rate risk from the cost of deficit finance. Indeed, this was certainly an important motivation for some governments to make it for a timely entry into EMU in 1999. If a country with a profligate government joins a pre-existing monetary union with a credible, stability oriented central bank, the government is likely to benefit in this way. But if several countries form a monetary union, it cannot be true that all governments benefit in the same way. Put somewhat differently, country-specific exchange rate risk is replaced by the corresponding risk associated to Euroland as a whole. And if Euroland incorporates similarly profligate countries, nothing much will have changed. In the EMU case, however, we do observe that the risk-premia on government bonds have fallen for *all* countries, although not by the same amount since yields have converged to a common level.[38] In any case, if we start off from a situation where pre-existing imperfections give rise to excessive budget deficits and public debt, then what governments perceive as a benefit actually worsens the situation, a classic second-best-type effect. Conversely, if governments are facing higher risk-premia being in the Union than they did before, this second-best effect is actually a gain to society.

The aforementioned empirical finding of negligible yield spreads may reflect the presence of a second effect of monetary union. Suppose that prior to the monetary union governments had deliberately embarked on an excessive debt path, repeatedly easing their real debt burden by surprise inflation, based on an implicit contract between the government and the central bank. In a way,

---

37 See *Eichengreen/Wyplosz* (1998).

38 See *Boonstra* (2005).

such an implicit contract is similar to (a somewhat milder form of) the case where the government anticipates an ex-post bail-out that the central bank will not be able to resist to, because of its general responsibility for avoiding financial crises. In a monetary union, each national government faces a central bank which is disassociated with national interests, hence such a strategy seems more difficult to pursue ex ante. This suggests that the second effect works towards lowering deficits, thus delivering the second-best-type improvement alluded to above.

However, while it may now be more risky for governments to count on the central bank, the adverse effects of surprise inflation or bail-out are now partly external to the single country. They are felt by all countries of the union, and not just the electorate of the profligate government. Presumably, the benefits of the expenditure largely fall on the national electorate, while part of the cost are thus borne elsewhere. Moreover, if the no-bail out clause is deemed incredible ex ante, and if expectations are formed accordingly *throughout* the union in response to excessive borrowing in any *one* country, then this will inflict a cost on all countries of the union, even if the central bank resists the bail-out pressure ex post.[39] In a way, other countries are then held hostage and the pressure on the central bank increases accordingly. In this way, the monetary union introduces a "new" type of distortion with a direct detrimental effect, in addition to aggravating the pre-existing debt bias. The pre-existing bias will often be associated with political imperfections along the time dimension, such that the benefits and cost of debt-financed public expenditure are unequally distributed across present and future generations. Monetary union introduces an additional (static) distortion in the international dimension. In the context of the political debt bias, the distortion is hardly new, however, since it essentially corresponds to the free-rider-type failures usually identified as the key domestic reasons for excessive

---

[39] This is the oft-quoted Barro-Gordon problem which makes attaining credibility so difficult to start with, see *Barro/Gordon* (1983). It is perhaps worth pointing out here that fiscal policies are not the only, or even the most important, source of this problem. Witness for instance the pressure for low interest rates from almost all other segments of a typical European economy, including in particular the stock market. Indeed the SGP may even have the perverse effect of aggravating the concerns behind such pressure not directly related to fiscal policy. See *Canzoneri/Diba* (2001).

public deficits.[40]

Although we have now identified various effects that partly tend to offset each other, the aforementioned distortion *additionally* introduced by the monetary union does appear to constitute some justification for a fiscal constraint to be imposed on national governments forming the union. Whether a constraint of the type represented by the SGP is appropriate to deal with this distortion is a different matter. This line of reasoning may seem to take us back to the policy coordination issue addressed above, which is also concerned with international policy spill-overs. However, there is a fundamental difference. The present distortion is of long-run nature, it unambiguously leads to excessive deficits, and it is much less dependent on country characteristics and the peculiarities of idiosyncratic shocks.[41] Hence, a rule which is relatively rigid and does not allow for much flexibility in application seems more justified.

But there is an even more important difference. In the classic coordination case, there is a clear incentive for all countries to resolve the inefficiency of a non-cooperative policy game, since by definition all would gain. "Leviathan-type" governments may have questionable political objective functions, but even they are interested in avoiding *political inefficiencies* through coordination efforts. Whether something like the SGP is the appropriate solution is, of course, a separate question, and I have argued above that it probably isn't. By way of contrast, an SGP-like rule does seem quite helpful for correcting the distortion that monetary union introduces with respect to excessive deficits, but whether "Leviathan-type" governments would be interested in it seems less clear cut. While it is true that they would avoid receiving negative spill-overs from other countries' excessive debt paths, they would at the same time stand to lose from being constrained themselves. A net gain for all governments may, but need not, arise. Remember that we have defined an SGP-like rule to be self-imposed, and to be enforced through explicit consent by governments.

---

40 See for instance *Alesina/Perotti* (1996).

41 The distinction between short-run, business-cycle-related coordination issues on the one hand, and long-run implications of excessive debt positions on the other is also emphasized in *Uhlig* (2003), although his long-run view concentrates on insolvency issues and financial crises, rather than the relatively mild problem of political or market-induced debt bias that I discuss in this section. I will turn to insolvency and crisis in the next chapter of this paper.

The case for a SGP-like institution is further strengthened if the excessive debt path is due to a *time-inconsistency problem* in the strict sense of the word. This arises if a benevolent government would ex ante want to abstain from an excessive deficit path, but is unable to commit itself to an efficient path, because there is an ex post incentive to devaluate debt through surprise inflation. International obligations would obviously help, but barring monetary union there is no apparent incentive for countries to bear the cost of enforcing such an international agreement. Monetary union, with the aforementioned externalities, may provide sufficient incentives. Notice that there are *two* types of incentives involved. An incentive for governments to mutually commit themselves to certain limits is not enough. For a successful Pact, there also needs to be an ex-post incentive to actually bear the cost of punishing (as opposed to the cost of being punished for) deviant behavior. While benevolent governments that suffer from a time-inconsistency problem may have both types of incentives, "Leviathan-governments" may not even have an incentive to enter an agreement ex ante, as I have argued above. The relevance of this line of reasoning for the SGP is obvious.[42]

VI. Long-run sustainability

To address long-run sustainability of fiscal policy, the intertemporal dimension needs to be made explicit. In this section, I define a path of deficits and debt as sustainable if it satisfies the government's intertemporal budget constraint, or the solvency condition. Excessive deficits as defined in the preceding section need not be economically unsustainable. If they are, then the inter-country spillover effects that derive from monetary union may become particularly severe. Scenarios with outcomes such as direct bail-outs, outright government default, or financial crises and contagion enter the picture. These may appear somewhat far-fetched for present-day European economies, but the monetary constitution of an economy, or a monetary union, must contain provisions for ex ante unlikely events. Indeed, the likelihood of such events importantly hinges on the monetary constitution. Extreme scenarios have repeatedly been brought up in the run up to European Monetary Union, and the SGP has been regarded as an important safeguard against such events.[43]

---

42 A formal analysis is offered by *Beetsma/Uhlig* (1999).

43 Witness the oft-quoted "war-scenario" brought up by *Feldstein* (1997)

Its proponents have always argued that credibility of the European Central Bank is inconceivable without such a safeguard.

Formally, the long-run solvency, or intertemporal budget restriction for fiscal policy emerges as the solution to the equation of motion for government debt, if a "no-Ponzi-game condition" is applied. Writing B for the nominal level of contractual government net debt and i for the short-run nominal interest rate, and denoting the instantaneous rate of change by a dotted variable, the *dynamic* government budget constraint is

$$\dot{B} = G - T - \dot{M} + iB, \tag{1}$$

where G and T denote nominal government expenditure and revenue, respectively, while $\dot{M}$ denotes seigniorage revenue from the issuance of high-powered money. Although largely ignored by the SGP, it is important to distinguish between consumption expenditure and investment expenditure, and between general tax revenue and revenue deriving directly from the public capital stock. Following *Buiter* (1999a, 2003) and *Buiter/Grafe* (2003), we thus write

$$G = G_C + G_I \text{ and } T = T_X + T_K, \tag{2}$$

where G_C and G_I denote consumption and investment expenditure, while T_X and T_K, respectively, denote tax revenues and direct cash revenues from the public capital stock. Denoting real GDP by Y and the price level by P, and using lower case letters to indicate GDP-ratios we thus have

$$b = B/PY \text{ and } \dot{b} = \dot{B}/PY - (\pi + \gamma)b, \tag{3}$$

where π and γ are the rate of inflation and the rate of growth of real GDP. In terms of GDP-ratios, the dynamic budget constraint becomes

$$\dot{b} = g_C + g_I - (t_X + t_K) - \dot{m} + (\rho - \gamma)b, \tag{4}$$

where $\rho = i - \pi$ denotes the real rate of interest. Notice that in this equation $\dot{m}$ is defined as $\dot{M}/PY$, instead of the change in real money balances $d(M/PY)$. For simplicity, I assume perfect foresight, hence the rate of inflation is always known with certainty. In equation (4), the term $g_C + g_I - (t_X + t_K)$ represents the primary government surplus relative to GDP. This will be denoted by $-s$ below.

It is important to realize that this view of the government's

---

in order to warn against detrimental effects of EMU.

budget constraint is comprehensive in that it includes the central bank. This is necessary for a consistent treatment if money supply is organized as a state monopoly, and it does not compromise the idea of central bank independence from the government. Whether or not seigniorage revenue $\dot{m}$ is readily available to the government, or available at all, is a separate issue, but conceptually, it is an integral part of the government budget constraint. The central bank's profit appears as part of the government's capital income t_K. The term $t_X + t_K$ represents what *Buiter* (2003) calls the long-run "deep pockets" of the government, while $\dot{m}$ represents the short-run "deep pockets" of the central bank.

There is a dynamic relationship between investment expenditure g_I and capital income t_K. Following *Buiter* (1999a), we may define a "cash rate of return" of the government capital stock, denoted by K, such that

$$T_K = \kappa(K_G P) \text{ and } \dot{K}_G = G_I / P - \delta K_G \tag{5}$$

where K_G denotes the real government capital stock, with a rate of decay equal to δ. This assumes a uniform composition of all macroeconomic variables and, therefore, a uniform price level *P*. Writing k for K_G / Y, we have $\dot{K}_G / Y = \dot{k} + \gamma k$, which implies $g_I = \dot{k} + (\gamma + \delta)k$. Since $t_K = \kappa k$, we may then rewrite the *dynamic* budget constraint as

$$\dot{b} - \dot{k} = g_C - t_X - \dot{m} + [\gamma - (\kappa - \delta)]k + (\rho - \gamma)b \tag{6}$$

$$= g_C - t_X - \dot{m} + (\rho - \gamma)(b - k) - (\kappa - \rho - \delta)k. \tag{7}$$

In this equation, $b - k = (B - PK_G)/(PY)$ is what *Buiter* (1999a) calls the "net tangible liabilities" of the government, again relative to GDP. It is the excess of contractual debt over the government capital stock, which generates real government revenue according to a rate of return κ.[44] Applying the interest burden of debt to net liabilities (instead of government debt), as we do in equation (7), then implies that the government capital stock contributes to the primary surplus only if the "cash rate of return" on the government

[44] A significant part of the government capital stock may in fact generate services that are private goods. The term κk captures the direct fees that the government charges for such services. But it also captures the profit of the central bank which is an integral part of the public capital stock.

capital stock is larger than its rate of decay plus the real interest rate, i.e., if $\kappa - \rho - \delta > 0$. This is intuitive.

Of course, the relationship between the government capital stock and the government's ability to extract revenue extends well beyond the direct cash rate of return. There are important indirect effects of *k* on the tax base of the economy and, more generally, on the government's ability to extract revenue from the economy through general taxes. Modeling this relationship is beyond the scope of this paper, but it is an important aspect to bear in mind when judging the economic sense of the SGP. Obviously, political preferences will play a decisive role as to how large a society wants the government capital stock to be. Generally, the last two decades have witnessed a medium term tendency to reduce *k* in virtually all EU member countries. But it is still important in the present context to realize that the EU leaves the size of *k* to the member state. Accordingly, the SGP should allow for this in its "numerology".

Imposing the "no-Ponzi-game condition", we may write the budget constraint in *intertemporal* form as

$$b(v) = \int_v^\infty \left[s(u) + \dot{m}(u)\right] e^{-\Gamma(u)} \, du, \tag{8}$$

where $s(u) = t_X(u) + t_K(u) - \left[g_C(u) + g_I(u)\right]$

and $\Gamma(u) = \int_v^u \left[\rho(z) - \gamma(z)\right] dz.$

In these expressions all variables are expected values at time *v* for time $u > v$. For simpler writing, I abstain from separate notation for expectational terms. The term $s(u)$ denotes the primary surplus, and $\Gamma(u)$ denotes the discount factor deriving from the interest rate path between time *v* and time *u*. A completely analogous formulation of the intertemporal budget constraint may be derived from (5). It is omitted here for lack of space.

What are the principle options for maintaining long-run solvency as given in (8)? The fiscal theory of the price level (FTPL) holds that solvency of a government can always be attained by an appropriate price level that reduces the real value of nominal debt to the present value of the future stream of real primary surpluses that the government may determine exogenously, according to its objective function, and given a stream of seigniorage determined by the central bank. This amounts to rewriting $b(v)$ in (8) as $\left[P(v)Y(v)\right]/B(v)$, treating contractual nominal debt $B(v)$ and real income $Y(v)$ as given, and then solving the equation for $P(v)$.[45] In other words, an instantaneous jump in the price level ensures intertemporal solvency.

This view is reminiscent of the fundamental solution to the problem of equity evaluation. But there is an important difference. Valuation of equity derives from a *no-arbitrage condition*, while a government's *intertemporal solvency condition* derives from a dynamic budget constraint. It can therefore be argued that an endogenous adjustment of the price level to formally meet the solvency condition for an *arbitrary* future stream of primary surpluses amounts to a violation of the budget constraint for a key actor of the economy. In other words, it amounts to (partial) default.[46] The same does not hold true for equity revaluation, where an unforeseen event simply leads to a violation of a no-arbitrage condition, but no violation of any budget constraint.

Whatever the merit of the FTPL, the key question here is where in the solvency condition for government finance an adjustment is sought, in order to ensure that it is met. Moreover, to be relevant for the present issue the answer to this question must depend on whether or not a country belongs to a monetary union. If it does, the next and final question is whether an SGP-like arrangement is an appropriate instrument to ensure solvency in an *efficient* way. In this latter regard, of course, cross-country spill-overs akin to the ones considered in the preceding section play a role. Thus, the relevant question regarding the SGP is not whether it is a rule that, if adhered to, guarantees solvency, but whether solvency is achieved in a first-best way.

Partial government default implies that an endogenous "default-discount-factor" on $B(v)$ is introduced in equation (8).[47] Bail-out that avoids this default implies an adjustment via a corresponding instantaneous adjustment in $\dot{m}(v)$, i.e., *Buiter's* short-run "deep pockets" of the central bank. Barring both default and bail-out, fiscal adjustment requires an appropriate plan of austerity that generates a corresponding present value of additional future primary

45 See also *Canzoneri/Diba* (2001).

46 See *Buiter* (1999b) who argues that any theory allowing for an arbitrary violation of budget constraints is ill-posed. On this account, as well as a series of anomalies in the resulting equilibrium, he therefore strictly refutes the fiscal theory of the price level.

47 See *Buiter* (1999b).

surpluses $s(u)$ in (8), i.e., *Buiter's* long-run "deep pockets" of the government. It should be noted that the solvency constraint as such still leaves degrees of freedom regarding the timing and structural details of the austerity plan.[48]

Obviously, *if* a government default in country A has adverse effects also in country B, then country B has an incentive to impose a rule avoiding insolvency and thus the risk of default. If the rule fails and insolvency occurs, then it *may* have an interest in avoiding default ex post by means of a bail-out, depending on how it weighs the bail-out-cost against the cost it stands to bear from country A's default. It is often argued that the bail-out cost has to do with higher inflation. This is a misconception. Any use of the central bank's "deep pocket" is subject to monetary equilibrium. In other words, the central bank moves along the money demand schedule. But for a single bail out, this implies a one-time jump in the price level caused by the aforementioned instantaneous adjustment in $\dot{m}(v)$.[49] Inflationary effects proper would result only in case of *repeated* default in short intervals, which seems a very remote scenario. Indeed, historical experience suggests that bail-outs are sometimes followed by periods of lower inflation, or even deflation.[50]

Surprising price level jumps caused by a bail-out always erode the real value of nominal asset holdings. This also happens to holders of government debt in case of default. But the distributional implications are obviously different. With a bail-out the effect is more widely dispersed than with default. Relative to government default, a bail-out is thus a policy of redistribution in favor of agents holding government debt. In some cases, this difference can be of vital political importance. For instance, if low-income

[48] Formally, yet another option would be to adjust the future stream of seigniorage revenue with a present value equal to the default value of the debt in question. However, any increase in high-powered money will – other things equal – affect the general price level, and with perfect foresight this will lead to a rise in the price level at time v, which is what will happen with direct bail-out as well. Of course, the time pattern of price level increases will be different under alternative policies of seigniorage revenue, with different intergenerational distribution effects. But I do not pursue this any further in the present paper.

[49] Or, equivalently, from corresponding adjustments in future streams of seigniorage $\dot{m}(u)$; see preceding footnote.

[50] See *Eichengreen/Wyplosz* (1998).

households hold mandatory individual accounts towards their old-age pension, and if these accounts are invested in government bonds, then a government default is most likely to have unwelcome distributional consequences. This has happened in Argentina where it had the additional effect of discrediting a recent pension reform policy.[51]

In any case, there is a further strategy which in most cases will dominate both, the fiscal rule and the bail-out. This is for country B to avoid *systemic* consequences for its own financial system from country A's default by means of regulatory provisions, for instance regulations that seek to avoid excessive exposure to country A's government debt.[52] It is usually argued that such regulation should focus on the lending institutions, particularly banks. However, it could also, partly at least, focus on the borrowing government, increasing transparency towards a better identification of government-specific risks, and increasing the dispersion of these risks across lending institutions. All of this may be, and probably is, relevant even absent monetary union. For the necessity of a fiscal rule to follow from monetary union, one would need to show that the likelihood of default and systemic consequences is increased through monetary union. The arguments that seem relevant here are of the free-rider-type that have already been presented in the preceding chapter. Without going into further detail, it seems clear, however, that a fiscal rule, even if it is successful in avoiding insolvency, is likely to be second-best. This has repeatedly been pointed out in the context of the SGP.[53]

VII. Interpreting the "numerology"

Generally, one would expect that the Stability and Growth Pact makes most sense if interpreted as a rule to ensure long-run sustainability of government finances within the EU.[54] Yet, the Pact makes

---

51 See *The Economist*, Feb. 19, 2005.

52 Inasmuch as default in country A leads to higher risk-premia on newly issued government debt also in country B, the spill-over is pecuniary in nature and the issue is one of redistribution; see *Buiter/Grafe* (2003). The problem is, of course, of a different nature if default and contagion leads to a systemic instability and financial crisis.

53 For instance by *Eichengreen/Wyplosz* (1998) and *Buiter/Grafe* (2003).

54 It may be worth pointing out at this stage that with some minor qualifications the deficit rules are also meant to apply for EU-member-countries that do not participate in the monetary union; see

surprisingly little reference to the intertemporal nature of the solvency constraint. While the Maastricht criteria incorporate a debt-related condition that is supposed to be met prior to entry, the SGP which governs government finances thereafter looks only at a single flow magnitude, viz. the consolidated deficit of the general government relative to GDP: $d = g - t + ib$. It specifies two reference levels: $d \leq 0.03$ and $\tilde{d} \leq 0$, where $\tilde{d}$ is the cyclically adjusted deficit. We may relate these criteria to the above solvency condition by rewriting the dynamic budget constraint as

$$\dot{b} = d - (\pi + \gamma)b - \dot{m} \tag{9}$$

where $(\pi + \gamma)$ is nominal income growth.

Although nowhere explicitly mentioned in the Pact, an economically meaningful interpretation of the medium-run ceiling $\tilde{d} \leq 0$, against the benchmark of the intertemporal solvency condition, is to assume that it relates to the steady state. This implies a steady state debt-ratio

$$\tilde{b} = -\tilde{d}(\pi + \gamma). \tag{10}$$

This follows from equation (9) by setting $\dot{b} = 0$ and $\dot{m} = 0$. If interpreted in this steady state form, the reference value for the cyclically adjusted deficit ties the long-run debt-ratio to the long-run deficit-ratio. Given this implication of the cyclically adjusted criterion which was newly introduced in the SGP, it was thus entirely consistent to not uphold the Maastricht entry condition of $b \leq 0.6$ for member countries of the EMU. It would simply be redundant.

One frequently finds interpretations of the SGP according to which the deficit ceiling $d \leq 0.03$ rests on a conviction that the debt-ratio should not exceed the “Maastricht level” of 60 percent, plus the assumption that nominal income growth will be around 5 percent. The preceding analysis shows that this interpretation is flawed. The long-run debt-ratio is governed by the reference value for the cyclically adjusted deficit, $\tilde{d} \geq 0$, and it implies $\tilde{b} \leq 0$. In turn, the deficit criterion simply reflects certain assumptions about the business-cycle sensitivity of public finances, and the severity of recessions in a typical European economy.[55] It can probably be interpreted to also allow for a certain amount of fiscal reaction to

---

Buiter/Grafe (2003).

55 See *Canzoneri/Diba* (2001).

country-specific shocks not related to the business cycle. One may, of course, question these implicit assumptions, but in my view this is a minor problem with the theoretical underpinning of the Pact.

The real problem lies with the requirement that cyclically adjusted public finances should be "close to balance or in surplus". If the above steady state interpretation meets the intentions of the Pact, this implies non-positive long-run debt levels for all countries. In practice, if member countries adhere to the medium term reference value of $\tilde{d}=0$, then they will sooner or later approach very low debt levels.[56] Over the cycle, b evolves according to $\dot{b}=-(\pi+\gamma)b$, hence all countries would see their debt-ratios fall more or less quickly, depending on their initial historical debt levels, and on their nominal income growth (assuming it is positive).

One might now argue that such a run-down of debt levels is exactly what should happen, and is therefore a welcome and intended effect of the SGP, due to the above mentioned debt bias that has emerged in post-Bretton-Woods Europe which might be a risk for the early period of EMU.[57] However, there are two problems. One is that such a scenario implies an especially restrictive fiscal stance for countries with high initial debt levels and strong nominal growth, and a much less restrictive position for countries with low debt levels and low growth. It is not clear, a priori, whether this asymmetry across countries is justified on economic grounds.[58] The second problem is more fundamental: Why should all member countries have a zero, or even negative, long-run level of government debt?

Given the significant role that governments play as investors, this implication seems highly questionable. It does not imply a zero steady state public capital stock, but it does put a long run restriction on this stock, which may be derived as follows. Taking equation (4), and setting $\dot{b}=0$ and $b=0$, as required from the steady state interpretation of $\tilde{d}=0$, and ruling out long-run seigniorage, we obtain

---

[56] *De Grauwe* (2003) calculates that with nominal income growth rates equal to 5 percent, debt-ratios of all EMU countries would drop to below 20 percent over the next twenty years.

[57] See *McKinnon* (1997).

[58] See *Buiter/Grafe* (2003).

$$g_C - t_X + g_I - t_K = 0 \,. \tag{11}$$

Taking account of public sector capital accumulation as given in (5), and focusing on the steady state where $\dot{k} = 0$ and, therefore, $g_I = (\gamma + \delta)\widetilde{k}$, we arrive at

$$(\gamma + \delta - \kappa)\widetilde{k} = t_X - g_C \,. \tag{12}$$

These equations assume that the "close to balance" condition of the SGP is met with equality. Barring any SGP-restriction, the steady state condition is

$$(\gamma + \delta - \kappa)\widetilde{k} = t_X - g_C + (\rho - \gamma)\widetilde{b} \,, \tag{13}$$

where $\widetilde{b}$ is the unconstrained steady state government debt-ratio.

The optimal size of the public capital stock is defined by the condition that the marginal social return of public capital is equal to the social opportunity cost of adding and maintaining a further unit to the public capital stock. A detailed analysis of various ramifications of this condition may be found in *Buiter* (1999a). For the present purpose, we may denote the *marginal* social return by ξ, so that the optimal long-run public capital stock satisfies the first order condition

$$\xi(\widetilde{k}) = \gamma + \delta + \rho, \tag{14}$$

where it is assumed that ξ depends on the public capital coefficient $k = K_G/Y$. Assuming that the second order condition $\xi'(\widetilde{k}) < 0$ is fulfilled, this equation determines a unique optimal public capital stock $\widetilde{k}^*$. The question now is whether, and in what sense, the SGP-condition (12) might be a binding constraint, leading to a non-optimal public sector capital stock.

In principle, the government can always subjugate "net-of-consumption-taxation", i.e., $z = t_X - g_C$, to maintain a socially optimal long-run public capital coefficient $\widetilde{k}^*$. But with a very low cash–rate-of-return κ, this might inflict a large static cost in the form of a high net-tax-ratio $z = (\gamma + \delta - \kappa)\widetilde{k}^*$. Alternatively, the government may let static considerations related to z dominate the policy, which might imply a public sector capital stock that deviates from $\widetilde{k}^*$, as determined by (14). In a sense, the requirement of a zero debt-ratio $\widetilde{b}$ effectively "shuts off" accumulation of public sector capital from capital markets. The government is unable to pursue a fiscal policy that *simultaneously* satisfies optimality conditions related to the *static* burden of taxation t_x and benefits of public consumption g_c, and *intertemporal* optimality with respect to public investment. To do so requires the ability to run a long-run debtor or creditor position. Of course, the SGP is an asymmetric restriction and it may, therefore, not be binding. But with a low cash-rate of return of the public sector capital stock, reflecting the public goods nature of services generated by this stock, it is likely to be so.

Accepting some "ad-hocery", the potential problem of a binding "close to balance" condition may be seen as follows. Suppose that some static consideration related to the burden of taxation and benefits of public consumption expenditure determines the desired long-run magnitude of net taxation z^* that the government is able and willing to extract from the economy. It seems reasonable to assume that, other things equal, this is increasing and concave in k: $z^* = z^*(k)$, with $z^*{}' > 0$ and $z^*{}'' < 0$. Notice that z^* could, in principle, also be negative, at least over certain ranges of k. Let us assume that the government, faced with the requirement that $\tilde{b} = 0$, lets these considerations dominate its fiscal policy. Assume, moreover, that the cash-return on the public capital stock is falling in k, $\kappa = \kappa(k)$ with $\kappa' < 0$. It then follows from (12) that the debt-restriction from the Pact implicitly determines a long-run public sector capital stock $\tilde{k}^P$ which satisfies

$$\kappa(\tilde{k}) = \gamma + \delta - z^*(\tilde{k}) / \tilde{k}\ . \tag{15}$$

The outcome may be a sub-optimally large public capital stock, or one that is too large. The higher the cash-rate-of-return of public capital, and the higher the desired "net-of-consumption" tax-ratio, the higher – other things equal – the Pact-determined public sector capital stock $\tilde{k}^P$. Figure 4 depicts a case with a low $\kappa(k)$-schedule, relative to the $\xi(k)$-schedule, where $\tilde{k}^P < \tilde{k}^*$.

Figure 4: long-run public capital stocks and debt levels with and without a „close to balance" restriction on periodic budgets

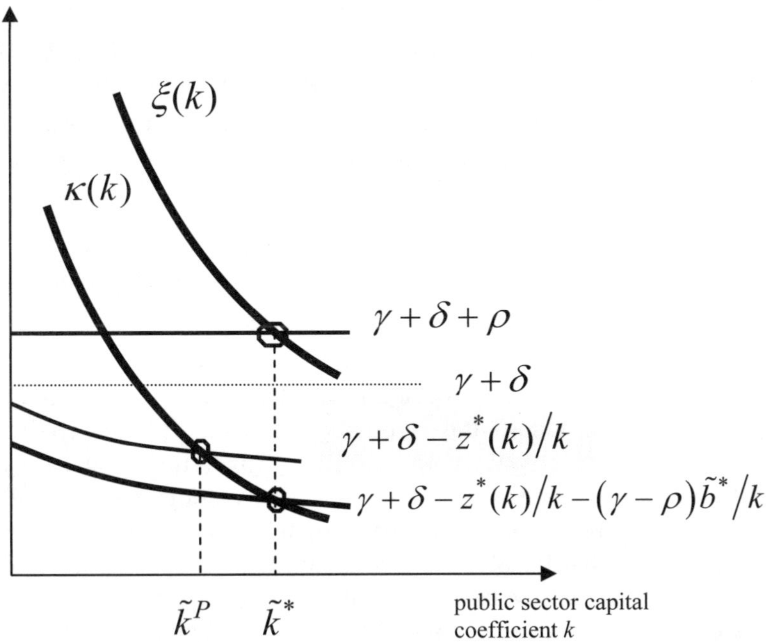

If there is no Pact-related restriction on the long-run debt-ratio, the corresponding condition reads as

$$\kappa(\tilde{k})=\gamma+\delta-z^*(\tilde{k})/\tilde{k}-(\gamma-\rho)b/\tilde{k}\,. \tag{16}$$

Now, the government may aim for the socially optimal capital stock $\tilde{k}^*$ in line with (14), and the condition (16), which incorporates the static optimality condition relating to z^*, then determines whether or not the country's long position involves government debt. In figure 4, endogenous determination of $\tilde{b}^*$ means that the line $\gamma+\delta-z^*(k)/k-(\gamma-\rho)\tilde{b}^*/k$ is drawn in such a way that it intersects with $\kappa(k)$ at the point $\tilde{k}^*$, and the vertical difference between this line and the line $\gamma+\delta-z^*(k)/k$ reflects the long run-debt position. A possible interpretation of the case depicted is that $\rho<\gamma$, in which case $\tilde{b}^*>0$. The "close to balance" condition would thus be binding. The intuition here is that the Pact determined capital stock is too low and if the real interest rate is lower than the real growth rate, then a long-run debtor position of the government allows to maintain a higher public sector capital coefficient. An alternative interpretation would be one where $\rho > \gamma$, whence $\tilde{b}^* < 0$ and the condition is not binding. A different case (not drawn) where the condition might become a binding constraint is one where (15) leads to $\tilde{k}^P > \tilde{k}^*$, and where $\rho > \gamma$. The intuition here is that, because of a high cash-rate of return κ and or a high desired net tax ratio z^*, a zero long-run debt-ratio would imply a sub-optimally large public sector capital stock. With $\rho > \gamma$, the burden of long-run debt would force the capital stock down to its socially optimal level k^*.

While admittedly somewhat ad-hoc, this line of reasoning highlights a fundamental shortcoming of the SGP. It rests on a view of government where the intertemporal role of fiscal policy is limited to strict *consumption* smoothing over the business cycle. And it ignores, partly at least, the role of government as an *investor*. The ultimate rationale for a government to engage in consumption smoothing is that fiscal deficits and surpluses over the course of the business cycle imply borrowing and lending terms that are better than what private agents would be able to obtain for themselves, say due to liquidity constraints. A further rationale is to smooth the distortionary effect of taxation, thereby alleviating the overall excess burden over the business cycle.[59] The Pact, by allowing a 3 percent deficit, allows for such a Keynesian role of fiscal policy over the business cycle, assuming certain numbers of key parameters of a typical European economy. But by enforcing a non-positive long run debt-ratio, it treats the public investment role of government in an asymmetric way, thus risking a sub-optimal level of the long-run public sector capital stock.

VIII. Conclusions

A brief look at the history of fiscal policy during the past decade has revealed that the fiscal *Maastricht criteria* for EMU entry have had a remarkable disciplinary impact on fiscal policy in all member

---

[59] See *Buiter* (1999a) for a more detailed presentation of these arguments for Keynesian fiscal policy oriented towards the business cycle.

countries of the EU, but the success of the *Amsterdam Stability and Growth Pact* is severely in doubt. While fiscal policies in European countries have not yet returned to the precarious positions of the mid nineties, it cannot be said that the SGP has lived up to the expectations of a self-enforcing device of lasting fiscal discipline in the EMU. Indeed, it is often perceived as a major nuisance, and doubts about its necessity abound. Against this background, I have attempted to readdress the theoretical justification of an SGP-like fiscal rule in an EMU-type monetary union.

I have argued that the relevant question is not whether such a fiscal rule is necessary, or at least useful, to ensure fiscal prudence in general, but whether a supra-national restriction of national fiscal policies is a necessary ingredient of a monetary union that deliberately, and supposedly for good reasons, abstains from even moderate degrees of fiscal centralization. *Conventional theory of currency unification* suggests that the EMU would need flexible and unrestricted national fiscal policies, rather than a SGP. Nor does empirical evidence indicate that SGP-like rules are prevalent in other monetary unions with comparable characteristics.

However, conventional theory is ill-posed to address the true concerns underlying the SGP. These have to do with various government failures that plague fiscal policies of European economies. The Pact needs to be judged against theory focusing on these failures. Modern macroeconomic theory suggests three types of arguments that may be brought up in support of an institutional agreement like the SGP: arguments related to the inefficiency of non-cooperative policy equilibria, arguments related to the political failures behind excessive government deficits as observed in post-Bretton-Woods Europe, and finally, concerns about the long-run solvency of fiscal policy, and the associated risk of government default. In this paper, I have argued, that the SGP *may* be a useful device in all three respects, but a convincing theoretical justification implies that, given politically feasible options, the Pact is a first-best solution to the underlying distortions, or at least that it avoids unnecessary costs.

As regards *policy coordination*, the verdict is that the Pact is a rather poor instrument to resolve inefficiencies of non-cooperative fiscal policies. Barring nominal rigidities, interest-rate spill-overs from government borrowing are pecuniary externalities that entail distributional effects and do not, as such, involve inefficiency. Inefficiency may arise if there are nominal rigidities, but fine-tuned efforts of macroeconomic policy coordination require a degree of flexibility that seems almost anathema to the principal orientation of the SGP. Nor does it contribute in an indirect way to dealing with these inefficiencies, since all SGP-procedures are applied on a strict one-for-one basis. Indeed, it is perfectly possible that the SGP may even work in the wrong direction. Inefficiencies may also arise in the form of violating rules of optimal taxation, due to monetary union. But here again, the usefulness of the Pact seems in doubt. Whether it has the (unintended) effect of alleviating inefficient taxation across the EMU very much depends on the leader-follower-structure of the game played by governments and the central bank. Policy coordination is, thus, at most a second-best (or even third-best) rationale for the SGP.

On *excessive deficits*, there are two questions that need to be answered. One is why private capital markets fail to exert sufficient discipline on governments, such that non-market measures seem warranted to complement the disciplinary force of markets. And the second is whether the Pact is likely to alleviate, or aggravate, the type of distortions that lead to the alleged tendency of excessive deficits. Distortions may be present both in capital markets and in the political system. The issue here is not whether in Euroland such distortions have in fact lead to overly high levels of public debt that need to be corrected (they probably have), but whether monetary union worsens the problem and, if so, whether the Pact is a first-best instrument of correction. I have argued that the answer is most likely to be negative. However, I have also argued that monetary union introduces a new distortion of its own that leads to excessive deficits. This runs along the lines of the Barro-Gordon problem of time-inconsistency and the cost of central bank bail-out, where the pact does find some theoretical justification.

A public deficit need not be economically unsustainable in the sense of violating the *solvency constraint* in order to be excessive, but if it is, then the specter of bail-out and financial crises becomes immediately relevant. Proponents of the SGP have always argued that it is an important safeguard for the monetary union against such disastrous events. However, the solvency-constraint is an inherently intertemporal concept, and I have argued that the SGP makes very little explicit reference to the intertemporal aspects of public finances. While the medium-run criterion of a public budget which is "close to balance or in surplus" does ensure solvency, I have argued that it is hardly an efficient way to avoid the systemic consequences of insolvent public finance positions. I have shown that this criterion, together with the 3 percent reference value of short-run annual deficits, represents a somewhat odd view which restricts the role of government to Keynesian policies related to consumption smoothing, and pays only insufficient attention to the role of government as an investor, aiming at an efficient level of the public sector capital stock.

References

Alesina A. / Perotti R. (1995), The political economy of budget deficits, in: IMF Staff Papers 42, 1995, pp. 1-32.

Baily M. N. / Kirkegaard J. F. (2004), Transforming the European Economy, Washington, D.C. 2004, Institute for International Economics.

Barro R. J. / Gordon D. B. (1983), Rules, discretion and reputation in a model of monetary policy, in: Journal of Monetary Economics 12, 1983, pp. 101-121.

Beetsma R. / Uhlig H. (1999), An analysis of the Stability and Growth Pact, in: Economic Journal 109, October 1999, pp. 546-571.

Boonstra W. (2005), Proposals for a better Stability Pact, in: Intereconomics 14, Jan./Feb. 2005, pp. 4-9.

Buiter W. H. (2003), Ten commandments for a fiscal rule in the E(M)U, in: Oxford Review of Economic Policy 19, 2003, pp. 84-99.

Buiter W. H. (1999a), Notes on 'A Code for Fiscal Stability', in: Oxford Economic Papers 53, 1999, pp. 1-19.

Buiter W. H. (1999b), The Fallacy of the Fiscal Theory of the Price Level, Cambridge 1999, Mass: NBER Working Paper 7302.

Buiter W. H. / Grafe C. (2003), Patching up the Pact: Some Suggestions for Enhancing Fiscal Sustainability and Macroeconomic Stability in an Enlarged Union, in: *Buti M.* (ed.), Monetary and Fiscal Policies in the EMU, Cambridge: Cambridge University

Press 2003, pp. 92-156.

Buiter W. H. / Corestti G. / Roubini N. (1993), Excessive deficits: sense and nonsense in the Treaty of Maastricht, in: Economic Policy 16, April 1993, pp. 58-100.

Buti M. / Sapir A. (1998), Economic Policy in the EMU, Oxford: Clarendon Press 1998.

Buti M. / Eiffinger S. / Franco D. (2003), Revisiting EMU's Stability Pact: A pragmatic way forward, in: Oxford Review of Economic Policy 19, 2003, pp. 100-111.

Canzoneri M. B. / Diba B. T. (2001), The Stability and Growth Pact: A delicate balance or albatross?, in: *Hughes Hallett A. / Mooslechner P. / Schuerz M.* (eds.), Challenges for Economic Policy Coordination within the European Union, Boston: Kluwer Academic Publishers 2001, pp. 127-142.

Casella A. (2000), Tradable deficit permits: efficient implementation of the Stability Pact in the European Monetary Union, in: Economic Policy 29, April 2000, pp. 323-361.

De Grauwe P. (2003a), The Economics of Monetary Union, 5th ed., Oxford: Oxford University Press 2003.

De Grauwe P. (2003b), The Stability and Growth Pact in Need of Reform, University of Leuven: mimeo 2003.

Eichengreen B. / Wyplosz Ch. (1998), The Stability and Growth Pact: more than a minor nuisance?, in: Economic Policy 26, April 1998, pp. 67-113.

Eichengreen B. (1998), European Monetary Unification: A Tour d ' Horizon, in: Oxford Review of Economic Policy 14, 1998, pp. 24-40.

Eijffinger S. C. W. (2005), Reform of the Stability and Growth Pact: Evaluating the European Commission's Communication of September 2004, in: Intereconomics 14, Jan./Feb. 2005, pp. 10-13.

Feldstein M. (1997), EMU and International Conflict, in: Foreign Affairs 76 (6), 1997, pp. 60-73.

Gros D. (2005), Reforming the Stability Pact, in: Intereconomics 14, Jan./Feb. 2005, pp. 14-17.

Hefeker C. (2005), Will a revised Stability Pact improve fiscal policy in Europe?, in: Intereconomics 14, Jan./Feb. 2005, pp. 17-21.

Masson P. R. (1996), Fiscal dimensions of EMU, in: Economic Journal 106, July 1996, pp. 996-1004.

Mc Kinnon R. I. (1997), EMU as a Device for Collective Fiscal Retrenchment, in: American Economic Review 87, May 1997, pp. 227-229.

Moesen W. / van Rompuy P. (1990), The Growth of Government Size and Fiscal Decentralization, Paper prepared for the IIPF Congress, Brussels 1990.

Ongena H. / Winkler B. (2001), Fiscal Policy in EMU, in: *Artis M. / Nixson F.* (eds.), The Economics of the European Union, Oxford: Oxford University Press 2001, pp. 314-352.

Uhlig H. (2003), One money, but many fiscal policies in Europe: what are the consequences?, in: *Buti M.* (ed.), Monetary and Fiscal Policies in the EMU, Cambridge: Cambridge University Press 2003, pp. 29-64.

Von Hagen J. / Eichengreen B. (1996), Federalism, fiscal restraints, and European Monetary Union, in: American Economic Review 86, May 1996, pp. 134-138.

Waltraud Schelkle[1]

Problems with the Pact

I. Introduction

The message of *Wilhelm Kohler's* nuanced and rich paper is not pleasant. I read it as: "The Pact is bad economics." He refuses to be summed up in that way but this seems what it amounts to in plain English. What arguments does he provide for this verdict, even if he does not endorse it?

The Pact is bad economics because it addresses problems with fiscal policy in Europe and elsewhere in a counterproductive way. These problems are, as the author rightly emphasizes, real problems and should be dealt with, but obviously in a constructive way. He discusses four flaws of the Pact:

1. The Pact can be justified neither by traditional Optimum Currency Area (OCA) arguments nor by what he calls the incentive-augmented OCA theory, and what I will call below "the Political Economy of sub-optimal currency areas". Based on evidence from fiscal federations, he argues that the Pact is not a self-enforcing contract between fiscal authorities in a decentralised setting.
2. The Pact is bad economics because it does not address the inefficiencies of non-cooperative behaviour in a monetary union. This is, at first sight, a counterintuitive claim since the architects of the Pact apparently had not much faith in the cooperative behaviour of member states. Yet, it is true that the Pact is not about

[1] Comment on the paper by *Wilhelm Kohler*.

cooperation at all but a disciplinarian device for fiscal consolidation in each member state.

3. The Pact with its initial focus on the 3 percent deficit criterion does not ensure long-term solvency of fiscal policy according to any of the criteria that economic theory has come up with. The norm of 'close to balance or in surplus' has gained prominence only recently and is in any case too strict to be credible, basically for the reason that *Paul De Grauwe* points out in his contribution: the norm implies in even weakly growing economies that public debt as a share of GDP converges to zero percent which is neither desirable economically nor likely to be feasible politically.
4. The only justification for the Pact that *Kohler* concedes is, in my view, flawed as well. He argues that the Pact's rigidity and one-size-fits all does indeed address the problem of time-inconsistent policies for which delinquent governments are likely to be less severely punished by markets in a monetary union. However, the fact on which his first criticism is based, namely that between four and six of the twelve EMU members have been or are de facto in breach of the Pact, indicates that it is not a self-enforcing Pact. Inflexibility has proven to be not good enough: the Pact cannot be good economics if it fails on incentives, especially if one is so obsessed with micro foundations as the Barro-Gordon tradition of time-consistent policymaking is.

Unfortunately for a commentator, I cannot help but agree with his analysis and the verdict that results from it. Thus, I note briefly what I have learnt from reading this excellent paper, highlight the arguments that I have not seen in the literature to be so clearly and meticulously spelled out and then move on to the question where we go from here.

His critique is original in that he puts 'SGP-like institutions' (fiscal constraints imposed on members of a monetary union as a safeguard of the monetary union) to the standard test of welfare economics: is it a first-best instrument to deal with market or government failures? He refrains from using that simply to forward his own pet reform but simply to make the analytical points in which respect the Pact fails a standard test of economic theory. This is obviously a most effective critique in that the Pact tends to be presented by its proponents as based on sound economics and even the critics use to attack the Pact for being based only on economic considerations but negligent of political considerations.

Even those of us who were critical of the original Pact might concede that perhaps it was unavoidable to make mistakes because the EMU is without precedent. Yet, *Kohler's* reading of the authors actually suggests that there has been experience one could have drawn on, namely from comparative fiscal federalism.[2] That evidence showed, first, that fiscally decentralised countries have less SGP-like constraints on the lower tiers of government because they are not incentive-compatible. The evidence also shows, secondly, that when shocks occur fiscal deficits increase more in countries that are fiscal more centralised. Both pieces of evidence undermine a fundamental rationale of the Pact since the Pact is based on the very assumption that we need constraints to ensure fiscal discipline in the presence of fiscal decentralisation.

Wilhelm Kohler points out the paradox that the Pact is based on the notion of pervasive government failure, yet the remedy it tries to implement is more government policy (surveillance of each other). The Wagnerians among us are reminded of Siegfried's sword that is supposed to heal the wound that it cuts. Alas, this is Germanic mythology. Yet, it reveals the irony that the Pact's proponents think it is all about enlightened good economics in its heroic battle against the political forces of evil and yet their arguments follow the logic of Germanic mythology. The more general point is that the Pact is built on mainstream Political Economy where good economics (sound fiscal policy) is always bad politics (no bribes for special interests) and bad economics (lax fiscal policy) is good politics (lots of bribes). I read this argument as suggesting that bad economics is also bad politics, i.e. the inconsistent theoretical underpinning of the Pact is a problem for its political acceptance and thus implementation or self-enforcement.

Where do we go from here? I think the theoretical underpinning for economic governance of EMU should come from the Political Economy of sub-optimal currency areas which ultimately all existing monetary unions are. It must be based on good economics and on a realistic notion of government. As I argued elsewhere the good economics which is also good political economy comes from an insurance approach to policy coordination which conceptualises a monetary union as a collective insurance pool.[3] This approach

---

2 See *von Hagen/Eichengreen* (1996) pp. 134-138; *Moesen/van Rompuy* (1990).

3 See *Schelkle* (2005) pp. 371-392.

would not try to tie governments' hands but give them an additional instrument. Such an insurance approach does not deny that there are problems of non-cooperative behaviour that need to be dealt with; in fact it throws light on the classical insurance problems of adverse selection and moral hazard in political economy. But this approach does not see all governments as crooks – if most of them were crooks, safe for the electorate only if handcuffed, then EMU was an irresponsible undertaking that is beyond repair. Rather, the structural legitimacy of European integration and the positive motivation of governments to share sovereignty can better be explained if we assume that governments are typically full of good intentions but weak in implementation. Thus they need support and additional incentives to live up to the promises for which they were elected into office. The following is just to indicate how such an insurance approach would address the problems that *Wilhelm Kohler* identified in present arrangements.

II. Cooperation and coordination

A common currency creates an insurance pool. The evidence that *Kohler* helpfully provides could for once indicate that this is not a symptom of market imperfection (implicit bail-out guarantee) but simply acknowledging the fact that a common currency *nolens volens* pools the good and bad risks. So you better apply standard insurance principles to prevent adverse selection and contain moral hazard. The original Pact, by contrast, provided perverse insurance in that the insured promises to pay extra should the insurance case arise; and it was lax on adverse selection as indicated by high public debt, obviously because one thought that discipline later on would be tough.

The essence of policy coordination as an insurance arrangement is that the cooperating governments form an insurance pool out of which a member country that experiences relatively hard times is compensated. Such compensation need not imply an insurance payment in the form of cash transfers from a central fund, but could instead be achieved by other members adjusting their policies to make it easier for the country in difficulty to stabilise its economy. An illustration would be fiscal stimulation by partner countries that creates higher demand for the unfortunate member's exports. Alternatively, the central bank could reduce interest rates in the knowledge that these rates may be too low for the other countries, obliging them to exercise countervailing fiscal restraint. The immediate implications of policy coordination as a collective insurance arrangement against aggregate income risks are, first, that the target is the appropriate *aggregate* fiscal stance so as to stabilise the pool (get the right policy mix). It also implies, secondly, *case-by-case evaluation* by an independent auditor to confirm that the member facing hard times has been hit by an exogenous shock. This is necessary because policy coordination, like any insurance scheme, is beset by moral hazard problems.

III. Long-term solvency

Insofar as an insurance approach gives governments an additional instrument for targeting both the level and the volatility of a policy objective such as employment, it should make achieving an instrumental goal like sustainable public debt easier as well. But ultimately, I think we should trust that national parliaments and political systems play the crucial role here. The sanctions that the insurance pool has for non-cooperative behaviour in this regard should not jeopardise that and provoke a political backlash against European integration. This is not to underestimate the potential for increasing interest rates from an irresponsible increase of government debt by a member state; but I am afraid the side-effects of the remedy will be more detrimental than any conceivable immediate effect on containing such behaviour.

To deal with moral hazard, political sanctions are in principle more appropriate than an Excessive Deficit Procedure which leads to pro-cyclical policies. Just to illustrate the idea, a government could lose its voting right in Ecofin as long as it does not comply with the stipulations. This would signal to domestic interest groups that the government loses its political leverage if it gives in to demands that are incompatible with EMU obligations. Political sanctions should be applied symmetrically, to deficits and surpluses, since they are equally unwarranted if collective stabilisation is the objective.

IV. Reform of the Pact

Suitably adapted, an insurance approach provides guidelines for reform of the SGP on both macroeconomic and political economy grounds. In *Schelkle* (2005), I argue in more detail that old and new Commission proposals are apt to make it more of an insurance arrangement.

An insurance approach calls for a strict implementation of entry rules that reveal good risks as well as for changing the working rules later on because the tying of hands in operating the union is counter-productive.[4] Entry rules must be strictly enforced to prevent adverse selection. Structural reforms such as making the central bank independent or – if deemed required for sustainable public finances, pension reforms – ensure that only economies that can live with the requirements of EMU enter the scheme. As regards working rules to contain moral hazard, the Commission has proposed (and got in the reform of March 2005) to give it – or an independent body – more discretion to introduce proposals to the Council on actions against national governments.[5] The Council must only be able to reject such proposals by unanimity, not by qualified majority as under the original rules. This is a sensible differentiation between the body that has decided whether the contingency has been met (the insurer) and the recipient of support (the insured) in the insurance arrangement that EMU policy coordination potentially amounts to.

A more emphatic role for the Commission would also facilitate consideration of the aggregate fiscal stance. In its response to the German draft in the mid-1990s, the Commission had proposed to take the aggregate into account when assessing the appropriate stance of national fiscal policies.[6] Targeting the aggregate stance would legitimise the constraints imposed by the SGP on national fiscal policies and increase moral pressure on governments that violate the rules. Yet the Council rejected it. This resulted in too little institutionalised concern for the stability of the union as a whole.

V. Conclusions

Finally, the Commission recognized early on that the Pact needs positive incentives for compliance if only to justify interference with national fiscal policy. As a result of research carried out by the Commission,[7] *Italianer* and collaborators devised a Community stabilisation mechanism, ie. a transfer scheme for pure stabilisation in

---

4 The idea is aptly summarised by *Khan/Sharma* (2001): "...in order to provide adequate safeguards, weaker ex post conditionality needs to be balanced with stricter ex ante pre-qualification."

5 See *European Commission* (2004).

6 See *Costello* (2001) pp. 116-117.

7 See *Italianer/Vanheukelen* (1993) pp. 493-510; *Italianer/Pisani-Ferry* (1994) pp. 155-194.

a monetary union; more recently, a study published by DG Ecfin also proposes a rainy day fund as part of a reformed fiscal framework.[8] It is recalled here to illustrate how an insurance fund might work, bearing in mind the political economy of fiscal policy coordination. The basic idea is simple. A member state would receive transfer payments in the fiscal year after a negative shock causes its unemployment rate to increase more than the average of unemployment rates in the other member states (excluding the respective country from this latter average). The amount of transfers would be proportional to the decline in income thus caused by the deviation of the country's unemployment trend from the others' average. This scheme has several features that prevent adverse selection and moral hazard. But most remarkably, the proposal is of the rule-based type.[9] From an insurance point of view, rule-based coordination has the obvious advantage that it delivers more security. If governments are risk-averse, security is by definition the welfare gain they derive from insurance: one Euro of transfer payments that a government can count on thanks to the rules is more valuable than one Euro that is the uncertain outcome of a bargain.

Reforms along these lines could be an entry point to more full-fledged fiscal coordination which I think is ultimately necessary for a stable and economically dynamic monetary union. While this is ultimately a political question, the contribution of *Wilhelm Kohler* gives us the criteria to judge whether the resulting arrangements stand the economic test. The original Pact, he lets us know in no uncertain terms, failed to do so.

References

Buti M. / Eijffinger S. / Franco D. (2003), Revisiting the Stability and Growth Pact: grand design or internal adjustment?, Economic Papers No.180, Brussels: European Commission, 2003.

Costello D. (2001), The SGP: How Did We Get There?, in: *Brunila A. / Buti M. / Franco D.* (eds.), The Stability and Growth Pact. The Architecture of Fiscal Policy in EMU, Houndmills, Bas-

---

8 See *Buti/Eijffinger/Franco* (2003) pp. 26-27.

9 See *Italianer/Vanheukelen* (1993) pp. 493-510.

ingstoke: Palgrave 2001, pp. 106-136.

European Commission (2004), Strengthening Economic Governance and Clarifying the Implementation of the Stability and Growth Pact, COM (2004) 581.

Italianer A. / Pisani-Ferry J. (1994), The regional-stabilisation properties of fiscal arrangements, in: *J. Mortensen* (ed.), Improving Economic and Social Cohesion in the European Community, Basingstoke & Hampshire: Macmillan 1994, pp. 155-194.

Italianer A. / Vanheukelen M. (1993), Proposals for Community stabilization mechanisms: Some historical applications, in: European Economy, Special No. 5, 1993, pp. 493-510.

Khan M. S. / Sharma S. (2001), IMF Conditionality and Country Ownership of Programs, IMF Working Paper WP/01/142, Washington DC: IMF 2001.

Moesen W. / van Rompuy P. (1990), The Growth of Government Size and Fiscal Decentralization, Paper presented at IIPF Congress, Brussels 1990.

Schelkle W. (2005), The Political Economy of Fiscal Policy Coordination in EMU: From Disciplinarian Device to Insurance Arrangement, in: Journal of Common Market Studies, vol.43 No.2, 2005, pp. 371-392.

von Hagen J. / Eichengreen B. (1996), Federalism, fiscal restraints, and European monetary union, in: American Economic Review vol.86, No.2 (P&P), 1996, pp. 134-138.

Part 4:
Economic Aspects of the Reform of the SGP

Marco Buti

Will the New Stability and Growth Pact Succeed? An Economic and Political Perspective

I. Introduction

While the Maastricht Treaty establishes the entry conditions for Member States to join the single currency, the Stability and Growth Pact (SGP) aims to make budgetary discipline a permanent feature of EMU. Consequently, the Pact is commonly interpreted as a major building block of EMU's architecture: the SGP "must rank as one of the most remarkable pieces of policy coordination in world history. Its construction makes it in some respects comparable to the founding of the Bretton Woods system."[1]

The SGP consists of a preventive arm, which is intended to strengthen the surveillance of budgetary positions and the surveillance and co-ordination of economic policies, and a dissuasive arm, which is intended to accelerate and clarify the excessive deficit procedure of the Treaty.[2]

Coming into force in 1998, six years after the Maastricht Treaty that had laid the constitutional foundations of EMU, the SGP was intended by its framers to strengthen the principles of budgetary discipline formulated in the Treaty so as to ensure that Member States would continue to abide by them, not just during the run-up to joining the single currency but beyond.

The approach chosen by the framers of the SGP was two-pronged:

First, the 3 per cent of GDP reference value for triggering the excessive deficit procedure should be treated as much as possible as a 'hard ceiling', the breaking of which would put in motion 'a quasi-automatic mechanism' for imposing sanctions, with escape clauses defined as narrowly as possible and legally binding deadlines for taking decisions imposed.[3] These features strengthened the role of the 3% deficit threshold, which had been introduced relatively late in the negotiations for the Maastricht Treaty and then hedged about with qualifications. As *Bini Smaghi* (2004) recalls, the report by the Chairman of the Monetary Committee on "The State of the Committee's Discussion on Excessive Deficits in EMU", dated 25 June 1991, stated that: "This procedure must address deficits representing gross errors of budgetary policy which jeopardize the stability of the Union or of a member state. It must

1 See *Artis* (2002) p. 155.

2 A detailed account of the legal aspects of the SGP is provided in *Cabral* (2001) pp. 193-157.

3 See *Stark* (2001) pp. 77-105.

be designed to identify such deficits and enforce their reduction. By its nature the initiation of this special procedure should not be a frequent event in full EMU." In the same vein, an expert closely involved on the Commission side in the Maastricht Treaty negotiations sums up the prevailing view of the excessive deficit procedure before the adoption of the Pact "... it is clear that the excessive deficit procedure is not a mechanistic procedure: the criteria or the judgment of the Commission are used to start a process which, after careful consideration of all the relevant aspects, may lead to the judgment that a Member State has an excessive deficit. Given the fact that, according to economic theory, an excessive deficit is difficult to define on the basis of strict criteria alone, this seems a balanced compromise."[4] Ensuring that breaches of the deficit ceiling would be a rare event would be the purpose of the so-called dissuasive arm of the SGP, which fleshes out the excessive deficit procedure foreseen by the Treaty (Art. 104), in particular by defining the exceptionality condition allowing a temporary breach of the 3 per cent of GDP threshold,[5] specifying the timetable for the correction of the excessive deficit and the adoption of decisions by the Council until the eventual imposition of sanctions for non-compliance, and the scale of such sanctions.

Second, Member States should commit themselves to a "medium-term budgetary objective of close-to-balance or in surplus", thereby providing on average a safety margin of 3 percentage points of GDP against breaching the 3 per cent deficit ceiling, enough to ensure that movements in the budgetary balance in response to cyclical fluctuations would leave the deficit under 3 per cent of GDP in all cases but a few rare recession episodes. This was to be the purpose of the so-called preventive arm of the SGP, which fleshes out the surveillance economic policies provisions of the Treaty, in particular by institutionalising the annual submission by Member States and examination by the Council of stability

---

4 See *Italianer* (1993) p. 86.

5 While the SGP provides a clear definition of the exceptionality and temporariness clauses, the closeness to the 3% of GDP threshold was not specified, the reason presumably being that no Member State wanted to anticipate at the time the level of the deficit which would be acceptable for qualifying for euro-area membership. Some ambiguity on how close the deficit should remain to the 3% of GDP reference value would also provide some flexibility in the definition of an excessive deficit.

programmes setting out their medium-term budgetary strategy to achieve and maintain the close-to-balance or in surplus objective, including the accompanying economic assumptions, and putting in place an early-warning mechanism for addressing recommendations in the event of a "significant divergence of the budgetary position from the medium-term objective, or the adjustment path towards it."

The SGP has been the subject of heated controversy among academics and opinion-makers ever since its inception. Opponents considered it "a vote of no confidence by European authorities in the strength of democratic institutions in the member states", even going beyond the conditions the IMF imposes on banana republics;[6] supporters saw it as "the price that must be paid for a common currency", noting that "stability between currencies has been possible only when countries have been prepared to relinquish some national sovereignty".[7]

Proposals for radical changes have been put forward, even going as far as the idea of abolishing the Pact altogether. The debate on a possible reform of the SGP accelerated after 2002, prompted by the failure of key Member States to respect its basic requirements. The final trigger for reform was the stalemate following the November 2003 ECOFIN Council's refusal to endorse the European Commission's recommendations to step up the excessive deficit procedure vis-à-vis France and Germany. Negotiations on the reform then started with a communication by the Commission in September 2004; a political agreement was reached by the ECOFIN ministers in March 2005 and the process was eventually concluded in July 2005 with a new legislative text.

The purpose of this article is to offer an initial evaluation of the SGP reform. Section 2 reviews the main fiscal policy developments in the early years of EMU which were at the basis of the crisis of the SGP 'mark I'. Section 3 describes the reformed SGP and an assessment of its main features. Section 4 presents some reflections on the political economy of the EU rules, comparing the new SGP with the Maastricht Treaty and the SGP 'mark I'. The final section concludes.

---

6 See *De Grauwe,* Financial Times, 25 July 2002.

7 See *Dr. Horst Siebert,* Financial Times, 6 August 2002.

II. Fiscal policy in the early years of EMU: a snapshot

The imposition of the Maastricht budgetary targets at the beginning of the 1990s undeniably launched a genuine process of consolidation. In most countries budget deficits declined substantially after 1993, the year which marked the entry into force of the Maastricht Treaty and in which the euro area registered the historically high deficit ratio of 5.5% of GDP. Aided also by lower interest rates thanks to reduced risk premia, the cyclically adjusted balance improved by 4.5 percentage points in the euro area between 1993 and 1999 (Figure 1), and was brought back below the 3% of GDP threshold in all Member States except Greece by 1997.

Figure 1: Cyclically adjusted balance of the euro area

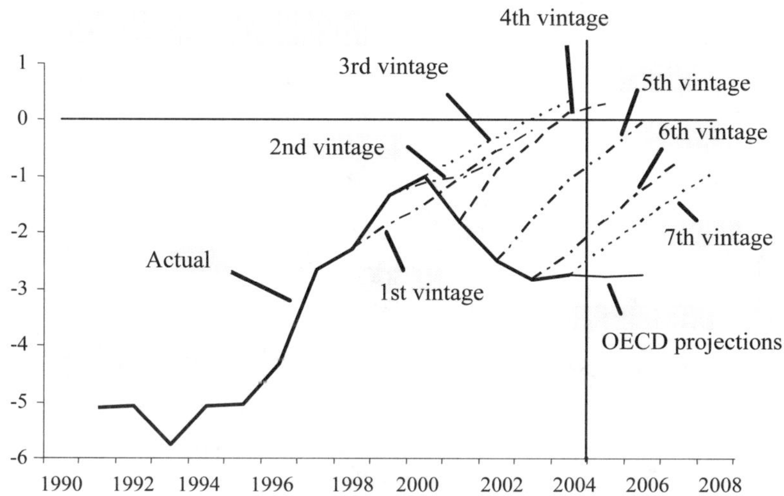

Source: *European Commission* (2005).

Some countries achieved spectacular turnarounds in fiscal performance. Italy managed to reduce its budget deficit by 7 percentage points of GDP between 1993 and 2000. Finland quickly regained control of its public finances after the recession of the early 1990s, posting – like Luxembourg – a surplus above 5% of GDP in 2000. In contrast, Germany and France, traditionally bastions of fiscal prudence, struggled to reduce budget deficits and keep control of public debt, fuelled in Germany by the costs of unification and in France by subdued economic performance in the first part of the period. In these countries public debt actually increased – though from a starting level below the 60% of GDP reference value.

The composition of the fiscal consolidation is shown in Figure 2, which decomposes the discretionary fiscal policy changes into changes in total revenue and changes in primary expenditure. The diagonal from top right to bottom left indicates the direction of the budgetary adjustment: the area above it marks an improvement in the cyclically adjusted primary balance, while the area below it indicates a structural deterioration. The diagonal from top left to bottom right marks the composition of the adjustment between expenditure changes and revenue changes.

Figure 2: Composition of the adjustment: 1993-1998 vs 1998-2004

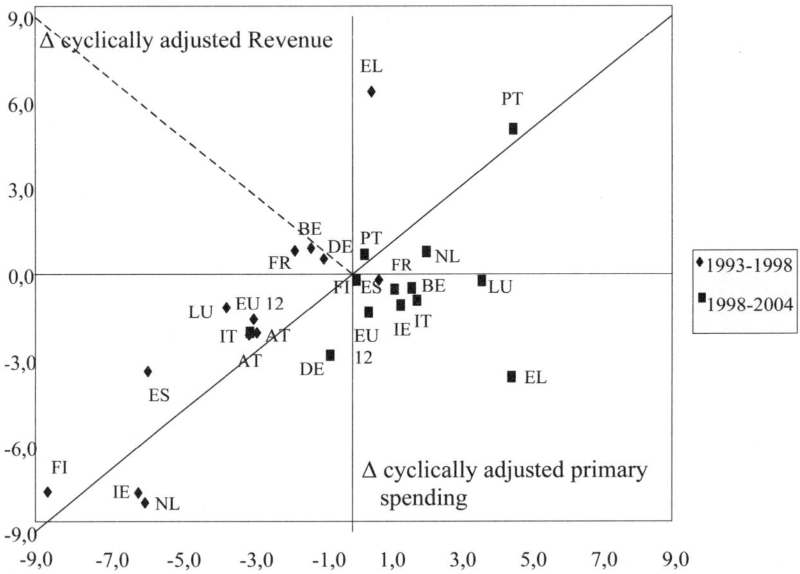

Source: *European Commission* (2005).

In the run-up to EMU practically all countries lie above the top right–bottom left diagonal, meaning that their cyclically adjusted primary balance improved during the period. Moreover, most of them pursued an expenditure-based retrenchment and several countries combined discretionary cuts in spending with a reduction in tax revenue, thus reducing the overall size of the public sector. Therefore, the composition of budgetary consolidation appears to have been of 'good quality', according to the criteria identified in the literature.[8]

While the retrenchment in the run-up to EMU is commonly considered a success, the SGP, which was supposed to consolidate Maastricht's achievements, has fallen short of its framers' expectations. At close to 3 per cent of GDP, the cyclically adjusted deficit of the euro-area members in the aggregate remains as distant from the close-to-balance objective as it ever has since the launch of EMU.

As shown in Figure 1 above, the cyclically adjusted balance for the euro area as a whole has progressively deteriorated in the years since 2000, falling well short of the commitments enshrined in the successive Stability Programme updates. The turnaround in both direction and composition of discretionary fiscal policy is confirmed by Figure 2, which shows that that the structural primary balances has deteriorated in most countries since the end of the 1990s: tax revenue has been reduced, while primary expenditure has started to climb again.

This analysis shows that the *de facto* suspension of the excessive deficit procedure in the cases of Germany and France after November 2003 (see below), which could have meant the amputation of the dissuasive arm of the Pact, had been preceded by a progressive loss of credibility of the preventive arm, as evidenced by persistent negative gaps between fiscal projections and the outcomes of successive rounds of stability programmes. However, the three largest countries in the euro appear largely to blame for this credibility gap, as their fiscal projections can be shown to suffer a significant tendency to under-predict actual deficits.[9] The small countries, by contrast, have managed as a group to achieve and maintain an underlying balance of their fiscal positions, something that has proved elusive for large countries.[10]

In sum, although the Maastricht process brought the unprecedented increase in non-war debt of the previous two decades to a

---

8 See, i.a. *Alesina/Perotti* (1996) pp. 461-467; *Perotti* (1999) pp. 1399-1436.

9 As shown in *Buti/van den Noord* (2004a), producing over-optimistic forecasts is particularly tempting in electoral periods as a way of increasing the room for manoeuvre of discretionary fiscal policy. See *von Hagen/Hallerberg/Strauch* (2004) and *Larch/Salto* (2005) for a more detailed discussion of this topic.

10 See *Buti/Pench* (2004) pp. 125-132.

halt, the SGP has apparently failed to eradicate the underlying – and ultimately unsustainable – deficit bias of fiscal policies. This bias manifests itself particularly through the continuation of the tendency to run expansionary policies or to fail to consolidate in good times, as can be seen from the deterioration of cyclically adjusted balances in the last upswing.

III. The reform of the SGP[11]

A. A new Pact

The failure of the SGP 'mark I' is epitomised by the repeated breaches of the 3 per cent of GDP deficit ceiling by individual Member States. Since 2002 six out of the twelve members of the euro area have been subject to the excessive deficit procedure; the early-warning mechanism has been invoked in four cases. Even more damaging to the credibility of the Pact than the frequency of the violations of the ban on excessive deficits has been the perceived disavowal of the original framework, and more specifically its enforcement mechanism, by key Member States. Already detectable in the apparent unwillingness of the Council to let the early-warning mechanism to run its normal course in the cases of Germany and Portugal in February 2002, the crisis of the enforcement mechanism of the Pact became manifest in November 2003 with the *de facto* suspension of the excessive deficit procedures initiated against Germany and France following the Council's failure to endorse Commission recommendations that the procedures be stepped up in accordance with the Pact's result-based approach to compliance.

While the debate in academic circles showed the depth of the divisions among economists, a certain consensus gradually emerged in the course of 2004 among the main policy players as to what changes were needed to the EMU fiscal framework. It was recognised that EMU needed numerical fiscal rules (since financial market discipline and national procedures were not deemed sufficient to ensure budgetary discipline) and that any radical changes to the rules introduced in 1992 (Maastricht Treaty) and 1997 (SGP) would be highly problematic. What *Buti et al* (2003) called "internal adjustment" of the existing framework rather than a radical overhaul

---

11 This section largely draws on *Buti et al* (2005). See also the Postscript in *Buti/Franco* (2005).

of the rules came to be regarded as the only feasible way forward. It was also acknowledged that complementary measures at the national level (such as better budgetary procedures and independent fiscal councils) would be highly desirable. The common menu of internal reforms included action to improve fiscal policy in good times, more consideration of public debt and long-term sustainability in assessing Member States' budgetary positions, a greater focus on cyclical developments and more transparency in fiscal data. Other aspects were more controversial: these included changes to the excessive deficit procedure and a stronger role for the Commission as enforcing agency.

The risks involved in embarking on a reform process under the pressure of unfavourable fiscal developments were also highlighted in the debate: the credibility of the framework itself could be endangered and the reform process could prove very long and uncertain. It was also noted that if the problem was primarily one of adherence to the rules, the priority should be to ensure rigorous implementation of the existing rules rather than to change them. At the same time, it was widely recognised that simply attempting to apply the existing rules after the watershed of November 2003 was not a viable option. Re-establishing a sense of ownership of the fiscal rules by all parties would be the precondition for their effective enforcement.

At the request of the European Council, in September 2004 the Commission issued a Communication suggesting a number of further changes to the Pact which, while preserving its overall architecture, aimed at avoiding pro-cyclical policies, especially in good times; better defined the medium-term objective by taking into account country-specific circumstances and reforms; gave greater prominence to the debt criterion; modified the implementation of the excessive deficit procedure, in particular by allowing more time to correct an excessive deficit under certain circumstances; and improved governance and enforcement.[12]

After a difficult and at times heated debate, an agreement was reached at the ECOFIN Council of March 2005. The guidelines of the reform were set out in a report which envisaged changes to both the preventive and corrective arms of the Pact.[13]

---

[12] See *European Commission* (2004).

[13] See *Council* (2005). These changes where subsequently translated into legislative amendments of the SGP regulations in July 2005. For a

On the preventive side (i.e. the medium-term targets and the adjustment path towards them), medium-term budgetary objectives (MTO) are now to be somewhat differentiated from one country to another on the basis of debt ratios and potential growth rates. Targets will be specified in structural terms, i.e. cyclically adjusted and net of the effects of temporary measures, and will range between a deficit of 1% of GDP and a small surplus. The latter will apply to high-debt, slow-growth countries. Implicit liabilities will also be taken into account in the future, once further technical analysis allows the Council to agree on criteria and methodological aspects. Major structural reforms with long-term fiscal benefits will be taken into consideration both when defining the adjustment path towards the medium-term objective and when considering temporary deviations from the target. A more detailed set of provisions also governs the path towards the medium-term objectives, though a minimum annual adjustment of 0.5% of GDP must be ensured.

On the corrective side (i.e. the application of the excessive deficit procedure), a modification was introduced in the definition of the "exceptional cyclical circumstances" which may justify the reference value for the deficit being exceeded: a breach of the threshold will now be considered exceptional if it results from a negative growth rate or an accumulated loss of output during a protracted period of very low growth relative to potential growth. When evaluating deficits exceeding the 3% limit, the Commission will take into account a number of factors ranging from cyclical conditions, through the implementation of the Lisbon agenda and policies to foster R&D and innovation, debt sustainability, the overall quality of public finances and financial contributions to international solidarity to fiscal burdens related to European unification. However, any excess over the 3% deficit threshold should remain limited and temporary. The implementation of pension reforms establishing a compulsory funded pillar will also be taken into consideration, especially when assessing whether an excessive deficit has been corrected.

While confirming that, as a rule, the deadline for the correction of an excessive deficit will remain the year after it is identified, the Council decided that the initial deadline could be set one year later if there were special circumstances, and could be revised at a later

---

detailed presentation of the new Pact, see *European Commission* (2005).

stage if unexpected adverse economic events with major unfavourable budgetary effects occurred.

The Council called for a stronger weight to be given to public debt, but was not able to agree on a quantification of the minimum debt reduction for countries with very high debt ratios, as suggested by the Commission.

The Council also outlined a number of steps to improve the governance of EU rules. It suggested closer co-operation between Member States, the Commission and the Council in the implementation of the Pact. It indicated the need to develop national budgetary rules and ensure that national parliaments are closely involved in the process. Finally, it called for reliable macroeconomic forecasts and budgetary statistics.

B. An evaluation of the reform

These changes got a mainly sceptical reception. Some commentators argued that, given the host of exceptions to the 3% rule and the greater discretion left to the Council, the Pact was, *de facto,* dead.[14] Even those traditionally critical of the old SGP, while appreciating the better balance between fiscal discipline and flexibility, viewed the reformed Pact as excessively prone to opportunistic interpretations and as having failed to tackle the root causes of fiscal imbalances.[15]

In reviewing the debate on the SGP, *Buti et al* (2005) highlight four critical issues that any effective reform of the Pact should tackle: (a) overcoming excessive uniformity, (b) improving transparency, (c) correcting pro-cyclicality, and (d) strengthening enforcement.

Table 1 provides a qualitative assessment of the main changes in the preventive and corrective arms of the SGP from these four perspectives. In the rest of this section, we provide an initial assessment of the 2005 reform and give some indications on where further progress is needed to ensure the effectiveness of the new rules.

---

14 See *Calmfors* (2005).

15 See *Coeré/Pisani-Ferry* (2005).

Table 1: Desirable improvement of the SGP: how the new Pact scores

2005 SGP REFORM	Overcoming excessive uniformity	Improving transparency	Correcting procyclicality	Strengthening enforcement
I. Governance				
Stability programme for the legislature		(+)		
Involvement of national Parliament				(+)
Reliable forecasts		(+)		(+)
Better statistical governance		+		+
II. Preventive arm				
Medium-term objectives	++	-		
Adjustment path	+		+	
Structural reforms	+	-		-
III. Corrective arm				
Exceptional circumstances	+		+	
'All other relevant factors'	+	- -		- -
Systemic pension reforms	+			-
Debt and sustainability	+	-	+	
Repeatability of steps	+	-	+	-
Overall assessment	+	-/+	+	-/+

Legend: ++ strong improvement, + improvement, - deterioration, -- strong deterioration. (+) improvement if effectively implemented at national level.

C. Overcoming excessive uniformity

The new SGP has introduced some elements of country-specificity in both the preventive and the corrective arm of the Pact. The close-to-balance rule of the original SGP, interpreted as broadly balanced budgets in cyclically adjusted terms, treated equally countries with different levels of public debt, implicit and contingent liabilities, and public investment needs.

In the early years of EMU, the only dimension on which countries were differentiated was the variability of the cyclical component of the budget balance: economies subject to higher business cycle volatility and having larger automatic stabilisers require a larger cyclical safety margin in order to avoid breaching the 3% of GDP deficit ceiling under normal cyclical circumstances.[16] In the new Pact, the articulation of the MTO has been extended to other dimensions, such as the financial fragility of the country, as embodied in the stock of public debt, and – in the future – the threat to long-term sustainability represented by the implicit liabilities of pension systems and the capacity of countries to 'grow out of their debt', measured by taking into account their potential growth (and therefore structural reforms which are intended to boost it).

The Council has taken a cautious approach by stipulating that, in order to safeguard the 3% deficit ceiling, the medium-term target should never exceed a deficit of 1% of GDP. This implies that countries with a relatively low stock of debt and estimated implicit liabilities will be allowed to have cyclically adjusted budget deficits of up to 1% of GDP. This solution is consistent, in most cases, with a prudent version of the golden rule.[17] In the case of structural reforms entailing frontloaded costs, deviations from the MTO are allowed, but only under strictly defined conditions. The debt ratios in high debt countries and in countries with expected rising expenditure levels should decline fast, helping to offset the burden of ageing in the future, while in the other countries deficit levels will ensure the maintenance of a small public debt. The solution should strengthen the political incentives to reduce the current and implicit debt at a faster pace.

In order to avoid moral hazard, commonly agreed estimates of implicit liabilities in EU countries will have to be computed, following the experience of the Economic Policy Committee's estimates of age-related public spending.[18] The use of long-term projections in the EU fiscal framework should be conditional on progress concerning the comparability, transparency and independ-

---

[16] See *Artis/Buti* (2000) pp. 563-592.

[17] As pointed out above, in the case of public investment, the right concept is that of net investment (hence taking into account amortisation).

[18] See *EPC* (2003).

ence of the projections. A variety of sustainability indicators could be used: tax-gaps, government net worth, and generational accounting. Since each indicator requires some arbitrary choices, it will be necessary to predefine the relevant assumptions and parameters and agree on a common set of indicators.

The new SGP also introduces elements of country-specificity in the corrective arm of the Pact. As argued below, whilst such changes may reduce excessive uniformity of the rules, they may in some instances increase their complexity, with negative implications for transparency and enforcement.

D. Improving transparency

Transparency has several dimensions: it includes accounting conventions, forecasting exercises and reporting practices.[19] Two aspects are particularly important. (i) Fiscal indicators providing a comprehensive view concerning current and perspective fiscal accounts and compliance with the rules should be available to monitoring institutions, the general public and financial markets. (ii) The design of the rules should allow for an unambiguous assessment of compliance. This calls for simple, well-defined rules.

Regarding the first aspect, the EU fiscal framework has been widely criticised for a lack of transparency,[20] manifested in a number of ways. First, the deficit indicator as defined by ESA-95 does not provide a full picture of countries' public finance imbalances. Second, the debt indicator (gross financial debt at face value) allows targets to be achieved via operations which do not improve fiscal sustainability, and tends to underestimate overall outstanding liabilities. Third, under the current system of national accounts, monitoring is hampered by delays in data provision and allows some manipulation of statistics with the result that the whistle is often blown far too late or only when the true data eventually surface. And lastly, the forecasts underlying stability programmes have frequently turned out to be over-optimistic.

The new SGP includes potentially important provisions leading to improved transparency, but also elements which work in the opposite direction.

In recent years, in order to meet the short-term targets, countries have frequently adopted one-off, cash-raising measures instead of

---

19 See *Kopits/Symansky* (1998).

20 See *Balassone/Franco/Zotteri* (2005), *Buti/Nogueira/Martins/Turrini* (2006), *Koen/van den Noord* (2005) and *von Hagen/Wolff* (2004).

making the necessary structural adjustment. The decision that compliance with the medium-term target as well as with the minimum annual adjustment of 0.5% of GDP is to be assessed in *structural* terms, by netting out the estimated effect of the cycle and one-off measures, will lead to improved transparency. In order to implement this, an agreed definition of one-off measures could complement the existing agreement on how to compute cyclically adjusted balances. However, given the current legislation and accounting conventions, the 3% rule has not been modified. Hence, in practice, one-off measures can still be used at the margin to avoid an excessive deficit. As to the abrogation of an excessive deficit, it will be important to focus on the *durability* of the adjustment, thereby reducing the incentives to use one-off measures to temporarily bring the deficit below the reference value without correcting the underlying imbalances.

As to public debt, the application of the fiscal rules will continue to focus on its definition in *gross* terms. However, this overlooks the fact that government assets can be sold to repay the debt and that there are non-financial liabilities. It is preferable to use both a gross and a net debt definition. On the basis of an agreed, transparent framework, governments could be required to provide estimates of off-budget liabilities, their net asset position and long-term budgetary trends.

The availability of high-quality statistics and timely fiscal indicators is still an issue. The problem of early detection of deviations from targets was vividly exposed in the case of Portugal in 2001. Even more serious has been the case of Greece, which in 2004 turned out to have had a deficit in excess of 3% of GDP since 1997. In Greece's case, but also in other countries, the yearly increase in public debt has frequently exceeded the deficit level as below-the-line operations have systematically contributed to debt growth.

The new Pact acknowledges the importance of high-quality, timely and reliable fiscal statistics and pledges to ensure the independence, integrity and accountability of both national statistical offices and Eurostat.[21] The availability of better statistics should be complemented by a more comprehensive surveillance of fiscal variables. One way forward would be to resurrect, in parallel with national accounts definitions, regular monitoring of cash flows.

21 On the importance of a reliable statistical framework for the application of EU fiscal rules, see *Balassone/Franco/Zotteri* (2003).

National authorities could be required to indicate ex ante cash figures broadly consistent with the ESA95 balance. In parallel, changes in the debt level (net of the effects of exchange rate changes and privatisation proceeds) could be closely monitored: if a significant departure from target is detected in financial flows, it would be up to national authorities to explain the difference.[22]

The overly optimistic forecasts that are common in some Member States can translate into higher-than-projected deficits, since government revenues quickly respond to changes in potential output whereas adjustments on the expenditure side normally require a lengthy process of political decision-making. The new Pact indicates that budgetary projections should be based on realistic, even cautious, macroeconomic forecasts. The *European Commission* (2004) proposed that stability programmes should be based on macroeconomic assumptions provided by the Commission. The Council decided that countries are still free to use their own assumptions, but that they give detailed explanations of any divergences from the Commission forecasts.[23]

While the above changes are a step towards improving the quality and availability of fiscal indicators, others are likely to negatively affect the second aspect of transparency mentioned above, namely the possibility to easily assess compliance with the rules.

As to the corrective part of the Pact, the most notable amendment is the specification of so-called 'other relevant factors' in the assessment of whether a deficit in excess of 3% of GDP can be considered 'excessive' in the sense of the Treaty. Such factors – ranging from the implementation of the Lisbon agenda and policies to foster R&D and innovation, through the overall quality of public finances and financial contributions to international solidarity, to fiscal burdens related to European unification – may give countries easy escape routes in the event of deficits in excess of the reference value. While there is an important safeguard in the provision that any excess over the 3% deficit threshold should remain limited and

---

[22] As initially proposed by the Commission, in the cases of application of the excessive deficit procedure to Greece, Portugal and Italy in 2005, the recommendation on issued by the Council included a mention on avoiding reliance on below-the-line operations.

[23] The case for independent forecasts is advocated by *Jonung/Larch* (2004).

temporary, such a long list of relevant factors runs the risk of blurring the assessment.

The preventive part of the SGP has also become more complex. The medium-term objectives are no longer defined ex ante, but are set by countries themselves in their programmes on the basis of commonly agreed criteria that might evolve over time.

E. Correcting pro-cyclicality

It is widely recognised that the original SGP did not provide sufficient incentives for countries to run prudent fiscal policies in good times, with the result that their room for manoeuvre was curtailed in bad times. The new agreement explicitly aims to correct pro-cyclicality by emphasising the importance of reliable macroeconomic forecasts, the commitment to stepping up consolidation in good times, relaxing the "exceptionality clause", making the timing of the correction of the excessive deficit a function of the prevailing cyclical conditions and foreseeing the guarded possibility to repeat steps of the procedure in the event of adverse shocks.

While these changes go in the right direction, it remains to be seen whether they go far enough in terms of sticks and carrots.

One possible way of stepping up peer pressure would be to use the early warning procedure of the SGP, not only in bad times when the deficit approaches the 3% ceiling, but also in good times when a significant divergence from structural targets is detected. The idea of an early warning procedure independent of the immediate danger of an excessive deficit was considered by the *European Commission* (2004). However, the new SGP, while providing for the possibility for the Commission to issue "policy advice" in this regard, did not accept the proposal.

Buti et al (2003) and *Sapir et al* (2004) have argued that the introduction of rainy-day funds may improve the incentives for prudent fiscal behaviour in good times. These funds, which would be used in times of recession and replenished in upturns, might increase the incentive for governments not to waste the surpluses in good times and increase the room for manoeuvre in bad times. However, establishing them would require a review of the current ESA accounting rules for computing budgetary statistics, so such a move, although interesting, is not unproblematic.[24]

---

[24] Alternatively, the Treaty protocol could be revised, mentioning that the 3% reference value refers to budget balances net of accumulation of assets in the rainy-day fund. However, if the fund were depleted after

F. Strengthening enforcement

A legitimate criticism of the Treaty and the old SGP is that enforcement is partisan: national authorities are supposed to apply the rules to themselves, and therefore have strong incentives for collusion and horse-trading. As indicated in table 1 and as is the case with transparency, the new Pact includes both some provisions which will strengthen enforcement and others which are likely to weaken it.

As *Buti et al* (2003) point out, enforcement is particularly problematic in the case of supranational fiscal rules applying to sovereign countries. Enhancing national ownership of the rules would mean that there was a better chance of them becoming self-enforcing.[25] In parallel, the Commission's role in enforcing the SGP should be strengthened.

On the first count (national ownership), the new provisions concerning governance – notably the involvement of national parliaments – go in the right direction, but are too modest. In particular, the suggestion to establish independent monitoring bodies at national level, which was mentioned in the initial proposals by the Commission,[26] was not accepted. On the second count (a stronger role for the Commission), the new Pact does not introduce any significant change either in voting or in the procedural arrangements. Evidently, the Council was not prepared to strengthen the authority of the Commission in the interest of the credibility of EU fiscal rules. On the contrary, there is a risk that provisions such as the considerations of 'other relevant factors' could work against effective enforcement of the rules by reducing transparency and increasing the possibility of collusion in the Council.

---

protracted deficits, the budget balance figure used in the SGP would quickly worsen, leading to difficulties in the implementation of the SGP.

25 As *Buti/Pench* (2004) argue, this is particularly important in the case of large euro-area countries where the threat of external sanctions is less effective.

26 See *European Commission* (2004).

IV. A political economy view: renewed ownership or green light for collusion?

Experience clearly shows that successful implementation of the new Pact will depend on political will. In order to assess whether the reformed rules incorporate adequate incentives for compliance, it is useful to it useful to identify what went wrong with the original SGP compared to Maastricht from the political economy standpoint. Table 2 sketches out a number of features which have been considered the basis of the success of the Maastricht process.[27] While the SGP 'mark I' can be easily assessed against those criteria, it is too early to do the same for the reformed Pact'. Therefore, the table presents two alternative prospective readings: an opportunistic 'collusive' deal and 'genuine' adherence to the revamped rules.

Table 2: The old and the new Stability Pact: two readings

	Old SGP	**New SGP: Collusion**	**New SGP: Genuine**
1. Public visibility	High but fading	On the way to oblivion	Medium
2. Clear incentives	Blurred	Easier to get away with	Better rationale
3. Political ownership	Small MS	High deficit MS: DE+FR+IT	Germany and virtuous MS
4. Constraining calendar	CTB a moving target	MTO de facto never	MTO by the end of Stability programme
5. Collegial culture	Acrimony prevailed	Mutual back-scratching	New collegiality based on trust

---

[27] See *Buti/Giudice* (2002) pp. 823-847; *Buti/van den Noord* (2004b) pp. 737-756.

A. Public visibility

With the Maastricht convergence criteria, the objective of meeting them became the centrepiece of government strategies in many EU countries. Public visibility was greatly facilitated by the simplicity of the 3% of GDP deficit criterion, which provided a clear signpost for economic policies regardless of the political colour of the government, especially in countries which entered the 1990s with very high deficits and looming unsustainability threats. The simplicity and the (largely) unambiguous definition of the fiscal requirements – especially that concerning the budget deficit – allowed the European Commission to effectively monitor them as an external agent entrusted by all Member States with the correct interpretation and implementation of the Treaty criteria. High visibility, together with easy monitoring, was also one of the reasons for preferring numerical targets over national procedural rules. The close-to-balance-or-in-surplus rule of the SGP enjoyed lower visibility than a simple deficit ceiling would have. The fact that, in the reformed Pact, the MTOs have to be set by national authorities (albeit within the range agreed upon by the Council) gives a better chance of renewed visibility – assuming a genuine implementation of the new rules. By contrast, a collusive approach would relegate the Pact to the back burner and, after an initial period of renewed interest, it would be likely to fade into oblivion.

B. Clear structure of incentives

The rewards and penalties linked with the Maastricht public finance requirements were very clearly laid out. Politically, meeting the convergence criteria would allow budgetary laggards to join the virtuous countries in the new policy regime, while failing to comply carried the penalty of exclusion from the euro area. This was considered too harsh a political sanction, especially for countries traditionally at the forefront of the process of European integration. Market incentives were therefore also crucial, notably because countries with high deficits and debt levels adopting a credible adjustment programme could enjoy a less costly and faster reduction of risk-premia in interest rates, which would help lower public finance imbalances. With the move to a single currency, the structure of incentives changed: the market incentives were reduced with the convergence of interest rates and the carrot of entry was eaten, while the stick of exclusion was replaced by the threat of sanctions under the SGP that might only materialise at a late stage, if at all. The experience of the early years of EMU showed that the Council was not prepared to use the 'nuclear option' of pecuniary sanctions, especially vis-à-vis large countries. The new Pact offers easier ways out, for instance by allowing repetition of the various steps of the EDP procedure. However, if applied genuinely, this stronger economic rationale may help justify increasing peer pressure on fiscal delinquents.

C. Political ownership

The whole debate on the fiscal requirements of EMU reflected Germany's concern with fiscal discipline: both the Maastricht fiscal criteria and the SGP clearly bear Germany's fingerprints. Strong macroeconomic stability came to be regarded as an essential precondition for Germany to agree to merge its monetary sovereignty into a single currency. The political ownership of the SGP shifted towards smaller countries with structural surpluses which, although numerous, have a relatively small weight in the euro area. This was sufficient to keep the Pact alive, but weakened the enforceability of the rules, especially vis-à-vis large countries. Germany holds again the key to a rigorous implementation of the new rules. Renewed political ownership by Germany requires it to accept a strict application of the rules to itself, and thus to lead by example. If it does not do so, high deficit countries will take over, paying lip service to the EU rules but disregarding them in practice. Resistance by virtuous small Member States would in that case eventually be swamped in a collusive deal.

D. Constraining calendar

The Treaty set very clear deadlines for moving to the final stage of EMU. Countries willing to join with the first wave had no choice but to make the required consolidation effort to meet the convergence requirements. The SGP set very clear, short deadlines between the various steps of the procedure, but the 2003 November crisis over stepping up the EDP for France and Germany led to a stalemate. Moreover, the creation of sufficient margins under the 3% deficit ceiling was not linked to a specified calendar and, as discussed above, close-to-balance positions became a moving target. This would be the fate of the MTO if the collusive option under the new Pact were to prevail. But if the new rules are applied in earnest, the provision for non-EDP countries to achieve their MTO by the end of the Stability Programme period may hold.

E. Collegial culture

During the run-up to EMU, the convergence process facilitated the progressive building of a collegial culture of stability through personal contact amongst policy-makers and national and EU officials. This new climate facilitated peer pressure between national authorities and enhanced the role and authority of the European institutions. In the implementation of the SGP, however, this climate of mutual trust was replaced by acrimony between the Council and the Commission (which culminated in the Court appeal after the 2003 November crisis), and between large and small countries. Under the reformed Pact, if collusion prevails, the more complex setting would favour mutual back-scratching by fiscal sinners ('I help you now, you help me later'), whereas a genuine application of the new rules would favour the emergence of a new collegial atmosphere based on trust.

What are the chances that the new SGP will be applied in a rigorous manner? According to most academics and policy commentators – even those fiercely critical of the old Pact – the new rules bear the imprint of collusion as a birthmark. However, while a certain degree of scepticism may be justified, we should not write off the Stability Pact 'mark II' too quickly. At EU level, the loss of reputation that its failure would entail for the ECOFIN Council and, especially, the Eurogroup, not to mention the Commission, would be enormous. At national level, the key to its success is held by large countries – first and foremost Germany. We will not have to wait for long before the jury comes back with its verdict.

V. Conclusions

The EU fiscal policy framework aims to balance fiscal discipline and fiscal stabilisation in a context in which countries ultimately remain responsible for national fiscal policy.

Clearly, the Stability Pact 'mark I' had a number of drawbacks – particularly its asymmetric incentives and lack of a long-term view. The reformed Pact goes some way towards correcting such problems while retaining the original architecture.

Some innovations allow greater flexibility in dealing with special circumstances and country-specific problems, while retaining a prudent approach to fiscal behaviour. If they are actually implemented, the steps being considered to improve fiscal transparency, enhance the quality of statistics and strengthen national budgetary institutions have the capacity reinforce the rules. On the other hand, the extended deadlines for correcting deficits and, more generally, the greater complexity of the new framework may lower the visibility of the fiscal targets and make monitoring less effective. Few changes have been introduced in the key provisions affecting enforceability of the rules.

A successful application of the new Pact will require increasing political accountability at national level. This applies to the provisions concerning governance, namely the use of reliable forecasts and the stronger role of national Parliaments. It would be a great help if independent national boards in charge of budgetary monitoring and assessment were created in all Member States. In due course, the Commission's initial suggestion to establish a "European semester", where the broad orientations for fiscal policy are agreed, followed by a "national semester" where these general orientations are translated into concrete policy actions, should be resurrected in order to increase coherence and visibility.

But, in the end, the major weakness of the old rules was poor enforcement mechanisms. Will the new rules be more effectively enforced? The fact that in the new Pact there is a greater margin for discretion but no independent enforcer may increase the incentives for collusion by the Council in subverting the implementation of the rules. If so, the lack of enforcement will persist or even be aggravated. However, as the new Pact has a stronger economic rationale and may improve national ownership and fiscal transparency, there may be a better chance of it becoming self-enforcing.

While the reformed SGP has been greeted with scepticism in many academic and policy circles, it would be wrong to assume that it is bound to become irrelevant. First, the reasons why fiscal rules were adopted in a monetary union of many sovereign countries in the first place are still valid. The future enlargement of the euro area to Central and Eastern European countries actually strengthens the need for a common fiscal framework.[28] Second, no viable alternative to a credible supranational rule has emerged from the debate on the reform of the Pact, since all the other potential solutions have foundered on serious criticism of one kind or another. Third, many countries will continue to need an external anchor to ensure sound fiscal policies leading to a reduction in debt levels also for purely domestic reasons – particularly the demographic shock which lies around the corner. Finally, it is likely that,

[28] See *Orbán/Szapàry* (2004).

as soon as serious imbalances emerge in some countries, threatening the stability of the euro area, the other euro-area members will step up the pressure for rigorous implementation of the rules.

Whether and when a call for stronger fiscal discipline will arise depends on politics, the key factor being renewed ownership of the rules. In the end, the new rules can be rigorously applied only if they are backed by key players and fully integrated in their national policy framework.

References

Alesina A. / Perotti R. (1996), Fiscal Discipline and the Budget Process, in: American Economic Review 86, 1996, pp. 461-467.

Artis M. J. (2002), The Stability and Growth Pact: Fiscal Policy in the EMU, in: *F. Breuss / Fink G. / Griller S.* (eds.), Institutional, Legal and Economic Aspects of the EMU, Springer: Wien-New York 2002, pp. 101-116.

Artis M. J. / Buti M. (2000), Close to Balance or In Surplus - A Policy Maker's Guide to the Implementation of the Stability and Growth Pact, in: Journal of Common Market Studies 38(4), 2000, pp. 563-592.

Balassone F. / Franco D. / Zotteri S. (2003), Fiscal Rules: Indicators and Underlying Statistical Frameworks, paper presented at the IIPF congress, Prague 2003.

Balassone F. / Franco D. / Zotteri S. (2005), EMU Fiscal Indicators: A Misleading Compass?, in: Empirica, forthcoming.

Bini Smaghi L. (2004), What Went Wrong with the Stability and Growth Pact?, paper prepared for the conference on Monetary Union in Europe: Historical Perspectives and Prospects for the Future, Copenhagen, December 2004.

Brunila A. / Buti M. / Franco D. (2001), The Stability and Growth Pact-The Architecture of Fiscal Policy in EMU, Basingstoke: Palgrave 2001.

Buti M. / Eijffinger S. / Franco D. (2003), Revisiting the Stability and Growth Pact: Grand Design or Internal Adjustment?, CEPR Discussion Paper 3692, 2003.

Buti M. / Eijffinger S. / Franco D. (2005), The Stability Pact Pains: a Forward-Looking Assessment of the Reform Debate, CEPR Discussion Paper 5216, 2005.

Buti M. / Franco D. (2005), Fiscal Policy in Economic and Monetary Union – Theory, Evidence and Institutions, Cheltenham: Edward Elgar 2005.

Buti M. / Giudice G. (2002), Maastricht's Fiscal Rules at Ten: an Assessment, in: Journal of Common Market Studies 40(5), 2002, pp. 823-847.

Buti M. / Nogueira Martins J. / Turrini A. (2006), From Deficit to Debt and Back: Political Incentives under Numerical Fiscal Rules, paper prepared for the Banca d'Italia Public Finance Workshop, Perugia, March 2006.

Buti M. / Pench L. (2004), Why Do Large Countries Flout the Stability Pact? And What Can Be Done About It?, in: Journal of Common Market Studies 42(5), 2004, pp. 125-132.

Buti M. / van den Noord P. (2004a), Fiscal Policy in EMU: Rules, Discretion and Political Incentives, in: Moneda y Crédito 218, 2004, pp. 265-307.

Buti M. / van den Noord P. (2004b), Fiscal Discretion and Elections in the Early Years of EMU, in: Journal of Common Market Studies 39(4), 2004, pp. 737-756.

Cabral A. J. (2001), Main Aspects of the Working of the Stability and Growth Pact, in: *Brunila / Buti / Franco* (eds.), The Stability and Growth Pact-The Architecture of Fiscal Policy in EMU, 2001, pp. 139-157.

Calmfors L. (2005), What Remains of the Stability Pact and What Next?, Sieps, Report n° 8, 2005.

Coeré B. / Pisani-Ferry J. (2005), Fiscal Policy in EMU: Towards a Sustainability and Growth Pact?, in: Oxford Review of Economic Policy, forthcoming.

Council (2005), Improving the Implementation of the Stability and Growth Pact, 7423/05, March 2005.

European Commission (2004), Strengthening Economic Governance and Clarifying the Implementation of the Stability and Growth Pact, COM (2004) 581, September 2004.

European Commission (2005), Public Finances in EMU – 2005, European Economy 3, 2005.

Italianer A. (1993), Mastering Maastricht: EMU Issues and How They Were Settled, in: *Gretscham K.* (ed.), Economic and Monetary Union: Implications for National Policy-Makers, Institute of Public Administration, Maastricht 1993, pp. 51-113.

Jonung L. / Larch M. (2004), Improving Fiscal Policy in the EU: the Case for Independent Forecasts, Economic Papers 210, European Commission 2004.

Koen V. / van den Noord P. (2005), Fiscal Gimmickry in Europe: One-Off Measures and Creative Accounting, OECD Economics Department Working Papers 417, 2005.

Kopits G. / Symansky S. (1998), Fiscal Policy Rules, IMF Occasional Paper 162, 1998.

Larch M. / Salto M. (2005), Fiscal Rules, Inertia and Discretionary Fiscal Policy, in: Applied Economics 37, 2005, pp. 1135-1146.

Orbán G. / Szapàry G. (2004), The Stability and Growth Pact from the Perspective of the New Member States, MNB Working Paper 4, 2004.

Perotti R. (1999), Fiscal Policy in Good Time and Bad, in: Quarterly Journal of Economics 114, 1999, pp. 1399-1436.

Sapir A. / Aghion P. / Bertola G. / Hellwig M. / Pisani-Ferry J. / Rosati D. / Viñals J. / Wallace H. (2004), An Agenda for a Growing Europe: Making the EU System Deliver, Oxford: Oxford University Press 2004.

Stark J. (2001), Genesis of a Pact, in: *Brunila / Buti / Franco* (eds.), The Stability and Growth Pact-The Architecture of Fiscal Policy in EMU, 2001, pp. 77-105.

Strauch R. / Hallerberg M. / von Hagen J. (2004), Budgetary Forecasts in Europe. The Track Record of Stability and Convergence Programmes, Working Paper Series, ECB 307, 2004.

von Hagen J. / Wolff G. B. (2004), What Do Deficits Tell Us about Debt? Empirical Evidence on Creative Accounting with Fiscal Rules in the EU, Deutsche Bundesbank Discussion Paper 38, 2004.

Paul De Grauwe[1]

Some Thoughts on Reforming the Stability and Growth Pact

I. Introduction

Before analyzing the problems and prospects of the Stability and Growth Pact (SGP) it is useful to remind ourselves of the fact that the SGP was primarily introduced for political reasons with little regard for economic analysis. The politics surrounding the SGP was influenced by German domestic conditions. There was first the need to placate the German public opinion which was very much hostile towards monetary union, by creating an image of budgetary toughness that everybody believed would be needed to discipline the "Club Med" countries. Second, there was the hidden political agenda of a number of ministers of finance from Northern Europe to keep Italy and other Southern countries out of the monetary union.

[1] Comment on the paper by *Marco Buti*.

This political atmosphere led to a set of rules that are ill-conceived and unenforceable, as has been shown by the repeated transgressions of the Pact by major countries.

A. The SGP is politically ill-conceived and unenforceable

Government spending and taxation within the EU is still very much the responsibility of national governments and parliaments. That is also the level at which democratic legitimacy is vested. The Pact now imposes an elaborate control and sanctioning system top down on the net effect (budget deficit) of this democratic decision making process and by European institutions that are perceived to lack the same democratic legitimacy as national governments and parliaments.

This lack of legitimacy should be understood here in a political sense. From a purely legal perspective the European institutions have legitimacy as they were created by treaties signed by democratically elected governments. What makes them lacking in political legitimacy is that the European institutions which take decisions about the budgetary process in the framework of the SGP do not face the sanctioning of the voters at the national level. And it is at the national level that voters express themselves about spending and taxes.

Such a system is bound to lead to conflicts, as it has in the past. It will continue to do so in the future as long as nation-states maintain sovereignty over taxation and spending. In short, the Pact exhibits so much political naiveté that I cannot imagine that those who invented this ever believed it would work.

B. The SGP is ill-conceived from an economic point of view

The 3% budget deficit rule (which is in fact part of the Maastricht Treaty but which is a cornerstone of the SGP) is not based on rational economic analysis. It is an arbitrary number. Thus, intelligent people (policy makers) will not subject themselves to a rule that is perceived to be unintelligent, especially when these policymakers face strong commitments vis-à-vis their electorate during a recession. They will set the rule aside.

The balanced budget rule of the SGP is equivalent to imposing government debt ratios to go to zero. This may make sense for Belgium, Italy and Greece which have excessive government debt levels, as a temporary strategy to reduce debt/GDP ratios to more sustainable levels. The problem is that it was forced on everybody as a permanent strategy. This makes as much sense as forbidding all firms to issue debt because some have issued too much debt in the past.

In addition, the requirement to bring the debt ratio to zero gives strong political incentives to reduce government investment. Governments are required by the Pact to finance all new investments by current taxation. A large part of the benefits of these investments, however, will be reaped by future governments. This gives incentives to governments today to reduce these investments and only spend on items that benefit the present voters. Thus the GSP is likely to lead to lower government investments and thus lower growth.

C. The SGP and the pension problem

An often heard argument is the following. Future pension liabilities are very high because of graying populations. Let us, therefore, reduce the government debt levels now, so that we create room for more spending on pensions in the future. In this view, the SGP is the right strategy because it forces countries to reduce their debt ratios in anticipation of future increases in the cost of old age.

This argument in fact implies that governments are now given strong incentives by the SGP to cut back on investment and to raise taxes, in order to finance future consumption (pensions). This strategy lowers the growth potential of Europe. It also lowers the incentives to introduce structural reforms in the pension systems.

II. How should the SGP be reformed?

Let us start from what the objective of the Pact should be. The only reason why we need a Pact is to avoid that countries get into a debt crisis. Such a debt crisis would harm everybody. This idea calls for targeting debt levels, not budget deficits (flows).

One important implication of targeting debt levels that are different from zero is that the 3% deficit ceiling cannot be maintained. Debt targeting and the 3% deficit ceiling are incompatible. In order to make this point clearer we show a table with the budget deficits that will stabilize the government debt ratios at different levels. In table 1 we assume that the nominal growth rate of GDP is 5%; in table 2 we assume this growth rate to be 4%.

Let us take an example. Suppose that the right debt ratio for Germany is 50%. This implies that the steady state deficit that Germany should aim at over the cycle is 2.5% (if the nominal growth rate is 5%) and 2% (if the nominal growth rate is 4%). But this implies that with every recession, because of automatic stabilizers, the deficit will exceed 3%. As a result, the maintenance of the 3% deficit ceiling in a debt targeting strategy robs that strategy from all flexibility to deal with recessions.

Table 1: Required deficits (%GDP) to reach different target debt ratios (nominal growth of GDP = 5%)

target debt ratio	10 %	20 %	30 %	40 %	50 %	60 %
required deficit	0.5 %	1.0 %	1.5 %	2.0 %	2.5 %	3 %

Table 2: Required deficits (%GDP) to reach different target debt ratios (nominal growth of GDP = 4%)

target debt ratio	10 %	20 %	30 %	40 %	50 %	60 %
required deficit	0.4 %	0.8 %	1.2 %	1.6 %	2.0 %	2.4 %

A. The reform of March 2005

The reform of the SGP that was adopted in March 2005 and which is described admirably well by *Marco Buti*, goes in the right direction. It makes a distinction between countries with low and high debt levels allowing the former to depart from the balanced budget rule and to stretch their return to the 3% norm over a longer period. In addition, the conditions under which countries can depart (temporarily) from the 3% rule are expanded.

Thus the reform goes in the right direction of targeting the debt levels and allowing more flexibility. However, by keeping the 3% rule but allowing for many exceptions, the reform has laid a minefield for future discussions and conflicts. In addition, it does not solve the political problem identified earlier, i.e. the disconnection between political responsibility and the monitoring of the Pact.

B. Who should be responsible for implementing debt targeting?

My answer is that national authorities should bear the responsibility of implementing debt targeting. The reason is that this is where the democratic legitimacy about taxation and spending is vested. Therefore the monitoring and control process should also be organized at the national level. A reformed Pact should then devise stronger national control systems, e.g. by independent national debt agencies.

Does this mean that there is no role for the European institutions and in particular for the European Commission? The answer is negative. The European institutions should focus on monitoring the extreme outliers in terms of debt ratios. Today, I can only see three countries that come close to being outliers, Belgium, Italy and Greece with debt levels that are close to, or exceed 100%. The others, however, should be left alone.

In other words it makes no sense for the European Commission to set up an elaborate monitoring and control system on all countries, most of which are far away from debt default. These countries should be trusted to use their national monitoring and controlling systems.

Thus, I favour a two-tier system. Countries staying within safe debt margins are left alone while the outliers are monitored by the European Commission.

III. Conclusion: From top-down to bottom-up

Mature democratic European countries have shown to be able to avoid debt crises in the last 50 years when the Stability and Growth Pact did not exist. There is no reason to believe that they cannot do so in the future. That's why there is a need to transfer the responsibility for budgetary discipline back into the hands of the member states, as long as democratic legitimacy concerning spending and taxing remains in the hands of national governments and parliaments.

Part 5:
Model Simulations of the SGP Fiscal Rule

Fritz Breuss / Werner Roeger[1]

Sluggish Growth and the SGP Fiscal Rule: Model Simulations[2]

---

1 The views in this paper are entirely those of the author and do not necessarily reflect those of the European Commission.

2 A shorter version of this chapter has been published in *Breuss/Roeger* (2005).

I. Introduction

In the last decade, many OECD countries have experienced with budgetary rules in order to help restore or safeguard fiscal sustainability.[3] The most prominent examples are the USA with the 1985 Balanced Budget and Emergency Deficit Control Act (Gramm-Rudman Act) which was relaxed and renamed in the 1990 Budget Enforcement Act (BEA) introducing caps on discretionary spending. The caps could be exceeded in the event of "emergencies". In the end most of its provisions elapsed in September 2002, without being extended or replaced.[4] In the United Kingdom, two fiscal rules were set out in 1997: the so-called "golden rule", which states that over the cycle current outlays, including the consumption of fixed capital should not be financed by borrowing; and a debt rule, or "sustainability investment rule", stipulating that over the cycle the ratio of net debt to GDP should not exceed a prudent level, defined for the time being as 40 per cent. Several other OECD countries have adopted new rules since the 1990s (e.g. New Zealand and Switzerland with its debt brake - "Schuldenbremse").[5]

In the European Union the Maastricht Treaty and the Stability and Growth Pact (SGP) put in place in 1997 by two regulations (1466/97 – surveillance - and 1467/97 – clarifying the excessive deficit procedure) and one resolution of the European Council set out conditions necessary to safeguard fiscal discipline in a common currency area.[6] The Treaty set the deficit hurdle for entry into

3 For an overview, see *OECD* (2002) pp. 117-136.

4 For an evaluation, see *Fatás/Mihov* (2004).

5 See *Brandner et al.* (2004).

6 See *Brunila et al.* (2001); *Buti/Giudice* (2002); *Emmerson et al.* (2003).

monetary union at 3 per cent of GDP, allowing for long-run debt convergence around 60 per cent of GDP (on the assumption of trend growth around 3 per cent and trend inflation around 2 per cent, which satisfies the Domar formula). The SGP – which introduced possible financial penalties for non-compliance with the deficit ceiling – , also calls for fiscal positions to be "close to balance" or in surplus over the medium run, which would asymptotically lead to zero net debt. These conditions are the minimum to achieve long-term fiscal sustainability in the individual countries. In practice, the emphasis has gradually shifted from the actual deficit measure to the cyclically-adjusted one, to avoid pro-cyclical budgeting. This approach was made very explicit in 2001 in the revised Code of Conduct on the format and content of the stability and convergence programmes.[7] Besides, some euro area member states have also put in place domestic "stability pacts" in order to promote fiscal discipline at sub-national levels.[8]

Although there are many efforts to justify the fiscal rules of the SGP theoretically[9] or to formulate optimal fiscal rules in general,[10] in practice there are no indisputable optimal criteria. Therefore any indebtedness target is bound to remain judgemental. However, rules not only have the purpose to safeguard long-run fiscal sustainability, they also limit the room for discretionary policy and hence increase macroeconomic stability. *Badinger* (2004) concludes from a cross-section and panel analysis for a sample of 20 OECD countries over the period of 15 years that discretionary fiscal policy has a significant and sizeable effect on volatility of GDP per capita;[11] but he did not find a direct effect on inflation volatility as postulated by *Rother* (2004).

Beyond their importance for ensuring sustainability, rules also have a role to play in communicating with the public. Therefore they should fulfil some criteria.[12] Rules should be credible but not overly rigid, simple to understand, perceived as binding and backed

---

7 See *European Commission* (2002) pp. 201-206.

8 Austria, Belgium, Germany and Spain; for Austria, see *Schratzenstaller* (2005) pp. 12-22.

9 For an overview, see *Breuss* (1998); *Brunila et al.* (2001); *De Grauwe* (2003).

10 E.g., see *Schmitt/Grohe/Uribe* (2004); *Annichiarico/Giammaroli* (2004).

11 Like *Fatas/Mihov* (2003).

12 See *OECD* (2002) p. 126.

by sanctions.[13] A way to alleviate the trade-off between credibility and flexibility is by improving transparency. In the EU, the requirement that member states submit annual stability and convergence programmes and their obligations to notify flow and stock outcomes twice a year is also meant to enhance transparency.

After a promising start the SGP seems not to have passed the "Elch" test during the low-growth or stagnation phase in Europe since 2001. The Excessive Deficit Procedure (EDP) according to Article 104 of the EC Treaty had to be initiated already against 4 EMU members (Greece, France, Germany and Portugal) and one non-member (Hungary). Whereas Greece and Portugal violated the rules ex-post,[14] France and Germany breached the 3% hurdle over four years, starting in 2002. Over the continuation of the EDP against both countries there was a legal row between the Commission and the ECOFIN resulting in a case before and the ruling of the *European Court of Justice* (2004).

Due to several shortcomings of the SGP a reform was overdue. The ECOFIN on 20 March 2005 and the European Council on 22 and 23 March 2005 agreed upon concrete reform steps aiming at more flexibility and practicability in implementing its rules, while retaining its two nominal anchors – the 3 percent of GDP reference value for the deficit and the 60 percent of GDP reference for the debt to GDP ratio.

In our contribution we do not put forward a new or alternative rule to the existing SGP rules but rather we want to study why the two largest EMU countries ran into the deficit troubles during the past recession and whether an alternative more SGP-like fiscal adjustment policy could have led to a better overall macroeconomic performance. For this purpose we reproduce the sluggish growth situation in some member states of the Euro area. Then we analyse fiscal policy under two alternative shock scenarios. One scenario views the sluggish growth period caused by a supply shock, one originating from a (negative) demand shock. For both types of shocks we analyse the response of the economy under two alternative fiscal rules: a) no SGP rule and b) the SGP rule. The exercise is

---

13 *Buti/van den Noord* (2004) show that the current difficulties of EMU's fiscal policy framework have little to do with its alleged fault lines and much to do with the resurgence of the electoral budget cycles.

14 For an overview of creative accounting in Europe, see *Koen/van den Noord* (2005).

carried out by simulations with the European Commission's QUEST model.[15]

The next section provides an overview of the model, its coverage and a brief description of its main features. In the third section we briefly describe the seven years experience with the SGP and the concrete reform proposals by the ECOFIN and the European Council. The fourth section discusses and presents the results of the model simulations of the alternative scenarios concerning the fiscal policy stance in case of a period of sluggish growth. Then tentative conclusions are drawn from our exercise.

II. The QUEST model

The QUEST model[16] is a New Neoclassical-Keynesian synthesis model, which combines the rigours of dynamic general equilibrium models with features of Keynesian style rigidities. The behavioural equations in the model are based on principles of dynamic optimization of private households and firms. Economic agents are assumed to maximize utility and profit functions subject to intertemporal budget constraints and consumption and investment decisions, therefore incorporate forward looking behaviours. Economic theory not merely determines the long-run model properties, but also drives its short run dynamics. The dynamic responses of the model have a theoretical basis, like the presence of adjustment costs and overlapping contracts, and adding ad hoc dynamics has been avoided as much as possible.

The supply side of the economy is modelled explicitly via a neoclassical production function. This assures that the long run behaviour of the model resembles closely the standard neo-classical growth model and the model reaches a steady-state growth path with a growth rate essentially determined by the rate of (exogenous) technical progress and the growth rate of the population.

There are two major departures from the neo-classical model in the long run. Because firms are not perfectly competitive but can charge markups over marginal cost in the long run, the level of economic activity will be lower than that predicted from a model with

---

15 In a recent model simulation exercise *Neck et al.* (2005) study the different combinations for co-operation between fiscal and monetary policy in the enlarged EMU.

16 This model description follows *Roeger/in't Veld* (2004). For a more detailed description, see *Roeger/in't Veld* (1997).

perfect competition. Also, a bargaining framework along the lines of *Pissarides* (1990) is used to describe the interaction between firms and workers. Labour market rigidities and therefore involuntary unemployment persist even in the long run and the model economy will therefore not reach steady state equilibrium with full employment. The short run behaviour of the model is influenced by standard Keynesian features since the model allows for imperfectly flexible wages and prices, liquidity constrained consumption, adjustment cost for investment and labour hoarding.

A. Private consumption

The specification of consumption and saving behaviour in the model is based on the concept of intertemporal utility maximisation of households, as formalised by *Blanchard* (1985) und *Buiter* (1988). It is a generalisation of the Permanent Income Hypothesis, since it allows for the analysis of consumption and saving behaviour of households under possibly only a finite planning horizon (positive probability of death). Consumers decide how much to consume and how much to save each period by maximising the present discounted expected utility from the consumption stream subject to their intertemporal budget constraint. Under the assumption of isoelastic or constant relative risk aversion (CRRA) utility, the consumption function, i.e. the optimal consumption rule for the household's optimisation problem, depends on human wealth H and financial wealth F; the marginal propensity to consume out of total wealth δ is a function of the rate of time preference θ, the probability of death p, the intertemporal elasticity of substitution σ and the real interest rate r at period t

$$C_t = \delta(\theta, p, \sigma, r_t)[H_t + F_t]P_t / PC_t \, . \tag{1}$$

Human wealth H is the present discounted value of the entire future stream of after-tax income ($L.w$ including benefits $U.ben$)

$$H_t = E_t \sum_{j=0}^{\infty} b_{tj} [(1 - t_l]L_{t+j} w_{t+j} + U_{t+j} ben_{t+j}$$

and financial wealth F equals the sum of the total equity wealth V, bonds (B), real money (M/P) and net foreign assets NFA

$$F_t = V_t + B_t + M_t / P_t + NFA_t \, .$$

Eq. (1) above assumes all consumers can freely substitute consumption today for consumption in the future at the going real interest rate. In reality, not all people may be able to borrow against their future income due to capital market imperfections and as a result they will not be able to smooth their consumption over time. These "liquidity constrained" consumers cannot achieve intertemporal optimisation and their consumption is better represented as a function of current real disposable income ("rule-of-thumb" consumers). In the model, total consumption is, therefore represented as the aggregation of the responses of two groups of consumers, one forward looking group of consumers who follow the optimal consumption rule (1) and another group that does not obey the life cycle/permanent income hypothesis and whose consumption depends on current disposable income

$$C_t = (1-\lambda)\delta(\theta, p, \sigma, r_t)\left[H_t + F_t\right] + \lambda Ydis_t \tag{1a}$$

where λ is the share of liquidity constrained consumption and *Ydis* current real disposable income.

Intertemporal substitution constitutes an important stabilising feedback, as a rise in interest rates can induce consumers to postpone consumption. When other components of aggregate demand rise, an increase in interest rates reduces consumption and the effect on total output is dampened. Consumption smoothing is an essential feature of this consumption specification. If households expect a temporary decline in their income, then according to this hypothesis, they will mainly react via a reduction in their savings rate. Alternatively, if they expect an increase in their future net income, e.g. because of credibly announced tax reductions, the current savings rate may also fall, i.e. consumption may already increase in the present period in anticipation of higher future income. The estimates used in the model lie within the range found in the empirical literature: the values for the share of consumption that is liquidity constrained is approximately 30%, while the elasticity of intertemporal substitution for that fraction of consumption that obeys the life cycle model is approximately 0.5.

B. Production

Firms operate in a monopolistically competitive environment. Private sector GDP Y_t is produced via a nested CES and Cobb Douglas production function with capital K_t, energy E_t and private sector employment L_t as inputs. The variable T_{Kt} represents an efficiency index for the fixed capital stock and the variable T_{Lt} represents labour augmenting technical progress. The following equation describes potential output $YPOT_t$ of the corporate sector under the assumption that all factors of production are fully utilised.

$$YPOT_t = \left(\left[aK_t^{-\rho} + (1-a)E_t^{-\rho} \right]^{-1/\rho} T_{Kt} \right)^{(1-\alpha)} (L_t T_{Lt})^{\alpha} \qquad (2)$$

Labour augmenting technical progress grows with an exogenous rate and the efficiency index for capital T_{Kt} is a function of the mean age of capital and captures embodiment effects resulting from current and past investment. Firms may not always operate at full or optimal capacity; therefore actual output can differ from potential output. The objective of the firm is to maximise the present value of its cash flow (total revenue minus costs), subject to a capital accumulation constraint and costs of adjustment associated with capital and labour. The solution of the maximisation problem gives the behavioural equations for investment, employment and energy.

C. Investment

Firms maximise profits by buying labour services from households and renting capital to produce output. The investment demand equation is the optimal rule for the firms' optimisation problem. The model specification is based on a framework that extends the neo-classical model of investment by incorporating adjustment costs. The neo-classical model of investment can be linked to Tobin's Q-model, which couples investment decisions to forward-looking stock market valuations of the firm. According to this hypothesis, investment is determined by the gap between the market value of a firm and the replacement value of its capital. The ratio between these two variables is referred to as *Tobins's Q*. This model can be derived from the neo-classical theory if it is assumed that investment is subject to adjustment costs, which are a convex function of the rate of change of the firm's capital stock. Firms face such adjustment costs when changing their capital stock, as there are disruptions to the existing production process: installation of new capital can be costly; workers may have to be retrained, etc. Convexity implies that these installation costs increase at an increasing rate and a too rapid accumulation of capital is more costly.

Total real investment expenditures are equal to investment purchases J_t plus the costs of installation. The unit installation costs are assumed to be a linear function of the investment to capital ratio. Total investment expenditure I_t can be written as

$$I_t = J_t \left\{ 1 + (\phi/2) \left\{ \frac{J_t}{K_t} \right\} \right\} \frac{PI_t}{P_t} \qquad (3)$$

where ϕ is the adjustment cost parameter, K the capital stock and PI_t / P_t denotes the relative price of investment goods relative to the GDP deflator.

The optimisation problem yields the following investment rule

$$I_t = \frac{1}{\phi}\left\{\frac{q_t}{PI_t / P_t} - 1\right\}K_t. \tag{4}$$

The shadow price of capital q is equal to the marginal product of capital plus any anticipated future events which are expected to influence the marginal product after period t. It is a function of current and discounted future expected profitability, including adjustment costs, and adjusted for profit taxes tc and monopoly rents. This representation of q allows us to interpret it as reflecting the present discounted value of the marginal revenue from current investment and illustrates the forward-looking nature of capital accumulation. Central to investment decisions are expectations about future demand conditions and costs. Estimates show that the adjustment costs amount to approximately 10% of total investment expenditure.

D. Labour market

The labour market specification is based on theoretical search models of the labour market as developed by *Pissarides* (1990). The basic incentive for search activities in the labour market by both workers and firms are the profit opportunities in present value terms, which are associated with a successful job match for both parties. Wages are determined by an implicit bargain at the individual level, i.e. the firm engages in Nash bargains with each individual worker by taking the wage of all other employees as given. Thus, wage contracts are set such as to maximise the product of their respective profit opportunities. In the case of households, this is given by the difference between the present value of labour income a household can earn in the case of a successful current job match (net wages) vs. the net present value of labour income in case of a failure (the reservation wage, i.e. unemployment benefits and/or the value of leisure). Arbitrage equations for the returns from their respective human capitals incorporate the expected capital loss from a job separation, and the expected capital gain from finding a job, depending on labour market tightness. For the firm, the return from a successful job match is given by the real pure profit of a firm per employee, the difference between the return of an occupied position and the costs of a vacant position. The wage rule is then the outcome of the maximisation of the product of both parties' profit opportunities and how much of the total return of a successful job match goes to each party depends on their relative bargaining position.

$$W_t = \frac{(1-\beta)}{(1-t_l)} Z_t + \beta \left\{ \alpha \frac{Y_t}{L_t} + \frac{P(\cdot) vc_t}{q(\cdot)} \right\} \tag{5}$$

Where β is the relative bargaining strength of workers, t_l the labour income tax rate and Z the reservation wage (unemployment benefits). The last term in brackets reflects the probability of finding and quitting a job for an unemployed/employed person and the vacancy cost incurred by the firm, and this is assumed to depend on labour market tightness (unemployment rate).

Nominal rigidities are introduced into the wage setting process through the assumption of wage staggering, as suggested by *Taylor* (1980). Contracts last for four periods (quarters) and at each date, exactly one quarter of all workers signs a new contract with firms. At each date t firms bargain with one quarter of the work force over a nominal wage contract, which will remain fixed for one year. Wage contracts in the current period are thus indexed to an average of the current price level and expected price levels for three consecutive periods. They are further determined by labour productivity Y / L, the reservation wage Z, vacancy costs vc and labour market tightness in the current and three consecutive periods.

This wage rule exhibits the feature that the importance by which the marginal product of labour and labour market tightness influence the level of current wage contracts, depends positively on the bargaining power of workers. As the bargaining strength of workers diminishes, firms can tie wages more narrowly to the reservation wage. The average nominal wage rate in period t is thus given by the average value of all wage contracts signed in the current and the previous three periods.

E. Pricing behaviour

The version used in this paper has a hybrid version of forward and backward looking pricing behaviour.[17] It derives price setting behaviour as the product of optimisation by monopolistically competitive firms subject to constraints on the frequency of price ad-

[17] See *Gali/Gertler* (1999) pp. 195-222.

justment. It allows for a 'cost-push' effect influenced by expected inflation, which makes inflation a forward-looking phenomenon. However, it is assumed that a fraction of firms uses a backward looking rule of thumb.[18]

F. Government

Governments follow exogenously given spending patterns. Government expenditure is divided into unemployment benefits, purchases of goods and services, government wages, investment expenditure, transfers to households and interest payments on government debt. Revenues are divided into labour income taxes (including social security contributions), corporate profit taxes, value added taxes, energy taxes and other receipts (lump sum tax).

A debt rule is imposed in order to make the evolution of the government budget sustainable. In default setting, it is lump sum taxes that adjust proportionally to the gap between the debt to GDP ratio and its target level b_0 according to

$$\Delta T_t = \Psi_1(b_0 - B_t / Y_t) - \Psi_2 \Delta(B_t / Y_t) . \tag{6}$$

G. Financial markets

Asset markets are assumed to be fully integrated across all the industrialised regions covered in the model, i.e. there is full capital mobility. Exchange rates between European currencies, US dollar and the yen are fully flexible. The exchange rate e, expressed as the amount of domestic currency per unit of foreign currency, is determined endogenously according to the following (uncovered) interest arbitrage relation with respect to the dollar

$$i_t^j = i_t^{US} + E_t\left[\frac{\Delta e_{t+1}}{e_t}\right] + risk_t . \tag{7}$$

The second term on the right hand side denotes the expected depreciation of the currency vis-a-vis the US dollar. The risk premium 'risk' is assumed to be exogenous and reflects, among other factors, the markets' perception of the risk differential between assets denominated in the two currencies.

The impact of shocks in the model depends to a large extent on the response of the monetary authorities and the expected future monetary stance. The model can be simulated under alternative monetary policy assumptions, and short term interest rates can be set to target the money stock, an inflation target, or in accordance to

---

[18] See *Gali et al.* (2001) pp. 1237-1262.

some formulation of a Taylor rule. The standard setting in the simulations for this paper is based on an agreed policy rule, which assumes that the monetary authorities adhere to an inflation forecast based rule

$$rs_t = rr^{eq} + \inf_{t+1} + a(\inf_{t+1} - \inf^{target}) + bGAP_t \quad (8)$$

where the equilibrium real rate is taken from the steady state model solution (here shocks were designed in such a way that the *ss* real interest rate was unchanged). The weight given to expected inflation ($a = 1$) is much larger than that to the output gap ($b = 0.25$). It is assumed that of the three EU member states not participating in EMU, Denmark follows the ECB and keeps the interest rate differential vis-a-vis the euro-area constant, while Sweden and the UK have an independent monetary policy and floating currencies against the euro.

H. International trade

The model consists of structural models for each of the EU member states, the United States and Japan, while the rest of the world is modelled through smaller trade feedback models, determining imports, exports and the evolution of net foreign assets.[19]

Table 1: Countries and Zones in the Quest II model (to be continued)

Complete country models		Zone trade-feedback models		
1. BE	Belgium-Luxembourg Economic Union (BLEU)	21. RO	The rest of the OECD	Korea, Iceland, Mexico, New Zealand, Turkey
2. DK 3. DE 4. GR 5. ES	Denmark FR of Germany Greece Spain	22. OP	OPEC	Algeria, Indonesia, Iran, Iraq, Kuwait, Libya, Nigeria, Qatar, Saudi Arabia, United Arab Emirates, Venezuela

[19] See Table 1.

Table 1(continued): Countries and Zones in the Quest II model

6. FR 7. IR 8. IT 9. NL	France Ireland Italy Netherlands	23. CE	Central and Eastern European Countries	Bulgaria, Czech Republic, Slovakia, Hungary, Poland, Romania, Slovenia, Estonia, Latvia, Lithuania
10. OS 11. PO	Austria Portugal	24. SU	Former Soviet Union	Russia, Ukraine, Rest of FSU-10
12. SF 13. SW 14. UK	Finland Sweden United Kingdom	25. DA	Dynamic Asian Economies	Hong Kong, Malaysia, Singapore, Taiwan, Thailand
15. US 16. JA 17. CA 18. AU	USA Japan Canada Australia	26. OA	Other Asia	Jordan, Nepal, Oman, Pakistan, Papua New Guinea, Philippines, Sri Lanka, Syria
19. NO 20. CH	Norway Switzerland	27. LA	Other Latin America and Africa	All countries of Latin America and Africa not listed elsewhere

It is assumed that each country or region produces a product which is an imperfect substitute for the products of other regions. Trade volumes are simple functions of demand and relative prices. Competitor's prices for each country are constructed as a weighted average of import prices, where the weights denote the share of the individual exporting country in total imports of the importing region. World demand for an individual country is defined as a weighted average of total imports with the weights representing the share of the exporting country in total imports of the importing country or region.

III. Seven years of experience with the SGP

A. Sluggish growth in Europe since 2001

The starting point of our analysis is the sluggish economic growth in some member states of the Euro area. The three large countries France, Germany, and Italy exhibited a period of slow growth over three years. In this period France and Germany were not able to keep their budget deficits below the 3%-SGP hurdle. Therefore, on 21 January 2003 the ECOFIN Council following the recommendation by the European Commission initiated the Excessive Deficit Procedure (EDP) under Article 104 of the EC Treaty.[20] The same happened with France on 3 June 2003. With the decision of 25 November 2003 the ECOFIN council stopped the EDP for both countries against the intention of the Commission. Therefore the Commission filed a suit against the ECOFIN before the European Court of Justice (ECJ). Its judgment was announced on 13 July 2004, declaring that on the one hand the ECOFIN has the right to decide against a recommendation by the Commission by qualified majority but on the other hand nullified the conclusions by the Council of 25 November 2003.[21] On 14 December 2004 the Commission decided (and recommended it to the ECOFIN council) that no further steps are necessary under the EDP because the budgetary forecasts for 2005 are plausibly showing that both countries will bring down the deficit below 3% of GDP.

Since the inception of EMU in 1999 we exhibited already EDPs against four Euro area members:[22] Portugal (November 2002 until April 2004), Germany and France (2003 to 2004) and Greece (after the announcement by Eurostat that it had faked its budgetary figures and due to the recent permanent breach of the SGP rules). The ECOFIN council initiated the EDP against Greece on 5 July 2004 and additionally on 1 December 2004 the Commission launched an infringement procedure against Greece to prevent incorrect or incomplete data transmission in the future. Base was a final Eurostat report for 1997-2003 showing that the government deficit in Greece has been revised upwards by 2.1% of GDP on average over that period, leading to the conclusion that the government deficit ratio has always exceeded 3% of GDP in the period.

After EU enlargement on 1 May 2004 the ECOFIN council initiated EDPs against six new member states (Czech Republic,

---

[20] Information about the framework and ongoing procedures in the context of the SGP and Fiscal Surveillance can be found on the website of the European Commission – DG Economic and Financial Affairs: http://europa.eu.int/comm/economy_finance/about/activities/sgp/main_en. htm (last visited May 2006).

[21] See *European Court of Justice* (2004).

[22] For a more comprehensive analysis of five years with EMU, see *European Commission* (2004a). A more recent evaluation of the EMU is done in *Breuss* (2006), chapters 11 and 12.

Cyprus, Hungary, Malta, Poland and Slovak Republic). On 5 July 2004 the ECOFIN council stopped the EDP against five countries, only in the case of Hungary the EDP continues with further budgetary surveillance.

Figure 1: GDP growth rates in % in selected Euro area countries

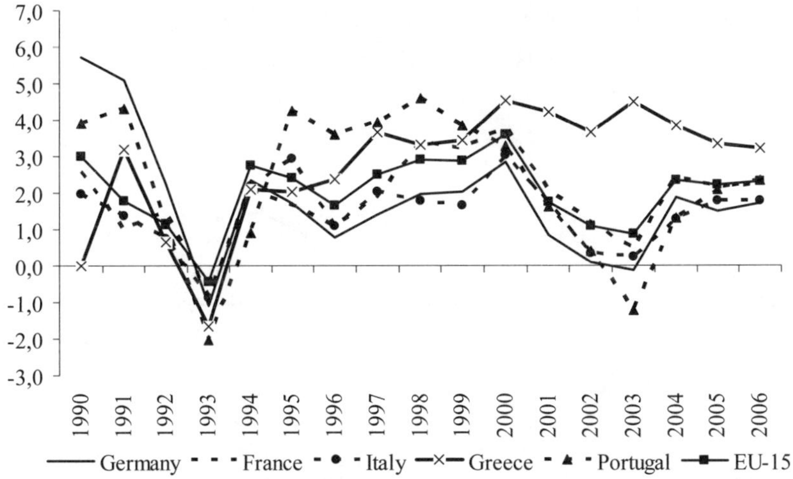

Source: *European Commission* (2004c).

Primarily we concentrate on the events in the three large Euro area countries France, Germany and Italy. However, we also show the performance of the two EDP countries Greece and Portugal in the following figures. The cyclical pattern of growth of real GDP was similar in the four countries; an exception is Greece. It exhibited a sustained high growth since the mid nineties (see Figure 1). Taking the output gap as business cycle indicator, one reaches at the same interpretation of the economic performance as shown with the GDP growth figures of Figure 1.

France's general government budget deficits exceeded the 3% SGP hurdle from 2002 to 2004 and according to the autumn forecast by the *European Commission* (2004c) a continuation of deficits at or above 3% of GDP in 2005 and 2006 is probable.[23] The budgetary situation in Germany was similar.[24] In both countries the performance of the structural deficit (cyclically adjusted)[25] was

---

[23] See Figure 2a.

[24] See Figure 2b.

[25] For the proper interpretation and use of cyclically-adjusted budget balances (CAP), see *Larch/Salto* (2003).

somewhat better, but also fell short of the 3% limit. In Italy the budget deficit hit the 3% limit in 2004 and will stay there in 2005 and 2006 according to the latest forecasts.[26] Despite an excellent GDP growth performance, Greece permanently surpassed the 3% deficit hurdle in the actual and cyclically adjusted budget balance. Portugal surpassed the 3% limit in 2001 and the forecasts expect deficits higher than 3% of GDP in 2005 and 2006.[27]

Figure 2a: France: Budget balance, actual and cyclically adjusted (in % of GDP)

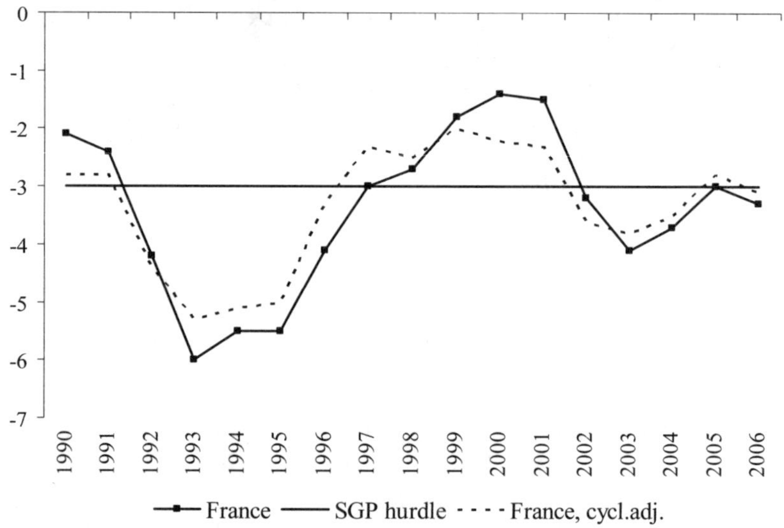

Source: *European Commission* (2004c).

---

[26] The short-term improvement in the actual budget balance figures in 2000 and 2001 was primarily due to the one-off proceeds relative to UMTS licenses, while the cyclically adjusted balances exclude these amounts. In 2000 these effects amounted to 50.8 bn DM in Germany, 13.8 bn Lira in Italy and 0.4 bn Pesetas in Portugal. In 2001 the UMTS effect amounted to 1.2 bn francs in France and 0.6 bn Drachma in Greece; see *European Commission* (2004c) p. 148; see Figure 2c.

[27] See Figure 2d.

Figure 2b: Germany: Budget balance, actual and cyclically adjusted (in % of GDP)

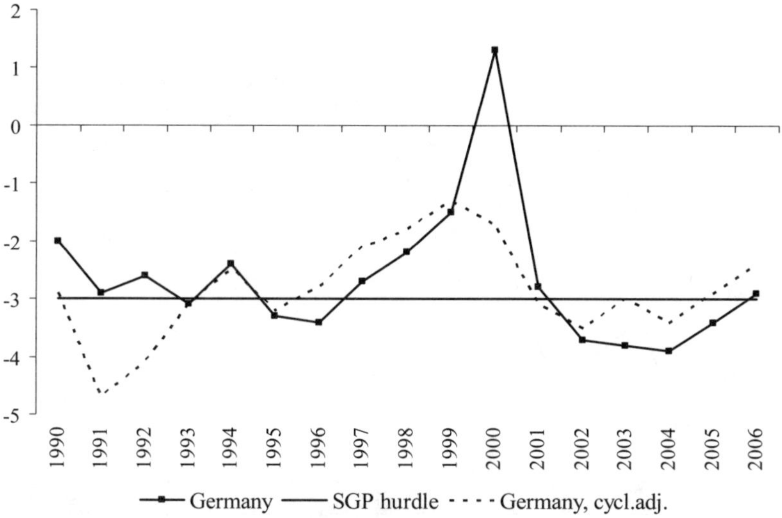

Source: *European Commission* (2004c).

Figure 2c: Italy: Budget balance, actual and cyclically adjusted (in % of GDP)

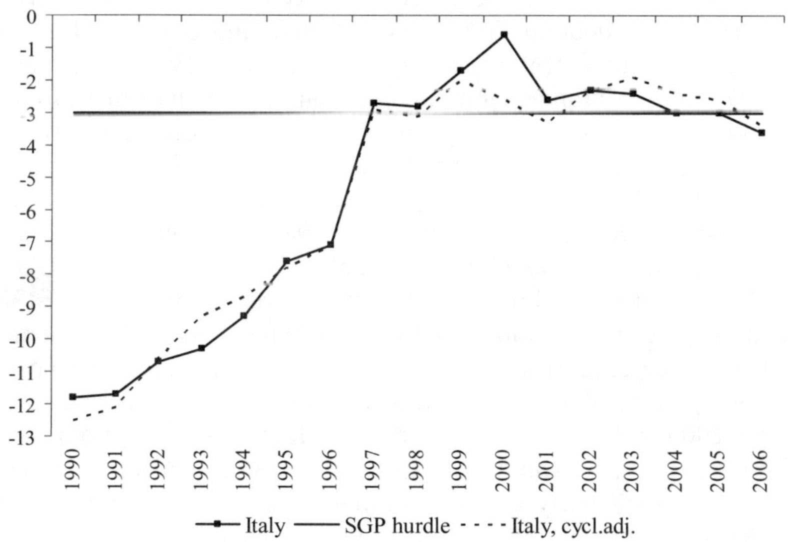

Source: *European Commission* (2004c).

Figure 2d: Greece and Portugal: Budget balances, actual and cyclically adjusted (in % of GDP)

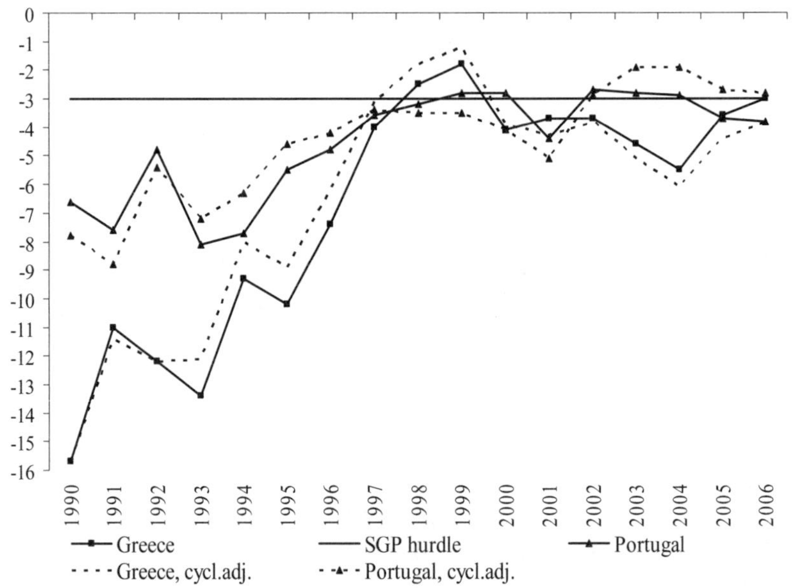

Source: *European Commission* (2004c).

When evaluating fiscal sustainability one looks at the performance of the debt to GDP ratio. Considering our four Euro area countries, some features stand out: First the level of the debt to GDP ratio in France, Germany and Italy is only half that of Greece and Italy. However, one also can detect a divergent dynamic. France, Germany and Portugal either stabilized or decreased its debt to GDP ratios during the run-up to the evaluation of the Maastricht convergence criteria in 1998. Since then we see an increasing trend, although the levels are still close to 60% of GDP. In Greece and Italy, although still at high levels of over 100% of GDP the debt to GDP ratios exhibit a declining trend.[28] In general we have three countries in the Euro area with still high and possibly unsustainable debt to GDP ratios. These are Belgium (the forecast for 2006 is 91%), Greece (110%) and Italy (104%). All other countries of EU-25 exhibit debt to GDP ratios around 60% or below. This is particularly true for the new member states. Only Cyprus (69%) and Malta (74%) are somewhat above this general tendency.

[28] See Figure 3.

Figure 3: Gross debt general government (in % of GDP) in selected Euro area countries

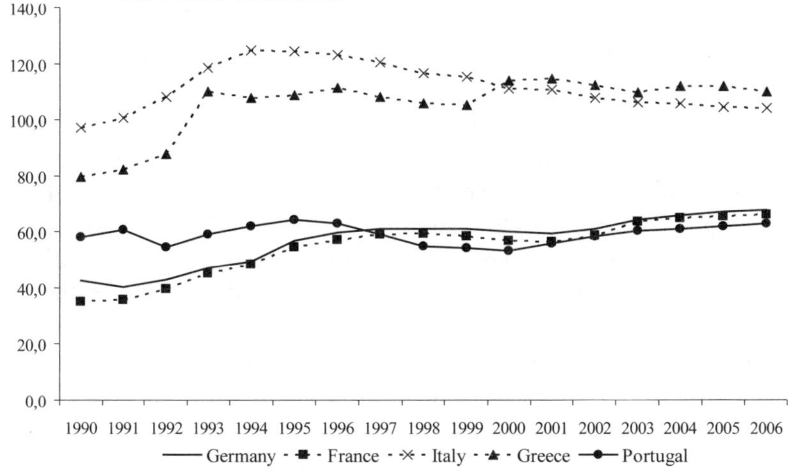

Source: *European Commission* (2004c).

B. The SGP mark II

Seven years of experience with the SGP have also highlighted its shortcomings. One important insight is the heterogeneity of the performance of the Euro are member states; either concerning GDP growth or budgetary stability. The "European business cycle" is still more a phantom than reality! The EU enlargement 2004 additionally will contribute to the amplification of the economic performance in the EU-25. The fact of the rather heterogeneous picture of the performance of public debt sustainability and - due to the protracted slowdown or "sluggish growth" period since 2001 - the non-compliance with the SGP fiscal rules of two major EMU players was the reason why the *European Commission* (2004b) was rethinking the economic governance and implementation of the SGP.[29]

The *ECOFIN* (2005) unanimously agreed to overhaul the present SGP by making proposals for "strengthening and clarifying" its implementation, "with the aim of improving the coordination and monitoring of economic policies according to Article 99 of the Treaty and of avoiding excessive deficits as required by Article 104(1) of the Treaty". These proposals were then introduced into

[29] Many of these suggestions were taken up by the *ECOFIN Council* (2005) on 20 March 2005 and were endorsed by the *European Council* (2005) on 22 and 23 March 2005.

the new Regulations (EC) No. 1055/2005 and No. 1056/2005 of 27 June 2005 (OJ L 174/1 and 174/5 of 7.7.2005) amending the old Council Regulations 1466/97 and 1467/97 and will – together with *ECOFIN* (2005) and *European Council* (2005) - form the "SGP mark II".

The Council, reviewing the SGP provisions, detected mainly five areas for improvements:[30] (i) enhance the economic rationale of the budgetary rules in order to improve their credibility and ownership; (ii) improve "ownership" by national policy makers (the Member States are responsible to implement the fiscal policies of their choice; the Council and the Member States respect the Commission's responsibility as guardian of the Treaty and its procedures); (iii) use more effectively periods when economies are growing above trend for budgetary consolidation in order to avoid pro-cyclical policies (this should help to better adhere to the medium term objective (MTO) for the Member States budgetary positions of "close to balance or in surplus" (CTBOIS)); (iv) take better account in Council recommendations of periods when economies are growing below trend and (v) give sufficient attention in the surveillance of budgetary positions to debt and sustainability.

Derived from this diagnosis the Council aims at clarifying the SGP rules in the following areas:

- Strengthening the preventive arm: In light of the increased economic and budgetary heterogeneity in the EU of 25 Member States, MTOs should be differentiated and may diverge from CTBOIS of individual Member States on the basis of their current debt to GDP ratio and potential growth. In cyclically adjusted terms (net of one-off and temporary measures), the range for the country-specific MTOs for euro area and ERM II Member States should be between -1 percent of GDP for low debt/high potential growth countries and balance or surplus for high debt/low potential growth countries. Hence, long-term fiscal sustainability is taken into account better than hitherto. However, in order to reach their MTO, Member States should pursue an annual adjustment in cyclically adjusted terms of 0.5 percent of GDP as a benchmark. In order to avoid pro-cyclical policies the Council demands a more symmetrical approach to fiscal policy over the cycle through enhanced budgetary discipline in periods of economic recovery.

---

[30] See *ECOFIN* (2005) p. 4.

• Improving the implementation of the Excessive Deficit Procedure (EDP): The EDP should remain simple, transparent and equitable. The guiding aim of the EDP is the prompt correction of an excessive deficit. Assistance and not punishment should be the purpose. Policy errors should be distinguished from forecast errors. In the end, the Council should have the power to apply sanctions. In evaluating whether an excess over the reference value is only "exceptional and temporary" – according to new proposals for "SGP mark II"[31] - the Commission should take into account a variety of "relevant factors". In this respect, the Council calls for a clarification of the relevant framework in the following lines: (i) a stronger link with the Lisbon targets for medium to long-run growth meaning considering expenditures to foster R&D and innovation;[32] (ii) fiscal consolidation efforts in "good times", debt sustainability, public investment and the overall quality of public finances; (iii) due consideration should be given to any other factors, such as budgetary efforts towards increasing or maintaining at a high level financial contributions to fostering international solidarity and to achieving European policy goals, notably the unification of Europe (e.g. costs of German unification; net-contributions to the EU budget); (iv) taking into account systemic pension reforms (net costs of the reform to the publicly managed multi-pillar system) for the initial five years after a Member State has introduced a mandatory fully-funded system, or five years after 2004 for Member States that have already introduced such a system.

The deadlines connected with the EDP will also be handled more flexibly. The deadline for adoption of a decision under Article 104(6) of the Treaty should be extended from three to four months, those under Article 104(7) from four to six months. The one month deadline for the Council to take a decision to move from Article 104(8) to Article 104(9) should also be extended to two months, and the two months deadline under Article 104(9) should be extended to four months. Also the deadline for correcting an excessive deficit should be extended to the second year after its occurrence. Under special circumstances, the initial deadline for correcting an excessive deficit could be set one year later, normally the third year after its occurrence.

---

31 See *ECOFIN* (2005) p. 15.

32 See also *Breuss* (2005).

In the light of the experience of the slow growth in Europe since 2001, the Council also considered the definition of "a severe economic downturn" given in Article 2(2) of Regulation 1467/97 as too restrictive. There it was defined – as a rule – as an annual fall of real GDP of at least two percent. The paragraphs (2) and (3) of Article 2 in Regulation 1467/97 are replaced in the new Regulation 1056/2005 by the following definition: The Commission and the Council, when assessing and deciding upon the existence of an excessive deficit ….., may consider an excess over the reference value resulting from a severe economic downturn as exceptional …. if the excess over the reference value results from a negative annual GDP volume growth rate or from an accumulated loss of output during a protracted period of very low annual GDP volume growth relative to its potential.

In anticipating the major changes in the "SGP mark II" this study – by using the method of model simulations - analyzes two aspects: (i) the consequences of a protracted period of very sluggish growth as experienced in Europe since 2001 for the fiscal policy stance in the largest euro area countries; and (ii) the long-run impact of potential GDP and debt sustainability of different fiscal policy adjustments (either adhering to the SGP rules or ignoring it).

IV. Simulating alternative fiscal policy strategies to overcome a slow growth period

The starting point of our exercise is the sluggish economic growth in some member states of the Euro area (in particular Germany) over the period 2001 to 2004. Our aim is to reproduce this cyclical downturn and study the pros and cons of sticking to the SGP. One important problem one faces when analyzing this economic situation is the uncertainty concerning the nature of the slowdown. At least two alternative interpretations seem possible.

Interpretation 1:

- The euro area has been hit by a negative supply shock in the form of weak growth of total factor productivity (TFP) over a period of three years. This view is consistent with the decline in TFP growth over a period of three years, which is unusual for pure cyclical variations in capacity utilization.

Interpretation 2:

- It is not 100% sure that the supply side interpretation is correct. There is evidence for weak private domestic demand. Consumer spending has been low in Germany, possibly related to structural and pension reform debates. Also there has been a significant decline in the investment rate (especially in construction). The more permanent nature of sluggish demand could have contributed to the unusual pattern of productivity growth.

It turns out that a proper assessment of the economic situation is crucial, since both interpretations have different medium term consequences. If the supply interpretation is correct then the current slowdown is associated with at least a permanent level shift of GDP. In case the demand interpretation holds, a cyclical recovery can be expected and GDP returns to the historic trend line.

A. Designing the simulation experiment

Supply shock: It is assumed that the decline in growth rates is temporary and that TFP growth returns back to pre 2001 growth rates. The supply shock is generated by a 1% reduction of TFP growth over a period of three years. After three years, TFP growth returns to the trend in the 90s. Notice, this means a permanent level shift of GDP.

Demand shock: It is assumed that private consumption declines exogenously at an increasing rate, starting with 1% of GDP in 2001 and ending with 4% at the end of 2003. Similarly for investment which is down by 0.5% of GDP in 2001 and where the shock ends with 2% at the end of 2003. Both shocks are reversed after three years in order to stress the pure cyclical nature of the economic downturn.

Both types of shocks are analyzed under two alternative fiscal rules:

- *Fiscal rule 1- No SGP:* Full working of automatic stabilizers (possibly violating the 3% deficit ceiling), which means no change in expenditure levels except for unemployment benefits and no change in tax rates. In order to avoid long run unsustainability, a debt rule is invoked after ten years which adjusts capital and corporate taxes in such a way as to stabilize the level of debt attained after ten years.
- *Fiscal rule 2- SGP:* Strict adherence to the 3% limit. This is achieved by a reduction in government spending in the recession.

B. *Simulation results*

1. Supply shock scenario

a) Results for Germany[33]

No SGP scenario:

- The growth rate shock lasts for three years and then returns to the historical growth rate.[34] That means potential and actual GDP is permanently down. With government expenditure and receipts hardly changed, this means that the fiscal deficit exceeds the 3% ceiling. Since the fiscal adjustment only occurs after ten years the deficit remains high and leads to an accumulation of government debt as a % of GDP by about 15% points.[35] Stabilisation of the government budget is eventually achieved via a tax increase. The additional tax burden is shared equally by capital and labour taxes which are increased by 2.5% points each.
- The supply shock has clear adverse short term effects on growth. Interestingly growth never returns fully to the historic growth path. This is related to the two negative long run effects of this policy, namely higher real interest rates and a larger tax burden[36] and the fact that the increase in taxes as well as the permanent increase in interest rates is understood by the private sector.

---

33 We only present results for Germany and Austria (as a representative neighbouring country). Results for France and Italy are similar.

34 See Figure 4 and Table I.A in the Appendix B.

35 See Figure 5.

36 The interest rate effect of a permanent increase of Government debt by 10% points is below ten basis points and is therefore at the lower end of available estimates.

Figure 4: Germany: GDP growth and potential output level after a TFP shock of 1% over 3 years

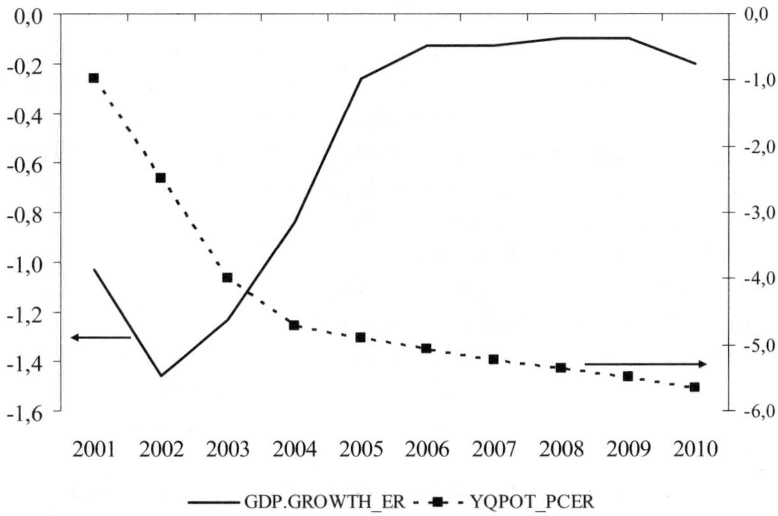

Source: Own simulations with the QUEST model.

Figure 5: Germany: Budget deficit (DEFTG) and debt to GDP ratio after the 3 years TFP shock

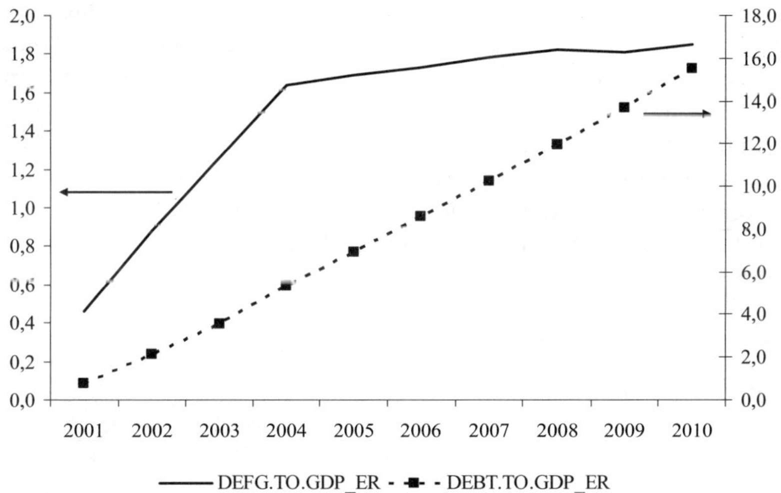

Source: Own simulations with the QUEST model.

Other features of the adjustment are the strong response of investment and consumption to the permanent output loss[37] and the anticipation of higher taxes. The strong response of private demand leads to an improvement in the trade balance. Also because of the negative response of aggregate demand the exchange rate depreciates initially, followed by an appreciation in the longer run because of the permanent decline in domestic output. The combination of negative supply and (induced) negative demand shock implies that inflation does not pick up strongly.

Alternative or SGP scenario:

- Fiscal policy responds to the slowdown in Germany, France and Italy with a rapid adjustment of government expenditure in order to stabilize government debt at the pre shock level. This is the response of a country which is close to 3% deficit and is then hit by a negative shock, i.e. there is no room for countercyclical fiscal policies.

Economic interpretation of the SGP results in comparison with those of no SGP:

- Obeying the SGP rules would have resulted in 1 percentage point higher potential output level in the medium to long-run.[38] The SGP approach would be only worse than the no SGP strategy in the first year of fiscal adjustment by around 0.1 percentage points. Thereafter it results permanently in a growth bonus of 0.1 percentage points annually.[39] In addition to more growth the SGP strategy would have resulted in an improvement of the budgetary situation in Germany: the budget deficit is reduced and the debt to GDP ratio increases only by 1 ½ percentage points, resulting in a better performance compared to the no SGP strategy as far as the debt to GDP ratio is concerned by around 14 to 15 percentage points.[40]

---

[37] See Figure 4.

[38] See Figure 6 and Tables I.B and I.C in the Appendix B.

[39] See Figure 6.

[40] See Figure 7.

Figure 6: Germany: Comparing the SGP with the no SGP scenario results: GDP growth and potential output level after a TFP shock of 1% over three years

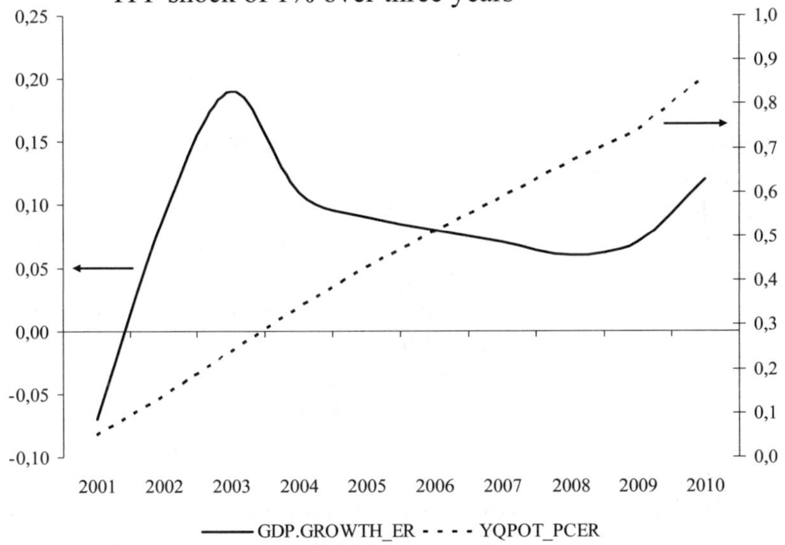

Source: Own simulations with the QUEST model.

Figure 7: Germany: Comparing the SGP with the no SGP scenario results: Budget deficit (DEFTG) and debt to GDP ratio after the three years TFP shock

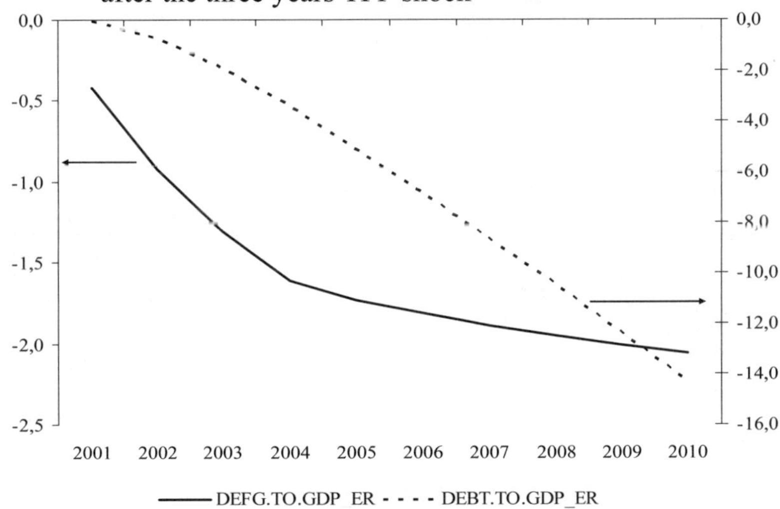

Source: Own simulations with the QUEST model.

b) Spill overs to neighbors – The case of Austria

The current SGP is looking primarily on the performance of a single Euro area country. This might be acceptable when evaluating a small country. If, however, a large country is scrutinized one should also consider the potential spill-over effects a large country might have. In order to study these additional effects we look at the outcome of the fiscal policy strategies in the three large Euro area countries on its neighbors. In order to make the presentation as simple as possible we only report the effects in Austria because Austria is highly connected with Germany and Italy and hence the spill-over effects are highest in this country.

Again the SGP strategy beats the no SGP fiscal approach. Only in the first year Austria would have suffered a small loss in real GDP growth by 0.2 percentage points. Thereafter, however the effects are always better in the SGP case.[41] Also potential output would be higher in the SGP scenario by ½ percentage points in the medium to long run.

The budgetary position would improve in Austria if the three largest Euro area countries would stick to the SGP strategy in order to overcome the economic crisis since 2001.[42]

Figure 8: Austria: Comparing the SGP with the no SGP scenario results: GDP growth and potential output level after a TFP shock of 1% over three years

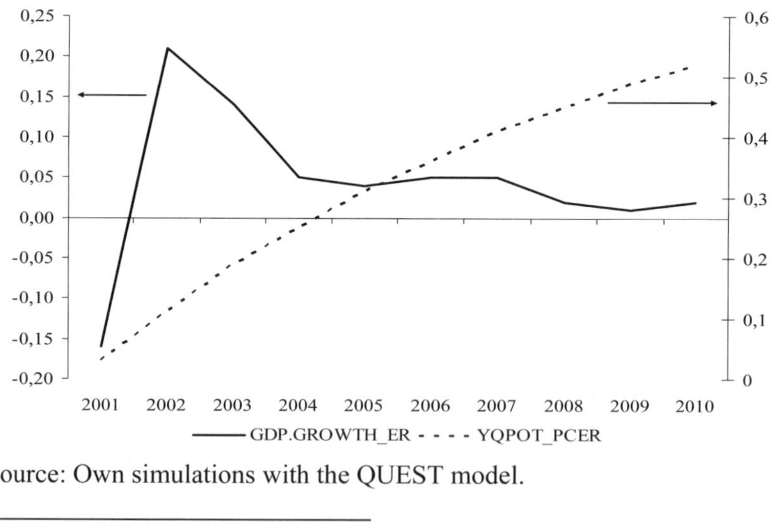

Source: Own simulations with the QUEST model.

[41] See Figure 8 and Table I.D in the Appendix B.

[42] See Figure 9.

Figure 9: Austria: Comparing the SGP with the no SGP scenario results: Budget deficit (DEFTG) and debt to GDP ratio after the three years TFP shock

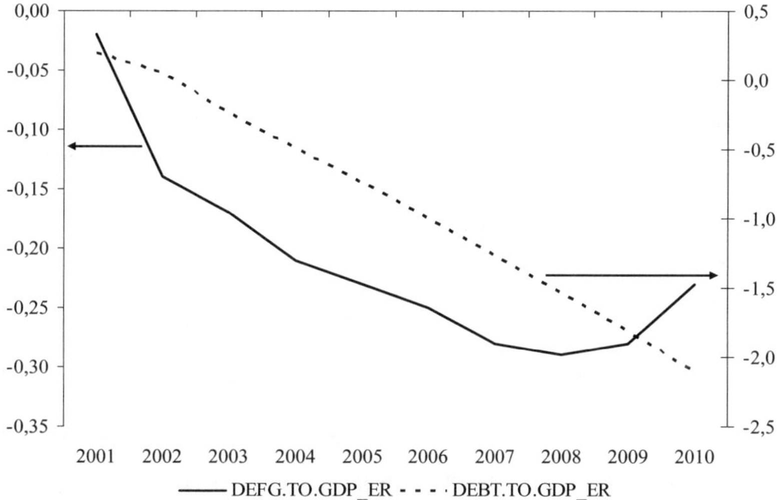

Source: Own simulations with the QUEST model.

2. Demand shock scenario

a) Results for Germany

No SGP scenario:

- We explore the following scenario: A group of countries (notably Germany) has been hit by a negative (private) demand shock, which leads to a reduction in GDP over three years (similar in magnitude to the decrease under the supply scenario). Notice, the shock is designed to be a typical demand shock (i.e. the shock is temporary!); this means that the recession is relatively short lived and investment recovers strongly in the third year.[43] A second feature which we want to highlight in this scenario is that not only is the negative demand shock temporary but it is followed by a positive demand shock after three years. In other words we want to stress a typical cyclical downturn with this scenario. This creates additional room for countercyclical fiscal policy, since any debt accumulated over the first three years will be eliminated (by a corresponding countercyclical policy in the following boom period).

[43] See Figure 10 and Table II.A in the Appendix B.

Figure 10: Germany: GDP growth and potential output level after a demand shock

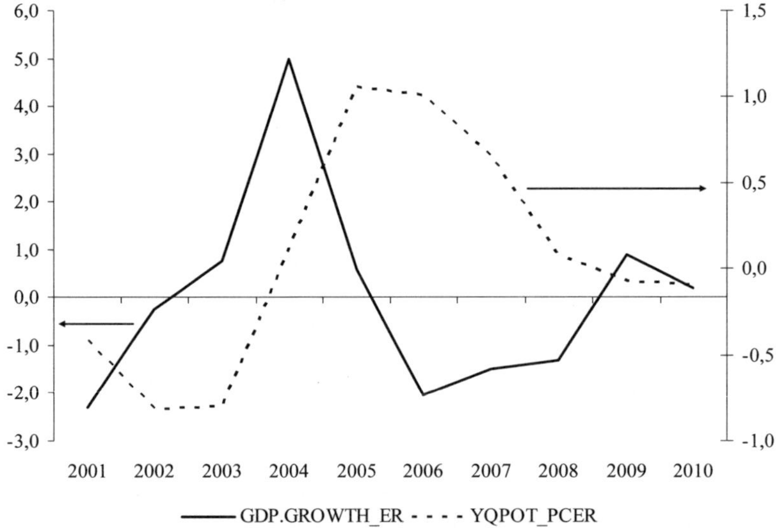

Source: Own simulations with the QUEST model.

The shock originates from private consumption. However since it leads to a decline in prices and a rise in real interest rates it also has negative implications for investment. The exchange rate starts to depreciate because of the negative demand shock in the Euro area as a whole. Importantly: the design of the shock experiment does not lead to a build up of debt with a strong countercyclical policy.[44]

[44] See Figure 11.

Figure 11: Germany: Budget deficit (DEFTG) and debt to GDP ratio after a demand shock

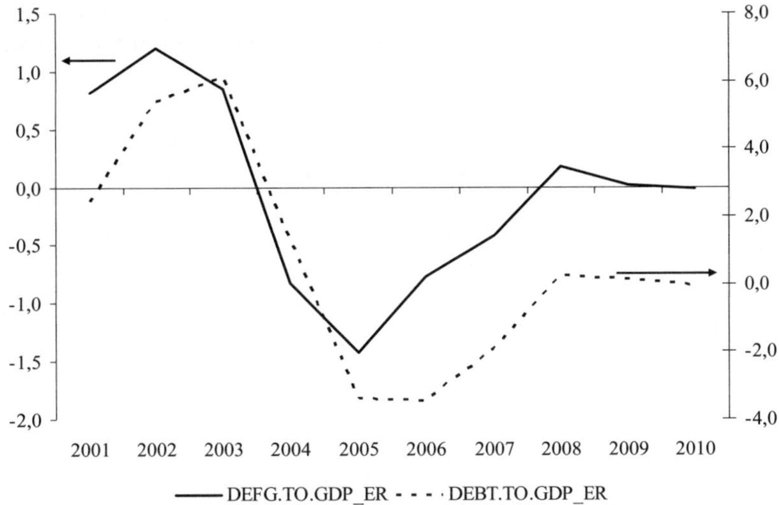

Source: Own simulations with the QUEST model.

SGP scenario:

- Here we assume that the short-term demand shock is adjusted with a SGP-like fiscal policy stance. That means that the short-term deterioration in the budgetary situation is counteracted by a cut in public expenditures.

Comparing the two demand shock scenarios with each other:

- With a temporary demand shock, countercyclical fiscal policy is more effective in stabilising the economy, though the fiscal multiplier[45] remains relatively small (below 50% of the change in the deficit). But, as can be seen from the comparison between the SGP and No SGP scenario, short run output stabilisation is achieved with practically no cost in terms of future output losses.[46] Also the budgetary performance is balanced in the medium to long-run.[47] Fiscal stabilisation is more effective in this case since the shock and therefore the fiscal response is only of a temporary nature. Because of the consumption smoothing motive of households, private con-

---

[45] There are several studies dealing with the importance of automatic stabilizers in Europe; see *Al-Eyd et al.* (2004), *Andrés/Doménech* (2003); *Barrell/Pina* (2004).

[46] See Figure 12 and the Tables II.B and II.C in the Appendix B.

[47] See Figure 13.

sumption responds less to a temporary fiscal shock. Secondly, there are no long run adverse income effects.

Figure 12: Germany: Comparing the SGP with the no SGP scenario results: GDP growth and potential output level after a demand shock

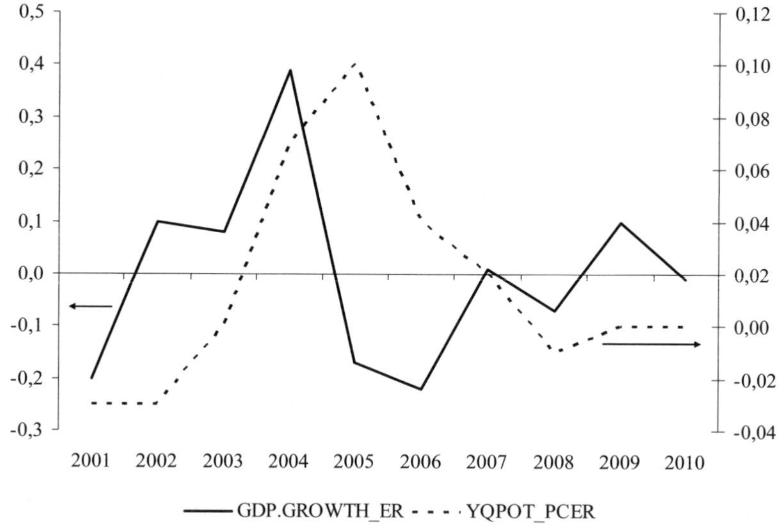

Source: Own simulations with the QUEST model.

Figure 13: Germany: Comparing the SGP with the no SGP scenario results: Budget deficit (DEFTG) and debt to GDP ratio after a demand shock

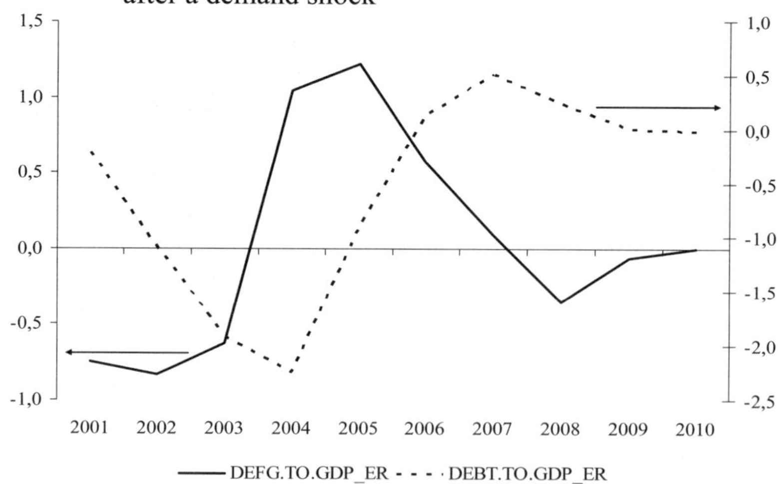

Source: Own simulations with the QUEST model.

b) Spill overs to neighbors – The case of Austria

Due to the small net effects in the three large Euro area countries the net spill-over effect (SGP minus no SGP strategy) after a demand shock in the large countries is neutral in the medium or long-run. This is the case in terms of real GDP[48] as for the budgetary performance.[49]

Figure 14: Austria: Comparing the SGP with the no SGP scenario results: GDP growth and potential output level after a demand shock

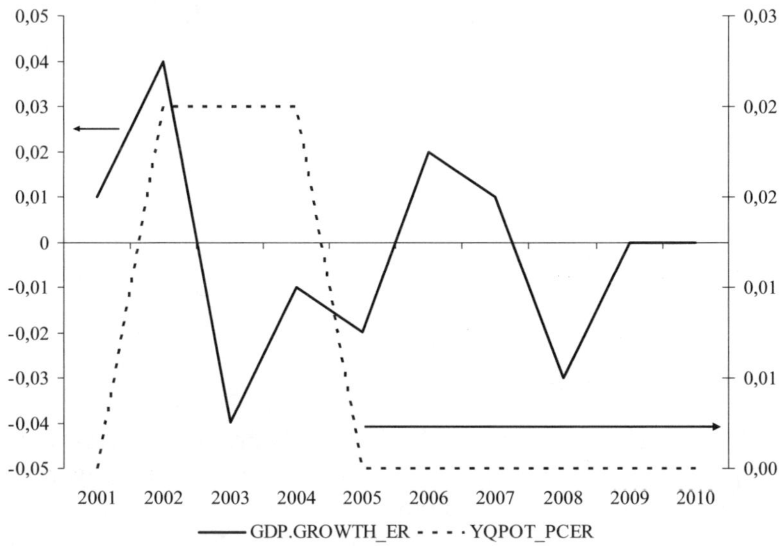

Source: Own simulations with the QUEST model.

48 See Figure 14 and the Table II.D in the Appendix B.

49 See Figure 15.

Figure 15: Austria: Comparing the SGP with the no SGP scenario results: Budget deficit (DEFTG) and debt to GDP ratio after a demand shock

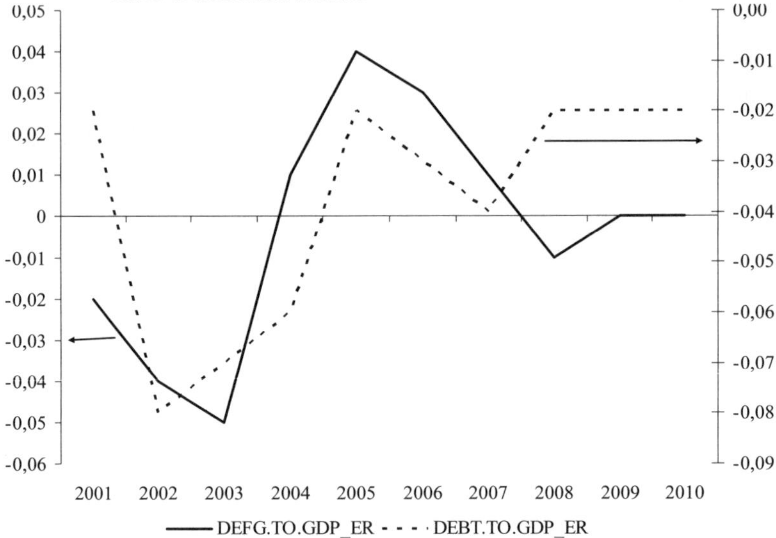

Source: Own simulations with the QUEST model.

V. Conclusions

In this paper we tried to study the advantage or disadvantage of applying the SGP fiscal rule in the case of a sluggish growth period which dominated the economic situation in Europe in the years after 2001. The debate about "refocusing the SGP" tried to improve the Pact exactly in view of the most recent bad experiences in France and Germany, struggling with the task to comply with the 3% deficit hurdle in the light of a slow but still positive growth over several years. The reform aims at improving the SGP in the following areas:[50] "(i) placing more focus on debt and sustainability in the surveillance of budgetary positions; (ii) allowing for more country-specific circumstances in defining the medium-term objectives of "close to balance or in surplus"; (iii) considering economic circumstances and developments in the implementation of the Excessive Deficit Procedure; (iv) ensuring earlier actions to correct inadequate budgetary developments."

With the Quest model we reproduced the downturn of the European economy since 2001 assuming two extreme interpretations: a)

[50] See *European Commission* (2004b) p.3.

on the one hand it could have been a consequence of a negative supply shock (TFP decline over three years) or b) a negative aggregate demand shock (reluctant consumption and investment demand) could have caused the slowdown. In any case we implemented these two shock scenarios in the three largest Euro area countries – France, Germany and Italy.

From our exercise we can draw the following tentative conclusions:

- *Supply shocks*

Obeying to a rule which forces the debt level back to the pre recession level (via cuts in government expenditure) gives the better permanent results (e.g. as measured by changes in private consumption or real GDP). This is in line with the SGP fiscal rules.

There is however a "small" cost in terms of current year output losses. This is to some extent model dependent and one could consider a sensitivity analysis with a few modifications to the model which make it less forward looking.

The SGP type rule is more favorable for neighbor countries, at least seen from a permanent perspective.

The long run effects of a lax fiscal policy response (no SGP rule), in terms of higher distortionary taxes and higher real interest rates are sizeable.

- *Demand Shocks*

With pure temporary demand shocks (which are followed by demand shocks going in the opposite direction) countercyclical fiscal stabilization (the no SGP scenario) does not seem to be harmful but to the contrary can contribute to stabilizing the economy.

A final judgment on fiscal rules and the SGP in particular must therefore be based on an analysis of the nature of recessions in the euro area. If recessions are fairly symmetric cyclical phenomena (followed by a boom of equal size) then countercyclical policies may be a good idea. If one believes that recessions in the euro area are of a more asymmetric nature, i.e. the economy does not fully return to the pre recession trend, then a more restrictive fiscal framework (the SGP scenario) may be more optimal.

References

Al-Eyd A. / Barrell R. / Holland D. / Hurst I. (2004), Fiscal Rules and Stabilisers in Europe, NIESR, June 2004.

Andrés J. / Doménech R. (2003), Automatic Stabilizers, Fiscal Rules and Macroeconomic Stability, Documento de Trabajo, No. 0314, Banco de España, Madrid 2003.

Annet A. / Decressin J. / Deppler M. (2005), Reforming the Stability and Growth Pact, IMF Policy Discussion Paper, PDP/05/2, Washington, February 2005.

Annichiarico B. / Giammaroli N. (2004), Fiscal Rules and Sustainability of Public Finances in an Endogenous Growth Model, ECB Working Papers Series, No. 381, August 2004.

Badinger H. (2004), Fiscal Rules, Discretionary Fiscal Policy and Macroeconomic Stability: An Empirical Assessment for OECD Countries, Europe Institute at WU-Wien, unpublished manuscript, November 2004.

Barrell R. / Pina A. M. (2004), How Important Are Automatic Stabilisers in Europe? A Stochastic Simulation Assessment, in: Economic Modelling, Vol. 21, No. 1, January 2004, pp. 1-35.

Blanchard O. J. (1985), Debt, deficits and finite horizons, in: Journal of Political Economy, 93, 1985, pp. 223-247.

Brandner P. / Frisch H. / Grossman B. / Hauth E. (2004), Eine Schuldenbremse für Österreich, Projektbericht, Wien, February 2004.

Breuss F. (1998), Sustainability of the Fiscal Criteria in Stage III of the EMU, IEF Working Papers, No. 29, Europe Institute, WU-Wien, August 1998.

Breuss F. (2005), Die Zukunft der Lissabon-Strategie, WIFO Working Papers, No. 244, Vienna, February 2005.

Breuss F. (2006), Monetäre Außenwirtschaft und Europäische Integration, Peter Lang: Frankfurt am Main 2006.

Breuss F. / Roeger W. (2005), The SGP fiscal rule in the case of sluggish growth: Simulations with the QUEST model, in: Journal of Policy Modeling, 27, 2005, pp. 676-780.

Brunila A. / Buti M. / Franco D. (2001), The Stability and Growth Pact: The Architecture of Fiscal Policy in EMU, Palgrave: Basingstoke-New York, 2001.

Buiter W. (1988), Death, birth, population growth and debt neutrality, in: The Economic Journal 98, 1988, pp. 279-293.

Buti M. / Giudice G. (2002), EMU's Fiscal Rules: What Can and Cannot be Exported?, European Commission, 30 April 2002.

Buti M. / van den Noord P. (2004), Fiscal policy in EMU: Rules, discretion and political incentives, European Economy, European Commission, Economic Papers, No. 206, Brussels, July 2004.

De Grauwe P. (2003), The Economics of Monetary Union[5], Oxford University Press: Oxford, 2003.

ECOFIN (2005), Improving the implementation of the Stability and Growth Pact, Council Report of the extraordinary ECOFIN meeting on 20 March 2005 to the European Council, 22-23 March 2005, Brussels, 21 March 2005.

Emmerson C. / Frayne Ch. / Love S. (2003), The Government's Fiscal Rules, The Institute for Fiscal Studies (IFS), Briefing Note No. 16, April 2001 (updated September 2003).

European Commission (2002), Public Finances in EMU 2002, European Economy, No. 3, Brussels, 2002.

European Commission (2004a), EMU after 5 Years, European Economy, Special Report, Brussels 1/2004.

European Commission (2004b), Strengthening economic governance and clarifying the implementation of the Stability and Growth Pact, Communication from the Commission to the Council and the European Parliament, Commission of the European Communities, Brussels, COM(2004) 581 final, 3 September 2004.

European Commission (2004c), The economy for the euro area, the European Union, and Candidate Countries in 2004-2006: Economic Forecast, Autumn 2004, European Economy, No. 5, Brussels 2004.

European Commission (2004d), The EU Economy: 2004 Review, Europäische Kommission, ECFIN (2004), REP 50455-EN, Brüssel, 26 October 2004.

European Council (2005), Presidency Conclusions of the Brussels European Council, 22 and 23 March 2005 (Luxembourg Presidency), Brussels, 23 March 2005.

European Court of Justice (2004), Judgment of the Court of Justice Clarifying the Powers of the Commission and the Council, Relating to the Excessive Deficit Procedure, Case C-27/04, Luxembourg, 13 July 2004.

Fatás A. / Mihov I. (2003), The case for restricting fiscal policy discretion, in: Quarterly Journal of Economics 4, 2002, pp. 1419-1448.

Fatás A. / Mihov I. (2004), The Macroeconomic Effect of Fiscal Rules in the US States, CEPR Discussion Paper Series, No. 4372, April 2004.

Gali J. / Gertler M. (1999), Inflation dynamics: a structural econometric analysis, in: Journal of Monetary Economics 44, 1999, pp. 195-222.

Gali J. / Gertler M. / Lopez-Salido J. D. (2001), European inflation dynamics, in: European Economic Review 45, pp. 1237-1262.

Joumard I. / Kongsrud P. M. (2003), Fiscal Relations Across Government Levels, OECD Economics Department Working Papers No. 375, Paris, 10 December 2003.

Joumad I. / Kongsrud P. M. / Nam Y-S. / Price R. (2004), Enhancing the Effectiveness of Public Spending: Experience in OECD Countries, OECD Economics Department Working Papers No. 380, Paris, 12 February 2004.

Koen V. / van den Noord P. (2005), Fiscal Gimmickry in Europe: One-Off Measures and Creative Accounting, OECD, Economics Department Working Papers, No. 417 (ECO/WKP(2005)) 4, Paris, 10 February 2005.

Larch M. / Salto M. (2003), Fiscal rules, inertia and discretionary fiscal policy, European Economy, Economic Papers, No. 194, European Commission, October 2003.

Neck R. / Haber G. / McKibbin W. J. (2005), Global Macroeconomic Policy Implications of an Enlarged EMU, in: *Breuss F. / Hochreiter E.* (eds.), Challenges for Central Banks in an Enlarged EMU, ECSA-Austria Publication Series, Vol. 9, Springer: Wien-New York, 2005, pp. 235-257.

OECD (2002), IV: Fiscal Sustainability: The Contribution of Fiscal Rules, in: Economic Outlook 72, Paris, December 2002, pp. 117-136.

Pissarides C. A. (1990), Equilibrium Unemployment Theory, Basil Blackwell: Oxford, 1990.

Roeger W. / in 't Veld J. (1997), QUEST II: A Multi-Country Business Cycle and Growth Model, Economic Papers, No. 123, European Commission, Brussels, 1997.

Roeger W. / in 't Veld J. (2004), Some selected simulation experiments with the European commission's QUEST model, in: Economic Modeling 21, 2004, pp. 785-832.

Rother (2004), Fiscal policy and inflation volatility, ECB Working Paper, no. 317, Frankfurt, 2004.

Schmitt-Grohe St. / Uribe M. (2004), Optimal Simple and Implementable Monetary and Fiscal Rules, NBER Working Paper Series, No. 10253, Cambridge, MA., January 2004.

Schratzenstaller M. (2005), A New Revenue Sharing Act and a New Stability Pact for Austria – No Fundamental Changes, in: Austrian Economic Quarterly, 1/2005, pp. 12-22.

Taylor J. B. (1980), Aggregate dynamics and staggered contracts, in: Journal of Political Economics 88, 1980, pp. 1-23.

Appendix A: Some facts on the nature of recessions in the Euro area:

Recessions and Productivity trends - Is there a level/growth shift after recessions?

- The following Figure A1 suggests that the supply interpretation is more correct for the euro area. Productivity growth has a concave shape and it is noticeable that trend productivity has a tendency to change direction right after recessions. Concerning the current situation, long period of strong growth would be required to bring the economy back to the 90s productivity trajectory.

Figure A1: The level of TFP and output gap in the Euro area

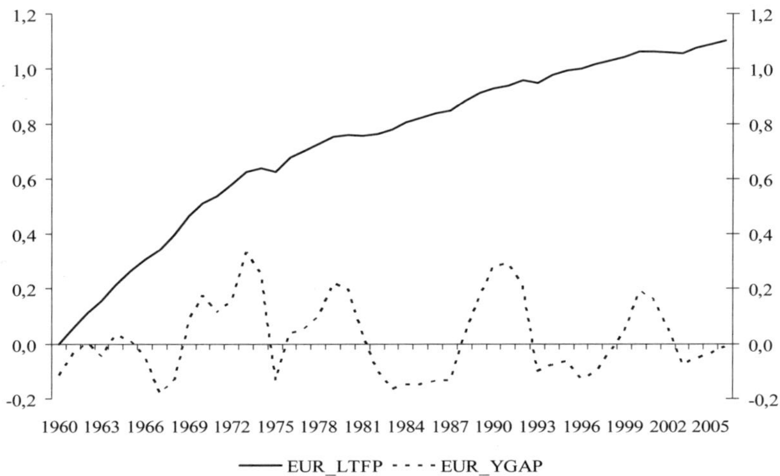

Source: *European Commission* (2004c).

The following Figure A2 shows this phenomenon more explicitly for labour productivity. Here we extrapolate forward at each recession (74, 81, 92, 01) the trend between the current and the previous recession the permanent output losses associated with recession episodes.

Figure A2: The level of productivity and output gap in the Euro area

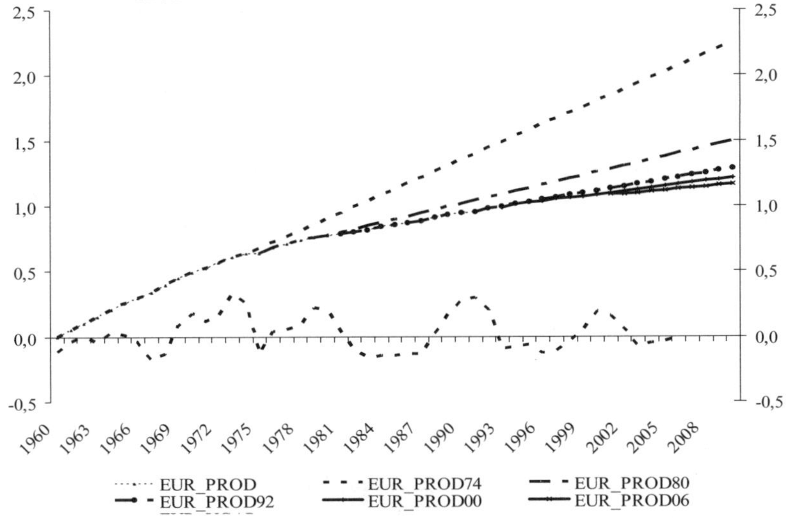

Source: *European Commission* (2004c).

Recessions and government expenditure shares:

- Another feature of fiscal policy that we highlighted in our supply shock scenario is the fact that there is a tendency for the fiscal expenditure share to increase after recessions.[51] This would arise naturally when there is a misperception about the nature of the recession (fiscal policy believes in a cyclical downturn followed by a boom while in fact previous GDP trends are not fully recovered after the recession).
- In the 70s and 80s there was a tendency for countries to come out of a recession with a permanently higher government expenditure share. This has changed in the 90s which was a period with more fiscal discipline. What will happen to government expenditure shares after this recession? DG ECFIN forecasts[52] assume that expenditure shares will not be permanently higher. See the examples of France, Germany and Italy in the Figures A3 to A5.

---

[51] For such analysis in more detail, see also *Joumard/Kongsrud* (2003) and *Joumard et al.* (2004).

[52] See *European Commission* (2004c).

Figure A3: Public expenditure shares in GDP and output gap in France

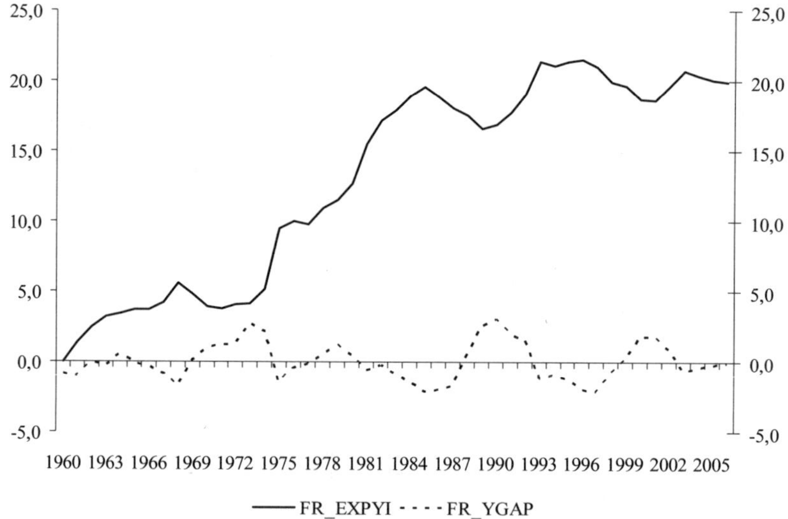

Source: *European Commission* (2004c).

Figure A4: Public expenditure shares in GDP and output gap in Germany

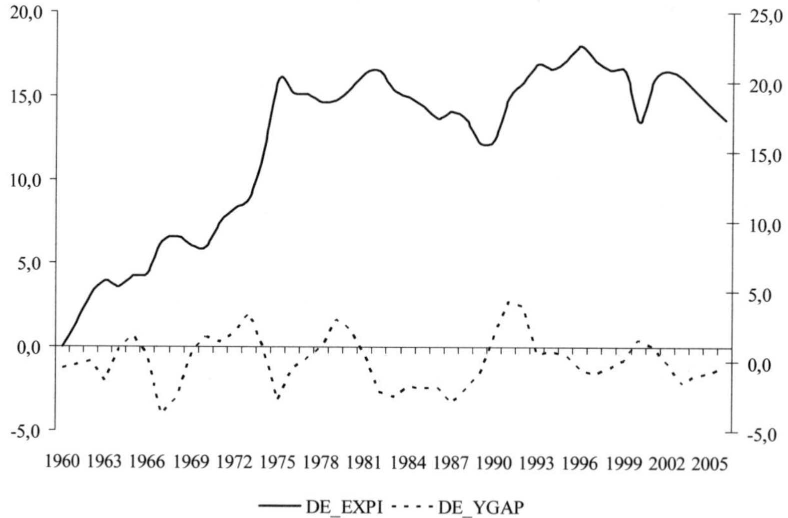

Source: *European Commission* (2004c).

Figure A5: Public expenditure shares in GDP and output gap in Italy

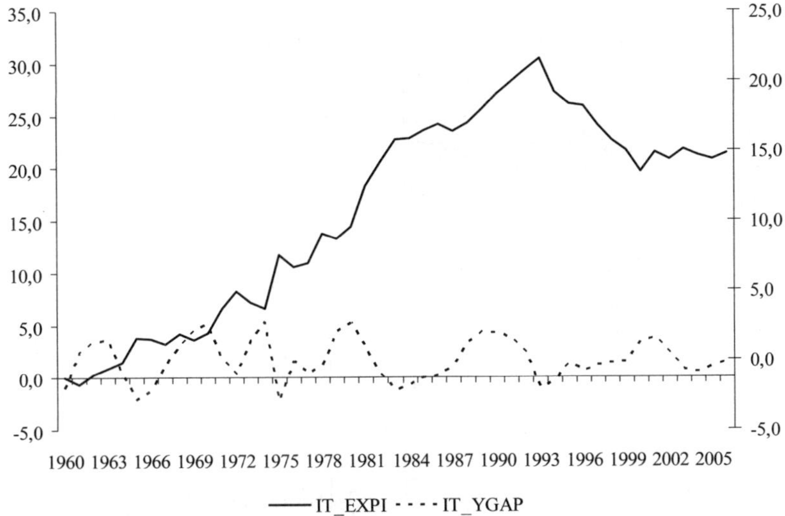

Source: *European Commission* (2004c).

Appendix B: Detailed simulation tables

Table I.A: Supply Shock Scenario: Germany
No SGP = Baseline

	2001A	2002A	2003A	2004A	2010A	2020A	2030A
TOTAL.GDP_PCER	-1.02	-2.46	-3.65	-4.45	-5.34	-7.39	-8.06
YQPOT_PCER	-0.98	-2.49	-3.99	-4.71	-5.65	-7.89	-8.56
PRIV.CONS_PCER	-2.92	-5.32	-5.89	-6.32	-6.44	-7.71	-7.69
PRIV.INV.I_PCER	-1.96	-5.12	-8.50	-10.27	-12.43	-14.34	-13.90
GOV.CONS_PCER	0.00	0.00	0.00	0.00	0.00	0.00	0.00
GOV.TRANS_PCER	0.00	0.00	0.00	0.00	0.00	0.00	0.00
EXPORTS.EX_PCER	0.96	0.45	-0.52	-1.22	-2.13	-4.58	-6.10
EXPORT.PRICES_PCER	0.77	1.27	1.49	1.60	1.54	1.25	1.08
IMPORTS.IM_PCER	-2.87	-5.36	-5.96	-6.22	-6.35	-6.29	-5.34
EMPLOYMENT_PCER	-0.11	-0.1	-0.10	-0.03	0.22	-0.89	-0.75
REAL.WAGE.COSTS_PCER	-0.74	-2.36	-3.77	-4.71	-5.72	-7.01	-7.80
PRICE.LEVEL_PCER	0.11	0.45	0.90	1.17	1.40	1.91	2.27
CONS.PRICE.LEVEL_PCER	0.55	0.81	1.12	1.31	1.37	1.41	1.47
IMPORT.PRICES_PCER	2.46	2.48	2.10	1.91	1.24	-0.68	-1.89
.NEER.PM1_PCER	2.24	2.60	2.24	1.94	1.34	-0.63	-1.85
DOLLAR.EXCH.RATE_PCER	6.37	6.15	5.42	5.04	3.59	0.19	-1.95
REER.PM.P_PCER	2.35	2.02	1.19	0.73	-0.16	-2.54	-4.07
LAB.TAX.REV.NOM_PCER	-0.73	-2.08	-3.01	-3.62	-4.19	-0.28	-0.64
VAT.TAX.REV.NOM_PCER	-2.39	-4.55	-4.83	-5.09	-5.16	-6.42	-6.33
GDP.GROWTH_ER	-1.03	-1.46	-1.23	-0.84	-0.20	-0.10	-0.05
INV.GDP_ER	-0.21	-0.57	-1.09	-1.36	-1.69	-1.63	-1.30
SHORT.RATE_ER	0.03	-0.55	-0.48	-0.01	-0.26	-0.05	-0.01
INFLATION.PGDP_ER	0.11	0.33	0.44	0.27	-0.00	0.04	0.03
INFLATION.PC_ER	0.55	0.26	0.30	0.19	-0.05	0.01	0.01
.INF.TARGET_ER	0.00	0.00	0.00	0.00	0.00	0.00	0.00
.INF.GAP_ER	0.21	0.40	0.44	0.15	-0.01	0.04	0.03
LONG.RATE.10YRS_ER	-0.16	-0.20	-0.16	-0.12	-0.13	-0.03	0.01
REAL.SHORT.RATE_ER	-0.24	-0.98	-0.87	-0.09	-0.25	-0.09	-0.04
VAT_ER	0.00	0.00	0.00	0.00	0.00	0.00	0.00
TL_ER	0.00	0.00	0.00	0.00	0.00	2.50	2.50
TC_ER	0.00	0.00	0.00	0.00	0.00	2.50	2.50
DEBT.TO.GDP_ER	0.75	2.11	3.58	5.30	15.49	17.19	17.12
DEFG.TO.GDP_ER	0.46	0.88	1.26	1.64	1.85	0.05	0.04
TRADE.BAL.TO.GDP_ER	0.78	1.63	1.77	1.82	1.75	1.34	0.74

Note: _PCER = cumulative percentage difference from base; _ER = absolute difference from base.

Table I.B: Supply Shock Scenario: Germany
SGP Scenario

	2001A	2002A	2003A	2004A	2010A	2020A	2030A
TOTAL.GDP_PCER	-1.10	-2.45	-3.45	-4.16	-4.58	-5.02	-5.29
YQPOT_PCER	-0.93	-2.36	-3.75	-4.38	-4.83	-5.28	-5.54
PRIV.CONS_PCER	-2.00	-3.80	-4.32	-4.75	-4.91	-4.82	-4.66
PRIV.INV.I_PCER	0.99	2.70	5.22	6.45	6.42	6.29	6.10
GOV.CONS_PCER	1.09	2.44	3.46	4.19	4.58	5.01	5.29
GOV.TRANS_PCER	1.11	2.44	3.45	4.16	4.58	5.02	5.29
EXPORTS.EX_PCER	0.39	1.07	1.62	2.29	3.25	4.01	0.06
EXPORT.PRICES_PCER	-0.12	-0.14	0.02	0.15	0.27	0.25	0.23
IMPORTS.IM_PCER	-1.26	-2.60	-3.17	-3.45	-3.35	-2.99	-2.61
EMPLOYMENT_PCER	-0.06	-0.03	0.08	0.17	0.47	0.57	0.58
REAL.WAGE.COSTS_PCER	-0.95	-2.61	-3.81	-4.62	-5.37	-5.87	-6.14
PRICE.LEVEL_PCER	-0.06	0.01	0.36	0.62	0.90	1.09	1.24
CONS.PRICE.LEVEL_PCER	-0.11	-0.09	0.14	0.32	0.48	0.54	0.60
IMPORT.PRICES_PCER	-0.32	-0.54	-0.81	-0.92	-1.17	-1.69	-2.08
.NEER.PM1_PCER	-0.28	-0.43	-0.72	-0.91	-1.14	-1.67	-2.07
DOLLAR.EXCH.RATE_PCER	-0.42	-0.70	-1.22	-1.39	-1.72	-2.31	-2.74
REER.PM.P_PCER	-0.26	-0.54	-1.17	-1.54	-2.05	-2.75	-3.28
LAB.TAX.REV.NOM_PCER	-1.06	-2.63	-3.38	-3.86	-4.07	-4.31	-4.43
VAT.TAX.REV.NOM_PCER	-2.11	-3.89	-4.19	-4.45	-4.45	-4.30	-4.09
GDP.GROWTH_ER	-1.10	-1.38	-1.03	-0.74	-0.08	-0.04	-0.02
INV.GDP_ER	0.02	-0.05	-0.38	-0.52	-0.41	-0.27	-0.17
SHORT.RATE_ER	-0.06	-0.52	-0.37	0.04	-0.09	-0.06	-0.05
INFLATION.PGDP_ER	-0.06	0.06	0.35	0.26	0.00	0.02	0.01
INFLATION.PC_ER	-0.11	0.01	0.23	0.18	-0.02	0.01	0.00
.INF.TARGET_ER	0.00	0.00	0.00	0.00	0.00	0.00	0.00
.INF.GAP_ER	-0.09	0.20	0.39	0.15	-0.01	0.02	0.01
LONG.RATE.10YRS_ER	-0.14	-0.14	-0.10	-0.07	-0.07	-0.05	-0.05
REAL.SHORT.RATE_ER	-0.01	-0.80	-0.73	-0.06	-0.08	-0.08	-0.06
VAT_ER	0.00	0.00	0.00	0.00	0.00	0.00	0.00
TL_ER	0.00	0.00	0.00	0.00	0.00	0.00	0.00
TC_ER	0.00	0.00	0.00	0.00	0.00	0.00	0.00
DEBT.TO.GDP_ER	0.70	1.40	1.67	1.86	1.15	0.06	-0.03
DEFG.TO.GDP_ER	0.04	-0.03	-0.05	0.03	-0.22	-0.18	-0.15
TRADE.BAL.TO.GDP_ER	0.53	0.90	1.05	1.10	0.94	0.60	0.30

Note: _PCER = cumulative percentage difference from base; _ER = absolute difference from base.

Table I.C: Supply Shock Scenario: Germany
Comparison SGP Scenario (I.B) minus No SGP Scenario (I.A)

	2001A	2002A	2003A	2004A	2010A	2020A	2030A
TOTAL.GDP_PCER	-0.07	0.01	0.21	0.31	0.80	2.56	3.01
YQPOT_PCER	0.05	0.14	0.24	0.34	0.86	2.83	3.30
PRIV.CONS_PCER	0.95	1.61	1.67	1.68	1.63	3.14	3.28
PRIV.INV.I_PCER	0.99	2.54	3.59	4.26	6.86	9.39	9.05
GOV.CONS_PCER	-1.09	-2.44	-3.46	-4.19	-4.58	-5.01	-5.29
GOV.TRANS_PCER	-1.11	-2.44	-3.45	-4.16	-4.58	-5.02	-5.29
EXPORTS.EX_PCER	-0.89	-0.84	-0.56	-0.40	-0.16	1.39	2.23
EXPORT.PRICES_PCER	-0.88	-1.40	-1.45	-1.42	-1.25	-0.99	-0.84
IMPORTS.IM_PCER	1.67	2.92	2.97	2.95	3.20	3.52	2.88
EMPLOYMENT_PCER	0.05	0.12	0.18	0.21	0.25	1.47	1.34
REAL.WAGE.COSTS_PCER	-0.22	-0.25	-0.03	0.09	0.37	1.22	1.80
PRICE.LEVEL_PCER	-0.17	-0.44	-0.53	-0.54	-0.50	-0.81	-1.01
CONS.PRICE.LEVEL_PCER	-0.65	-0.90	-0.97	-0.98	-0.87	-0.85	-0.86
IMPORT.PRICES_PCER	-2.72	-2.95	-2.85	-2.78	-2.38	-1.02	-0.20
IMPORT.PRICES.USD_PCER	3.91	3.75	3.68	3.57	2.89	1.52	0.61
.NEER.PM1_PCER	-2.47	-2.95	-2.90	-2.80	-2.45	-1.05	-0.23
DOLLAR.EXCH.RATE_PCER	-6.38	-6.46	-6.30	-6.12	-5.12	-2.50	-0.80
REER.PM.P_PCER	-2.55	-2.52	-2.33	-2.25	-1.89	-0.21	0.82
LAB.TAX.REV.NOM_PCER	-0.33	-0.57	-0.38	-0.24	0.12	-4.04	-3.82
VAT.TAX.REV.NOM_PCER	0.29	0.69	0.68	0.68	0.74	2.26	2.39
GDP.GROWTH_ER	-0.07	0.09	0.19	0.11	0.12	0.06	0.03
INV.GDP_ER	0.23	0.52	0.71	0.85	1.28	1.36	1.14
SHORT.RATE_ER	-0.10	0.03	0.11	0.04	0.17	-0.01	-0.04
INFLATION.PGDP_ER	-0.17	-0.27	-0.09	-0.01	0.01	-0.02	-0.02
INFLATION.PC_ER	-0.65	-0.25	-0.07	-0.01	0.03	0.00	-0.00
.INF.TARGET_ER	0.00	0.00	0.00	0.00	0.00	0.00	0.00
.INF.GAP_ER	-0.30	-0.20	-0.04	0.01	0.00	-0.02	-0.02
LONG.RATE.10YRS_ER	0.02	0.06	0.06	0.06	0,06	-0.02	-0.06
REAL.SHORT.RATE_ER	0.23	0.18	0.14	0.03	0.17	0.01	-0.02
VAT_ER	0.00	0.00	0.00	0.00	0.00	0.00	0.00
TL_ER	0.00	0.00	0.00	0.00	0.00	-2.50	-2.50
TC_ER	0.00	0.00	0.00	0.00	0.00	-2.50	-2.50
DEBT.TO.GDP_ER	-0.06	-0.71	-1.92	-3.43	-14.34	-17.12	-17.16
DEFG.TO.GDP_ER	-0.42	-0.92	-1.31	-1.61	-2.06	-0.23	-0.19
TRADE.BAL.TO.GDP_ER	-0.25	-0.73	-0.72	-0.72	-0.80	-0.74	-0.44

Note: _PCER = cumulative percentage difference from base; _ER = absolute difference from base.

Table I.D: Supply Shock Scenario:
Spill overs to neighbors – Austria: Comparison SGP minus No SGP

	2001A	2002A	2003A	2004A	2010A	2020A	2030A
TOTAL.GDP_PCER	-0.16	0.05	0.19	0.24	0.43	0.82	1.01
YQPOT_PCER	0.03	0.11	0.19	0.25	0.52	0.88	1.07
PRIV.CONS_PCER	0.87	1.96	2.17	2.24	2.19	2.41	2.14
PRIV.INV.I_PCER	0.70	1.65	2.06	2.31	2.63	2.72	2.76
GOV.CONS_PCER	0.00	0.00	0.00	0.00	0.00	0.00	0.00
GOV.TRANS_PCER	0.00	0.00	0.00	0.00	0.00	0.00	0.00
EXPORTS.EX_PCER	-0.55	-0.45	-0.32	-0.25	-0.06	0.40	0.65
EXPORT.PRICES_PCER	-0.83	-1.26	-1.21	-1.13	-0.90	0.17	0.58
IMPORTS.IM_PCER	1.06	2.28	2.52	2.60	2.62	3.02	2.82
EMPLOYMENT_PCER	0.02	0.08	0.11	0.12	0.09	0.09	0.06
REAL.WAGE.COSTS_PCER	-0.23	-0.16	0.06	0.12	0.36	0.78	1.00
PRICE.LEVEL_PCER	-0.17	-0.32	-0.27	-0.20	-0.06	0.85	1.04
CONS.PRICE.LEVEL_PCER	-0.72	-0.91	-0.88	-0.85	-0.66	0.23	0.53
IMPORT.PRICES_PCER	-1.90	-2.26	-2.23	-2.18	-1.90	-1.09	-0.60
IMPORT.PRICES.USD_PCER	4.79	4.48	4.34	4.20	3.40	1.44	0.20
.NEER.PM1_PCER	-1.54	-2.24	-2.25	-2.19	-1.94	-1.12	-0.62
DOLLAR.EXCH.RATE_PCER	-6.38	-6.46	-6.30	-6.12	-5.12	-2.50	-0.80
REER.PM.P_PCER	-1.73	-1.94	-1.97	-1.98	-1.84	-1.93	-1.63
LAB.TAX.REV.NOM_PCER	-0.38	-0.40	-0.10	0.03	0.40	1.73	2.12
VAT.TAX.REV.NOM_PCER	0.15	1.03	1.27	1.37	1.52	2.65	2.68
GDP.GROWTH_ER	-0.16	0.21	0.14	0.05	0.02	0.03	0.01
INV.GDP_ER	0.22	0.39	0.46	0.53	0.56	0.45	0.40
SHORT.RATE_ER	-0.10	0.03	0.11	0.04	0.17	-0.01	-0.04
INFLATION.PGDP_ER	-0.17	-0.16	0.06	0.07	0.11	0.03	0.01
INFLATION.PC_ER	-0.72	-0.20	0.03	0.03	0.10	0.04	0.02
.INF.TARGET_ER	0.00	0.00	0.00	0.00	0.00	0.00	0.00
.INF.GAP_ER	-0.28	-0.04	0.08	0.05	0.16	0.03	0.01
LONG.RATE.10YRS_ER	0.02	0.06	0.06	0.06	0.06	-0.02	-0.06
REAL.SHORT.RATE_ER	0.17	0.01	0.04	0.00	-0.02	-0.03	-0.06
VAT_ER	0.00	0.00	0.00	0.00	0.00	0.00	0.00
TL_ER	0.00	0.00	0.00	0.00	0.00	0.00	0.00
TC_ER	0.00	0.00	0.00	0.00	0.00	0.00	0.00
DEBT.TO.GDP_ER	0.20	0.05	-0.24	-0.49	-2.11	-0.32	-0.02
DEFG.TO.GDP_ER	-0.02	-0.14	-0.17	-0.21	-0.23	0.13	0.02
TRADE.BAL.TO.GDP_ER	-0.30	-0.89	-0.97	-1.01	-0.94	-0.73	-0.51

Note: _PCER = cumulative percentage difference from base; _ER = absolute difference from base.

Table II.A: Demand Shock Scenario: Germany
No SGP = Baseline

	2001A	2002A	2003A	2004A	2010A	2020A	2030A
TOTAL.GDP_PCER	-2.26	-2.52	-1.76	3.28	0.00	-0.21	-0.23
YQPOT_PCER	-0.42	-0.81	-0.80	0.12	-0.09	-0.23	-0.25
PRIV.CONS_PCER	-2.58	-6.29	-11.16	-4.32	-0.21	-0.61	-0.97
PRIV.INV.I_PCER	-4.36	-3.59	8.36	17.55	-0.48	-0.79	-0.41
GOV.CONS_PCER	0.00	0.00	0.00	0.00	0.00	0.00	0.00
GOV.TRANS_PCER	0.00	0.00	0.00	0.00	0.00	0.00	0.00
EXPORTS.EX_PCER	1.35	4.97	5.72	2.29	0.21	0.23	0.39
EXPORT.PRICES_PCER	-0.60	-2.50	-3.18	-1.60	-0.00	0.03	-0.02
IMPORTS.IM_PCER	0.41	-1.97	-6.01	-4.63	-0.45	-0.71	-0.94
EMPLOYMENT_PCER	-0.49	-0.81	-0.81	0.10	-0.00	-0.03	-0.04
REAL.WAGE.COSTS_PCER	-0.61	-1.89	-1.18	0.78	0.03	-0.19	-0.20
PRICE.LEVEL_PCER	-1.23	-4.28	-5.04	-2.01	-0.11	-0.09	-0.20
CONS.PRICE.LEVEL_PCER	-0.81	-3.26	-3.93	-1.82	-0.04	-0.02	-0.09
IMPORT.PRICES_PCER	1.10	1.65	1.03	-1.07	0.24	0.30	0.35
IMPORT.PRICES.USD_PCER	-1.33	-1.79	-1.61	0.59	-0.15	-0.17	-0.20
.NEER.PM1_PCER	0.00	1.65	1.42	0.28	0.25	0.29	0.35
DOLLAR.EXCH.RATE_PCER	2.46	3.50	2.68	-1.67	0.39	0.47	0.55
REER.PM.P_PCER	2.36	6.19	6.39	0.96	0.35	0.39	0.55
LAB.TAX.REV.NOM_PCER	-2.31	-6.85	-6.92	-1.17	-0.08	-0.31	-0.44
VAT.TAX.REV.NOM_PCER	-3.37	-9.34	-14.65	-6.17	-0.25	-0.62	-1.06
GDP.GROWTH_ER	-2.29	-0.26	0.77	5.00	0.18	-0.01	0.00
INV.GDP_ER	-0.48	-0.23	1.92	2.56	-0.10	-0.12	-0.04
SHORT.RATE_ER	0.23	0.02	-1.88	-1.52	-0.04	0.01	0.01
INFLATION.PGDP_ER	-1.24	-3.17	-0.79	3.05	0.07	-0.01	-0.01
INFLATION.PC_ER	-0.81	-2.52	-0.70	2.13	0.05	-0.01	-0.01
.INF.TARGET_ER	0.00	0.00	0.00	0.00	0.00	0.00	0.00
.INF.GAP_ER	-2.59	-2.57	0.31	5.26	0.14	-0.01	-0.01
LONG.RATE.10YRS_ER	0.03	0.01	0.01	0.20	0.01	0.01	0.01
REAL.SHORT.RATE_ER	2.94	1.94	-2.83	-6.90	-0.17	0.03	0.02
VAT_ER	0.00	0.00	0.00	0.00	0.00	0.00	0.00
TL_ER	0.00	0.00	0.00	0.00	0.00	0.00	0.00
TC_ER	0.00	0.00	0.00	0.00	0.00	0.00	0.00
DEBT.TO.GDP_ER	2.43	5.39	6.12	1.31	0.04	0.03	0.01
DEFG.TO.GDP_ER	0.82	1.20	0.85	-0.83	-0.01	-0.02	-0.01
TRADE.BAL.TO.GDP_ER	-0.11	1.17	2.70	2.22	0.16	0.25	0.34

Note: _PCER = cumulative percentage difference from base; _ER = absolute difference from base.

Table II.B: Demand Shock Scenario: Germany
SGP Scenario

	2001A	2002A	2003A	2004A	2010A	2020A	2030A
TOTAL.GDP_PCER	-2.46	-2.61	-1.78	3.67	0.02	-0.21	-0.23
YQPOT_PCER	-0.45	-0.84	-0.80	0.19	-0.09	-0.23	-0.25
PRIV.CONS_PCER	-2.80	-6.57	-11.32	-4.03	-0.18	-0.57	-0.93
PRIV.INV.I_PCER	-3.95	-2.62	9.29	17.21	-0.48	-0.80	-0.41
GOV.CONS_PCER	-2.45	-2.59	-1.77	3.66	0.02	-0.21	-0.23
GOV.TRANS_PCER	-2.50	-2.61	-1.78	3.66	0.02	-0.21	-0.23
EXPORTS.EX_PCER	1.42	5.19	5.90	2.27	0.21	0.23	0.40
EXPORT.PRICES_PCER	-0.63	-2.62	-3.30	-1.62	0.01	0.04	-0.02
IMPORTS.IM_PCER	0.15	-2.28	-6.21	-4.26	-0.43	-0.71	-0.94
EMPLOYMENT_PCER	-0.54	-0.87	-0.85	0.15	-0.00	-0.03	-0.04
REAL.WAGE.COSTS_PCER	-0.65	-1.98	-1.20	0.88	0.05	-0.20	-0.20
PRICE.LEVEL_PCER	-1.30	-4.47	-5.21	-2.00	-0.10	-0.09	-0.19
CONS.PRICE.LEVEL_PCER	-0.85	-3.41	-4.08	-1.83	-0.03	-0.01	-0.09
IMPORT.PRICES_PCER	1.15	1.69	1.01	-1.17	0.25	0.31	0.36
IMPORT.PRICES.USD_PCER	-1.41	-1.86	-1.64	0.68	-0.14	-0.17	-0.20
.NEER.PM1_PCER	0.00	1.71	1.42	0.22	0.25	0.31	0.36
DOLLAR.EXCH.RATE_PCER	2.59	3.62	2.70	-1.86	0.39	0.48	0.56
REER.PM.P_PCER	2.48	6.44	6.56	0.84	0.35	0.39	0.55
LAB.TAX.REV.NOM_PCER	-2.47	-7.17	-7.14	-1.01	-0.06	-0.31	-0.43
VAT.TAX.REV.NOM_PCER	-3.64	-9.75	-14.93	-5.91	-0.21	-0.58	-1.01
GDP.GROWTH_ER	-2.49	-0.16	0.86	5.39	0.17	-0.01	0.00
INV.GDP_ER	-0.34	-0.00	2.08	2.43	-0.11	-0.12	-0.03
SHORT.RATE_ER	0.18	-0.05	-1.99	-1.48	-0.03	0.01	0.01
INFLATION.PGDP_ER	-1.31	-3.30	-0.77	3.24	0.10	-0.01	-0.01
INFLATION.PC_ER	-0.86	-2.62	-0.70	2.27	0.07	-0.01	-0.01
.INF.TARGET_ER	0.00	0.00	0.00	0.00	0.00	0.00	0.00
.INF.GAP_ER	-2.73	-2.65	0.37	5.55	0.16	-0.01	-0.01
LONG.RATE.10YRS_ER	0.04	0.02	0.02	0.22	0.01	0.01	0.01
REAL.SHORT.RATE_ER	3.02	1.90	-3.02	-7.13	-0.18	0.03	0.02
VAT_ER	0.00	0.00	0.00	0.00	0.00	0.00	0.00
TL_ER	0.00	0.00	0.00	0.00	0.00	0.00	0.00
TC_ER	0.00	0.00	0.00	0.00	0.00	0.00	0.00
DEBT.TO.GDP_ER	2.21	4.30	4.21	-0.94	-0.05	0.01	0.01
DEFG.TO.GDP_ER	0.07	0.37	0.22	0.21	-0.01	-0.01	-0.01
TRADE.BAL.TO.GDP_ER	-0.02	1.28	2.80	2.08	0.15	0.25	0.34

Note: _PCER = cumulative percentage difference from base; _ER = absolute difference from base.

Table II.C: Demand Shock Scenario: Germany
Comparison SGP Scenario (II.B) minus No SGP Scenario (II.A)

	2001A	2002A	2003A	2004A	2010A	2020A	2030A
TOTAL.GDP_PCER	-0.20	-0.10	-0.02	0.37	0.02	-0.00	-0.00
YQPOT_PCER	-0.03	-0.03	0.00	0.07	0.00	-0.00	-0.00
PRIV.CONS_PCER	-0.23	-0.30	-0.17	0.30	0.03	0.04	0.04
PRIV.INV.I_PCER	0.43	1.01	0.86	-0.29	0.00	-0.01	0.00
GOV.CONS_PCER	-2.45	-2.59	-1.77	3.66	0.02	-0.21	-0.23
GOV.TRANS_PCER	-2.50	-2.61	-1.78	3.66	0.02	-0.21	-0.23
EXPORTS.EX_PCER	0.06	0.21	0.17	-0.02	0.00	0.00	0.00
EXPORT.PRICES_PCER	-0.03	-0.12	-0.13	-0.02	0.01	0.01	0.01
IMPORTS.IM_PCER	-0.26	-0.31	-0.22	0.39	0.02	0.00	0.00
EMPLOYMENT_PCER	-0.05	-0.06	-0.03	0.05	0.00	0.00	0.00
REAL.WAGE.COSTS_PCER	-0.05	-0.09	-0.02	0.10	0.01	-0.00	-0.00
NOM.WAGES_PCER	-0.12	-0.29	-0.20	0.11	0.03	0.01	0.01
BENEFITS_PCER	-0.03	-0.05	0.01	0.08	0.01	-0.00	-0.00
PRICE.LEVEL_PCER	-0.07	-0.20	-0.18	0.01	0.01	0.01	0.01
CONS.PRICE.LEVEL_PCER	-0.05	-0.15	-0.15	-0.01	0.01	0.01	0.01
IMPORT.PRICES_PCER	0.05	0.04	-0.01	-0.11	0.01	0.01	0.01
IMPORT.PRICES.USD_PCER	-0.08	-0.07	-0.04	0.09	0.00	0.00	0.00
.NEER.PM1_PCER	0.00	0.05	0.01	-0.05	0.01	0.01	0.01
DOLLAR.EXCH.RATE_PCER	0.13	0.11	0.03	-0.20	0.00	0.01	0.01
REER.PM.P_PCER	0.12	0.24	0.17	-0.12	-0.01	0.00	0.00
LAB.TAX.REV.NOM_PCER	-0.16	-0.35	-0.24	0.16	0.03	0.01	0.00
VAT.TAX.REV.NOM_PCER	-0.28	-0.45	-0.33	0.28	0.05	0.04	0.04
GDP.GROWTH_ER	-0.20	0.10	0.08	0.39	-0.01	0.00	0.00
INV.GDP_ER	0.14	0.23	0.16	-0.12	-0.00	-0.00	0.00
SHORT.RATE_ER	-0.05	-0.07	-0.11	0.04	0.00	0.00	0.00
INFLATION.PGDP_ER	-0.07	-0.13	0.01	0.18	0.03	-0.00	0.00
INFLATION.PC_ER	-0.05	-0.11	0.00	0.13	0.03	-0.00	0.00
.INF.TARGET_ER	0.00	0.00	0.00	0.00	0.00	0.00	0.00
.INF.GAP_ER	-0.14	-0.07	0.06	0.30	0.02	-0.00	0.00
LONG.RATE.10YRS_ER	0.00	0.01	0.01	0.02	0.00	0.00	0.00
REAL.SHORT.RATE_ER	0.08	-0.03	-0.19	-0.22	-0.00	0.00	0.00
VAT_ER	0.00	0.00	0.00	0.00	0.00	0.00	0.00
TL_ER	0.00	0.00	0.00	0.00	0.00	0.00	0.00
TC_ER	0.00	0.00	0.00	0.00	0.00	0.00	0.00
DEBT.TO.GDP_ER	-0.22	-1.09	-1.91	-2.24	-0.01	-0.03	-0.01
DEFG.TO.GDP_ER	-0.75	-0.83	-0.63	1.04	0.00	0.00	0.00
TRADE.BAL.TO.GDP_ER	0.08	0.12	0.09	-0.14	-0.01	-0.00	0.00

Note: _PCER = cumulative percentage difference from base; _ER = absolute difference from base.

Table II.D: Demand Shock Scenario:
Spill overs to neighbors – Austria: Comparison SGP minus No SGP

	2001A	2002A	2003A	2004A	2010A	2020A	2030A
TOTAL.GDP_PCER	0.01	0.05	0.01	0.00	0.00	-0.00	0.00
YQPOT_PCER	0.00	0.02	0.02	0.02	0.00	-0.00	0.00
PRIV.CONS_PCER	-0.00	0.06	0.05	0.02	-0.00	0.00	0.00
PRIV.INV.I_PCER	0.24	0.43	0.26	-0.27	-0.00	-0.00	0.00
GOV.CONS_PCER	0.00	0.00	0.00	0.00	0.00	0.00	0.00
GOV.TRANS_PCER	0.00	0.00	0.00	0.00	0.00	0.00	0.00
EXPORTS.EX_PCER	-0.06	-0.08	-0.08	0.11	0.00	-0.00	-0.00
EXPORT.PRICES_PCER	0.02	0.03	-0.02	-0.07	0.01	0.01	0.01
IMPORTS.IM_PCER	0.03	0.12	0.09	-0.00	-0.00	0.00	0.00
EMPLOYMENT_PCER	-0.00	0.01	0.00	0.00	0.00	0.00	0.00
REAL.WAGE.COSTS_PCER	0.01	0.03	0.01	-0.00	0.00	-0.00	0.00
NOM.WAGES_PCER	0.02	0.06	-0.01	-0.06	0.01	0.01	0.01
BENEFITS_PCER	0.01	0.02	-0.01	-0.00	0.00	-0.00	-0.00
PRICE.LEVEL_PCER	0.01	0.02	-0.02	-0.06	0.01	0.01	0.01
CONS.PRICE.LEVEL_PCER	0.01	0.00	-0.04	-0.06	0.01	0.01	0.01
IMPORT.PRICES_PCER	0.01	-0.04	-0.07	-0.07	0.01	0.01	0.01
IMPORT.PRICES.USD_PCER	-0.12	-0.15	-0.10	0.13	0.01	0.00	-0.00
.NEER.PM1_PCER	0.00	-0.02	-0.06	-0.08	0.01	0.01	0.01
DOLLAR.EXCH.RATE_PCER	0.13	0.11	0.03	-0.20	0.00	0.01	0.01
REER.PM.P_PCER	0.00	-0.06	-0.05	-0.00	-0.00	-0.00	-0.00
LAB.TAX.REV.NOM_PCER	0.02	0.06	-0.01	-0.06	0.01	0.01	0.01
VAT.TAX.REV.NOM_PCER	0.01	0.06	0.01	-0.04	0.01	0.01	0.01
GDP.GROWTH_ER	0.01	0.04	-0.04	-0.01	0.00	0.00	0.00
INV.GDP_ER	0.06	0.09	0.06	-0.07	-0.00	-0.00	0.00
SHORT.RATE_ER	-0.05	-0.07	-0.11	0.04	0.00	0.00	0.00
INFLATION.PGDP_ER	0.01	0.01	-0.04	-0.04	-0.00	0.00	0.00
INFLATION.PC_ER	0.01	-0.01	-0.04	0.03	0.00	0.00	0.00
.INF.TARGET_ER	0.00	0.00	0.00	0.00	0.00	0.00	0.00
.INF.GAP_ER	0.02	-0.01	-0.06	-0.02	0.00	0.00	0.00
LONG.RATE.10YRS_ER	0.00	0.01	0.01	0.02	0.00	0.00	0.00
REAL.SHORT.RATE_ER	-0.07	-0.05	-0.05	0.05	0.00	0.00	0.00
VAT_ER	0.00	0.00	0.00	0.00	0.00	0.00	0.00
TL_ER	0.00	0.00	0.00	0.00	0.00	0.00	0.00
TC_ER	0.00	0.00	0.00	0.00	0.00	0.00	0.00
DEBT.TO.GDP_ER	-0.02	-0.08	-0.07	-0.06	-0.02	-0.00	-0.00
DEFG.TO.GDP_ER	-0.02	-0.04	-0.05	0.01	0.00	0.00	0.00
TRADE.BAL.TO.GDP_ER	-0.05	-0.07	-0.07	0.06	-0.00	-0.00	-0.00

Note: _PCER = cumulative percentage difference from base; _ER = absolute difference from base.

Reinhard Neck / Gottfried Haber[1]

The SGP Fiscal Rule in the Case of Sluggish Growth: Some Alternative Simulations

I. Introduction

The paper by *Breuss/Roeger* (2005) investigates macroeconomic effects of the Stability and Growth Pact (SGP) in the Euro Area (EA). For this purpose, the authors undertake simulations with the QUEST Model of the European Commission, both without and with the assumption that the rules of the SGP are observed. After describing in some detail the main features of the QUEST Model, a macroeconomic multi-country model combining neoclassical and Keynesian features, they give a survey of macroeconomic developments in the European Economic and Monetary Union (EMU) during the last years, with special emphasis upon fiscal policies and the SGP. The core of the paper consists of a description and interpretation of the simulations with the QUEST Model. Differences between results under a supply and under a demand shock are pointed out. As a central conclusion, the authors give the SGP higher scores in the case of a supply shock than under a demand shock.

---

[1] Comment on the paper by *Fritz Breuss / Werner Roeger*. We are grateful to *Warwick J. McKibbin* for providing us with the MSG2 Model. Financial support of the Austrian National Bank (project no. 9152) is gratefully acknowledged. The views expressed need not be those of the Austrian National Bank.

The paper is concerned with a timely and important question in view of criticisms of the SGP and endeavours to reform its rules to prevent undesirable macroeconomic side effects. The methodology of simulating alternative (partly counter-factual) policy scenarios is appropriate to evaluate the virtues and vices of the SGP in terms of its macroeconomic effects. Of course, the results depend strongly upon whether the model used is a good approximation of the relations between the macroeconomic variables of interest, especially the fiscal policy variables and the main target variables of the EMU economies. This cannot easily be judged, especially when it comes to counter-factual simulations. Therefore it is desirable to check the robustness of the conclusions of such a simulation analysis by conducting similar experiments with one or more other models and compare the results with those of the original ones.

In this note, we do this by using the MSG2 Model, another multi-country macroeconomic model. In Section II, we give a short introduction to this model. Section III shows the results of simulations analogous to those performed by *Breuss/Roeger*. Section IV points out that there may be differences between temporary and permanent shocks that were not considered by *Breuss/Roeger*. A tentative "welfare" analysis is provided in Section V. Section VI concludes.

II. The MSG2 Model[2]

For the calculations in this paper, the McKibbin-Sachs Global Model (MSG2 Model), a dynamic, intertemporal, general-equilibrium model of a multi-region world economy, is applied. We use the European version MSGR44A. The theoretical background of the MSG2 Model is similar to that of the QUEST Model: Based upon microeconomic foundations by assuming that economic agents maximize intertemporal objective functions, the model exhibits a mixture of classical and Keynesian properties: partly rational expectations in combination with various rigidities allow for deviations from fully optimizing behaviour. In particular, nominal wages are assumed to adjust slowly in the major industrial economies. Nevertheless, the model solves for a full intertemporal equilibrium.

---

2 See *W. J. McKibbin / J. D. Sachs* (1991), Global Linkages. Washington, DC: Brookings Institution 1991.

McKibbin/Sachs (1991) describe the original version of the model in full detail.[3] The long run of the global economy is driven by a neoclassical growth model, with exogenous technical progress and population growth. Keynesian rigidities in the goods and labour markets in the short run and optimal decisions, conditional on expected future paths of the world economy, drive the short run of the model. Thus, the model captures long-run effects of shocks and short-run dynamics towards these long-run outcomes, with expectations formation providing a link between the long-run outcome and the short-run adjustment.

As the MSG2 Model is a fully specified dynamic general-equilibrium model, it incorporates both the demand and the supply sides of the major industrial economies. Stock-flow relations are carefully observed, and intertemporal budget constraints are imposed. For the long-run behaviour of the model, stock equilibrium rather than flow equilibrium is important. The short run of the model behaves in a way similar to the Mundell-Fleming model under flexible exchange rates and high capital mobility, but the future paths of the global economy are important in the short run because of the forward-looking behaviour in asset and goods markets. The assumptions of rational expectations in financial markets and of partially forward-looking behaviour in real spending decisions allow for the incorporation of the effects of anticipated policy changes.

The supply side of the model is specified in an internally consistent manner: Factor input decisions are based in part on intertemporal profit maximization by firms. Labour and intermediate inputs are determined to maximise short-run profits, given a stock of capital that is fixed within each period and adjusted according to a Tobin's q-model of investment, where Tobin's q evolves according to a rational-expectations forecast of future after-tax profitability.

The MSGR44A version of the MSG2 Model consists of models of the following countries and regions: the United States, Japan, Germany, the United Kingdom, France, Italy, Austria, the rest of the Euro Area (REA), Central and Eastern European economies (CEEC), the rest of the OECD (ROECD), non-oil developing countries, oil-exporting countries, and the former Soviet Union. For the last three regions, only foreign trade and external financial as-

---

3 Additional resources are available on the web, http://www.msgpl.com.au/ (last visited May 2006).

pects are modelled, whereas the industrial countries and regions are fully modelled with an internal macroeconomic structure. The basic theoretical structure for all industrial regions is the same, but institutional differences are taken into account, especially in modelling labour markets.

The MSG2 Model was fitted to empirical data by a mix of calibration techniques for CGE models and econometric time-series estimates. For the simulations described in this paper, the original MSG2 Model was modified by implementing the European System of Central Banks (ESCB) for the EMU. Money supply in all EA countries (twelve in reality, five in the model) is no longer available as an instrument, but monetary policy is conducted by the ECB, which acts independently of the instruments and goals of national fiscal policies. Therefore we have a single monetary authority in the EA (the ECB) and several national fiscal policy makers inside the EA.

III. The *Breuss/Roeger* Scenarios under the MSG2 Model

First, we replicate the scenarios simulated with the QUEST Model by *Breuss/Roeger*, using the MSG2 Model. As the two models have similar theoretical bases, structures and coverage, we expect them to deliver at least qualitatively similar results in the short run when subjecting them to comparable inputs. This is not necessarily the case for the long run, as the QUEST Model does not converge to steady state equilibrium with full employment, which the MSG2 Model does. Hence a comparison of the two models with respect to short-run and long-run effects is of interest.

As in *Breuss/Roeger*, we implement scenarios where the three largest EA economies are shocked: France, Germany and Italy. Shocks start in 2001 and are designed such as to correspond as closely as possible to those assumed by *Breuss/Roeger*. We consider a *supply shock*, where total factor productivity (TFP) falls below baseline values by 1 percent in the first year, 2 percent in the second year and 3 percent in all following years. This implies, as in *Breuss/Roeger*, a temporary reduction of TFP over a period of three years (2002 to 2004) and a permanent downward level shift of TFP. We also follow *Breuss/Roeger* in assuming a *demand shock* of the following size: autonomous private consumption falls below baseline values by 1 percent of GDP in the first year, 2.5 percent in the second year, 4 percent in the third year and returns to baseline values during the next three years (being back to baseline in 2006).

Autonomous private investment is reduced below baseline values during the same period by half of the amount (in percentage terms) of the reduction of autonomous private consumption.

Both shocks are analysed under the same types of fiscal rules as assumed by *Breuss/Roeger*. In the "No SGP"-version, we assume fiscal policy variables to remain at their baseline values, that is, a completely inactive fiscal policy. Automatic stabilisers work, but there is no discretionary or flexible-rule based reaction of policy-makers on the shock. Debt stabilisation is implemented in the MSG2 Model through an automatic adjustment of lump-sum taxes. Otherwise, tax rates and government consumption remain at their baseline values. By contrast, in the "SGP"-version, we keep the public-sector deficit at baseline values in all EA countries and regions. These values are below the 3 percent limit of the SGP; for instance, in 2001, the respective value is 2.7 percent of GDP for Germany. Government consumption is the instrument variable that is used to achieve this fixing of the public-sector deficit.

To complete the description of the scenarios, we have to make some assumptions about the other exogenous variables of the model. The most important one concerns monetary policy of the ECB. Here we assume the ECB to follow a rule of inflation targeting: money supply in the EA is adjusted such as to keep inflation rates at their baseline values in all scenarios considered. This seems a realistic assumption, given the commitment of the ECB to price stability. Moreover, in previous work with the MSG2 Model we found this monetary policy rule to deliver acceptable results under a variety of possible shocks. We also tried tentatively monetary targeting (keeping money supply at baseline values) and obtained not great differences to inflation targeting. Apart from these simulation inputs, all other exogenous variables of the model are kept at their baseline values. In particular, it is assumed that the other countries and regions of the model do not react upon the shock affecting France, Germany and Italy by changing their fiscal or monetary policies.

The resulting time paths of the level of real GDP, its growth rate, the public-sector deficit and the public-sector debt resulting from the TFP shock are shown in Figures 1 and 2 for Germany and Austria, respectively. These can be directly compared to Figures 4 to 7 (Germany) and 8 and 9 (Austria) in *Breuss/Roeger* to see the differences of the results from the two models. For easier comparisons between the two fiscal policy rules, both the No-SGP and the

SGP versions are shown in the same diagram for the respective variable here. Germany is chosen as the largest economy and Austria as a representative small EA economy, as in the *Breuss/Roeger* paper. All numbers are deviations from baseline values.

Figure 1: TFP Shock, Results for Germany

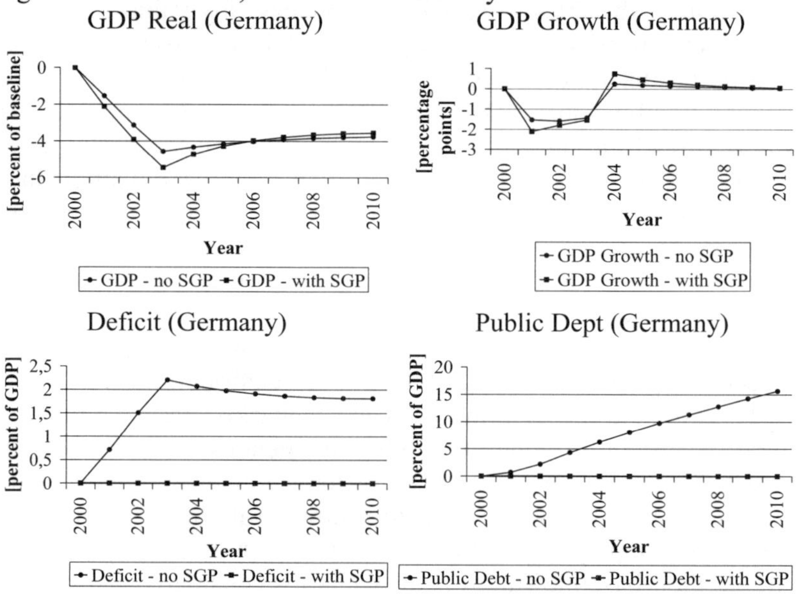

Figure 2: TFP Shock, Results for Austria

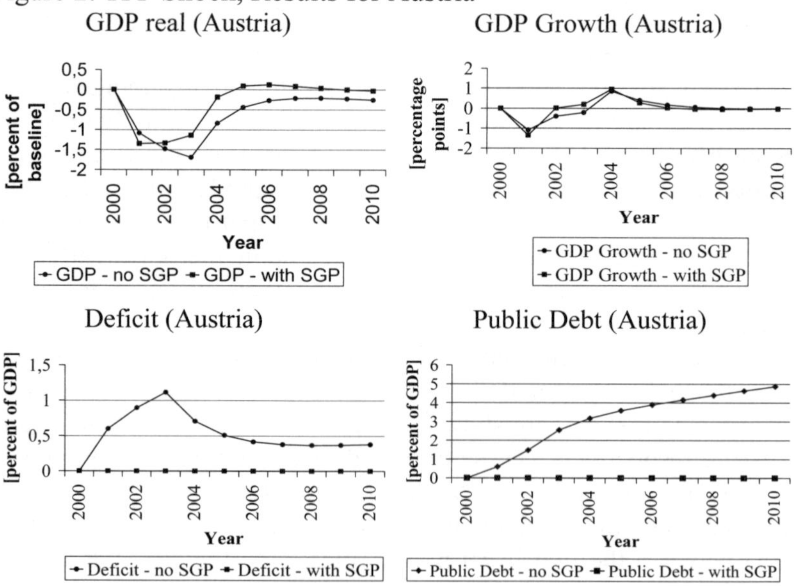

As can be seen from Figure 1, in the No-SGP version, GDP falls more quickly in the MSG2 Model than in the QUEST Model as reaction upon the TFP shock, but returns also more quickly to the baseline growth rate (overshooting it even slightly). In the long run, the level of real GDP remains below baseline by more than 3 percent. Public-sector deficit and debt show very similar behaviour in both models, again with a stronger short-run effect in the MSG2 Model. Note that the values of these two variables are nearly the same in both models in 2010 (the last year shown). The SGP version implies lower growth rates of GDP during the first three years of the shock and higher ones afterwards, which is a qualitatively similar behaviour as in the QUEST Model but with quantitatively stronger differences. According to the assumptions for this scenario, public deficit and debt are at baseline values in every period in the SGP scenario.

Figure 2 shows the spillover effects to Austria under both fiscal policy rules. As Austria has strong trade and financial relations to Germany, these effects are fairly strong, resulting in a decrease of Austrian real GDP by more than 1 percent below baseline during the first three years of the shock. With respect to the differences between the No-SGP and the SGP scenario, results are even more similar to those from the QUEST Model than for Germany: the SGP causes a slightly deeper recession in the first year but higher output in the following years than the No-SGP scenario. Permanent increases of public deficit and debt of non-negligible size occur in the No-SGP scenario, making it rather unattractive for Austria.

Next, we consider the effects resulting from the demand shock. Figures 3 and 4 show the main variables of interest as resulting from the MSG2 Model. Figure 3 (Germany) can be compared to Figures 10 to 13 in the *Breuss/Roeger* paper, Figure 4 (Austria) to their Figures 14 and 15. As in their analysis, the negative demand shock is temporary, and the entire shock scenario may be interpreted as a sequence of a negative and a positive shock, although the latter, in the framework of the MSG2 Model, results only in a return to the baseline (the path towards the steady state).

Figure 3: Demand Shock, Results for Germany

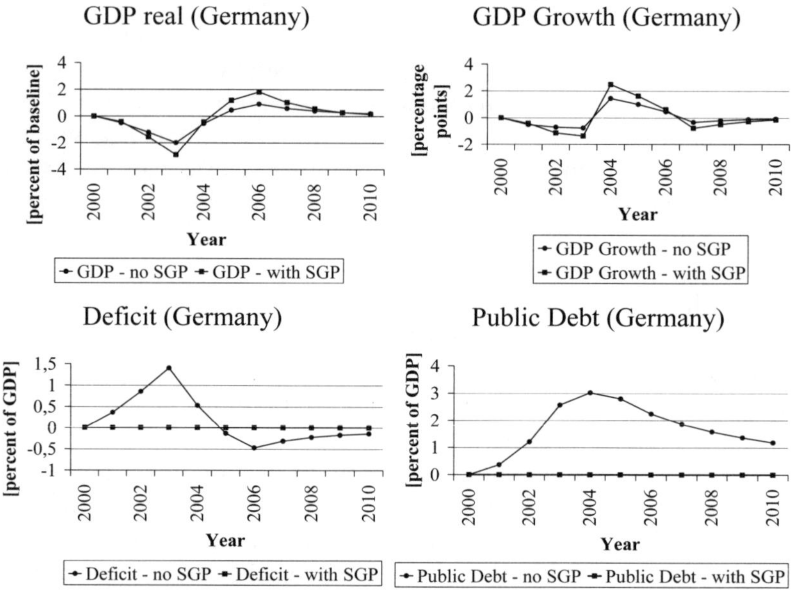

Although the reaction of GDP in Germany is qualitatively similar in both models, there are more pronounced quantitative differences now than in the case of the TFP shock. Under the demand shock, the MSG2 Model results in smaller effects on GDP than the QUEST Model, both during the first three years (where the effects are negative) and during the following years (where they are first positive and then result in damped oscillations). In the No-SGP scenario, the public deficit increases in a similar way in both models during the first three years but falls much less according to the MSG2 Model than according to the QUEST Model afterwards. This leads to higher public debt in the short and medium run in the MSG2 Model. Also the differences between the No-SGP and the SGP scenarios with respect to GDP, although with similar time profiles, are smaller in the MSG2 Model; hence it is not obvious which scenario is better for Germany under this kind of demand shock.

Figure 4: Demand Shock, Results for Austria

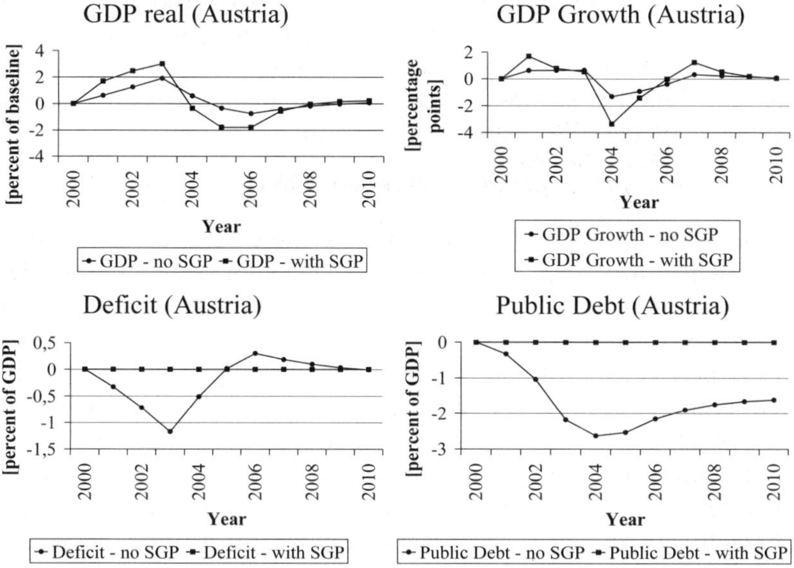

Spillover effects to Austria are, somewhat unexpectedly, positive during the first years and negative afterwards. This is due to the fact that the MSG2 Model has strong neoclassical features, including rational expectations. A reduction of demand in France, Germany and Italy, which is assumed to be expected by households and firms, results in quick reactions of prices, wages and real exchange rates which means that it acts like a shift of demand from French, German and Italian goods to those of other countries (including Austria) and hence increases in the latter's GDP. This effect can be seen in all countries of the model that are not directly affected by the demand shock. As a result, in Austria we can observe an improvement of public deficit and debt under the No-SGP scenario. Moreover, smaller oscillations of GDP occur in the No-SGP than in the SGP scenario due to Keynesian short-run fiscal policy effects. It is, however, questionable whether keeping the public deficit in Austria at baseline levels would be an adequate representation of the SGP requirement, because here this would mean a higher deficit with than without the SGP during most of the simulation period.

Altogether, our simulations with the MSG2 Model so far largely confirm most of the conclusions obtained by *Breuss/Roeger* with the QUEST Model. Under the TFP shock, we find short-run output losses but long-run gains from obeying the SGP, both for the countries directly affected by the shock and for the neighbour countries. Under the demand shock, results are less clear, and there seems to be some trade-off between fiscal goals (keeping the budget deficit below the SGP limit and avoiding fiscal imbalances) on the one hand and the desire to reduce the variability of output.

IV. Temporary versus Permanent Shocks

Breuss/Roeger conclude that for "symmetric cyclical phenomena" (which they equate with their demand shocks), countercyclical policies (and neglect of the SGP) may be preferable, while for more "asymmetric" recessions where "the economy does not fully return to the pre-recession trend" (their TFP shock), the more restrictive SGP scenario may be better. This assumes that demand shocks are always temporary and supply (TFP) shocks are always permanent (both with respect to the level variables; we do not consider shocks to growth rates here). But this is only a subset of possible scenarios. Logically, there are four possibilities: *temporary* and *permanent supply* shocks and *temporary* and *permanent demand* shocks.

This is not a pure matter of classification, but has also some empirical importance. Supply shocks that are temporary are rather frequent. For example, wars and environmental catastrophes (hurricanes, earthquakes, etc.) can be interpreted mainly as negative TFP shocks. But usually, after these exogenous shocks are over, sooner or later TFP growth overshoots and TFP level returns to its long-run path. The reconstruction period in Germany and Austria after the destructions of World War II is a case in point, but there are many more recent examples. On the other hand, negative demand shocks may be long-lived if not permanent. Shifts in preferences inducing shifts in demand for products from one country towards another one, for example, may be fairly permanent. Tourism is a sector where such shifts occur frequently, and often consumers cannot be persuaded even by intensive marketing to shift their preferences back once they have changed them.

This raises the question whether the adequate design of fiscal policy depends primarily upon whether shocks are coming from demand or from supply changes, or whether they are temporary or permanent. To get some idea on this issue, as a first step we can complement the analysis of the previous section by adding simulations of temporary supply shocks and permanent demand shocks. We use the same simulation design as before, but assume for the

TFP shock a return to the baseline level during the periods following the shock (2004 to 2006 in our case), i.e. a temporary TFP shock. For the demand shock, on the other hand, we assume that private consumption and private investment remain at lower levels forever.

Figures 5 and 6 show the result for the temporary supply shock for Germany and Austria, respectively, Figures 7 and 8 those for the permanent demand shock. As can be expected, each of these simulations shows some elements due to the temporary versus permanent character and some elements due to the demand versus supply shock character, respectively.

Figure 5: Temporary TFP Shock, Results for Germany

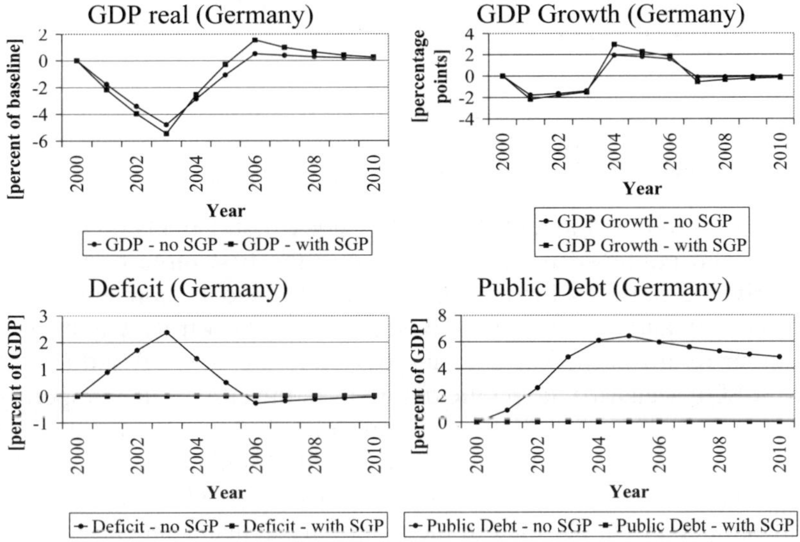

Figure 6: Temporary TFP Shock, Results for Austria

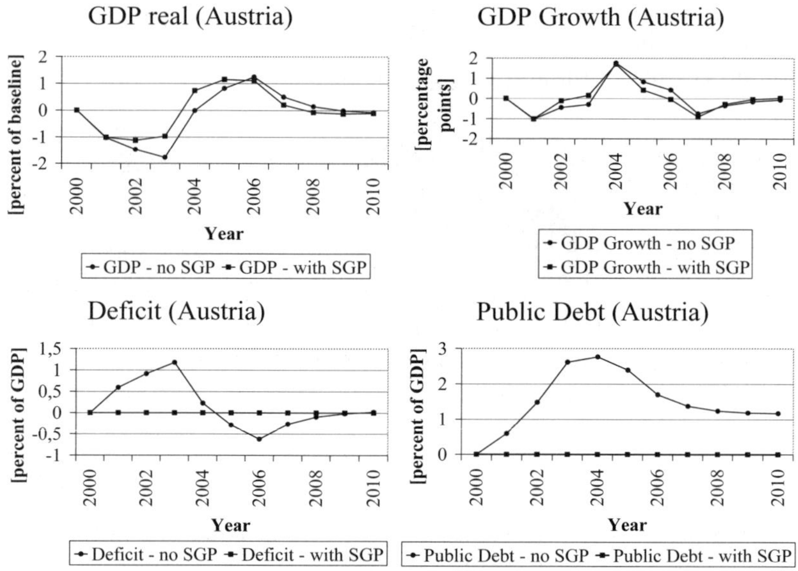

Let us look at the temporary TFP shock first. Effects on German GDP and public-sector variables during the first three periods are nearly the same as for the permanent TFP shock, both under the Non-SGP and under the SGP scenario. Afterwards, we have a similar return to the baseline and overshooting of GDP and (in the Non-SGP scenario) the public deficit as in the case of the temporary demand shock, again for both fiscal policy rules. The quantitative effects, in particular the amplitudes of the oscillations and (in the No-SGP scenario) the long-run level of public debt, are higher in the temporary supply than in the temporary demand shock scenario. Spillover effects to Austria are qualitatively similar but smaller as compared to the permanent TFP shock during the first three periods. Afterwards, we can observe similar behaviour as under the temporary demand shock, but stronger oscillations of GDP and (in the No-SGP scenario) lower public deficit and debt. A comparison of GDP between the No-SGP and the SGP scenario does not allow for an immediate evaluation.

Figure 7: Permanent Demand Shock, Results for Germany

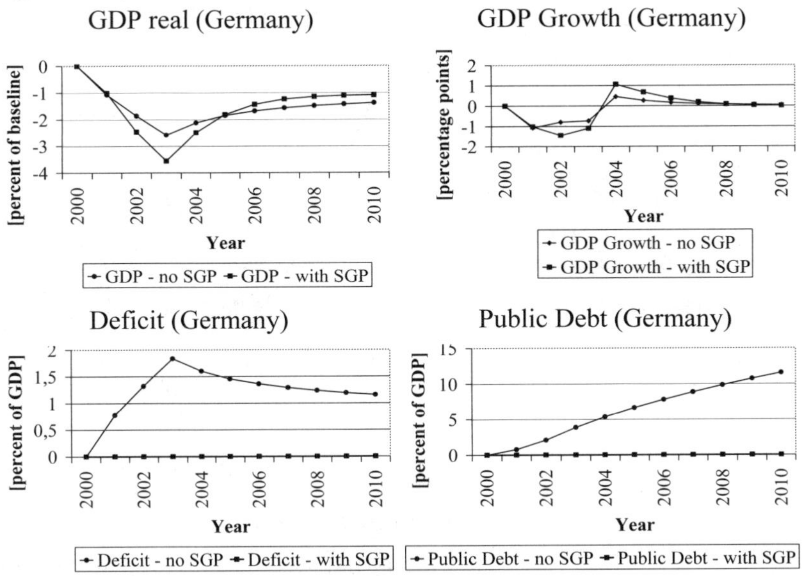

The effects of the permanent demand shock in Germany (and the other countries directly affected) may also be regarded as a mix of those of the temporary demand shock and those of the permanent supply shock. But here, the GDP effects in the short run are stronger than those of the temporary demand shock, and the same is true for the fiscal variables in the No-SGP scenario. Also the adjustment to the (permanently lower) GDP level is more unfavourable than under the permanent TFP shock, and public deficit and debt are always higher in the No-SGP scenario. Although GDP is lower with than without SGP in the short run, from the fifth period on it is higher, resulting in a permanently higher long-run level of GDP in the case of the SGP fiscal policy. On the other hand, the effects on Austria (and other not directly affected countries) are similar to those of the temporary demand shock (mostly favourable here) but stronger and, of course, permanent, leading to improved competitiveness. The "SGP scenario" would increase fluctuations and raise deficit and debt as compared to the "No-SGP" scenario, but in this case the interpretation of the scenario keeping the deficit at baseline as "SGP" is certainly inappropriate because the SGP does not require keeping public deficits at levels *higher* than those resulting endogenously without fiscal policy changes.

Figure 8: Permanent Demand Shock, Results for Austria

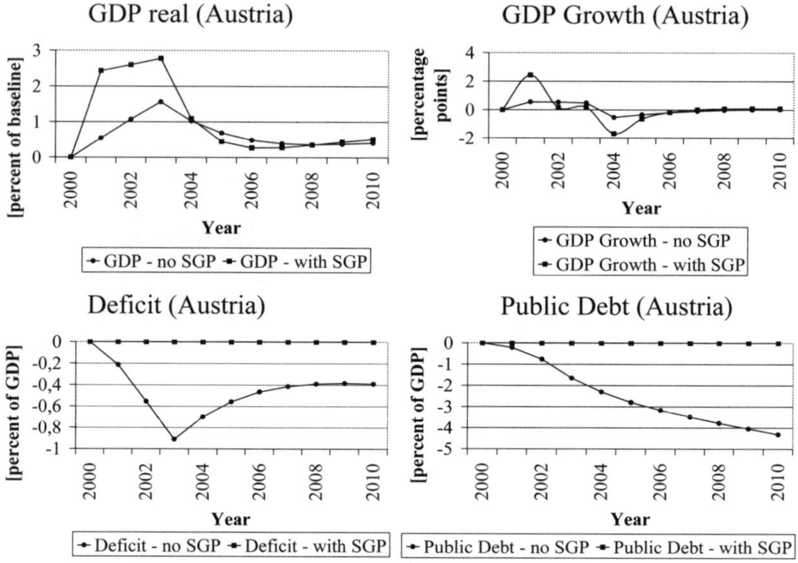

V. A "Welfare" Comparison

The previous sections leave us with the impression that it is very difficult to decide whether the SGP dominates a fiscal policy regime with less stringent or no rules on the public deficit or not. In any case, it seems to make a difference whether the shocks acting on the European economies are demand or supply side and whether they are permanent or temporary. Moreover, the results on the spillover effects to countries not directly hit by the shock show that it may also make a difference whether the shock is symmetric or asymmetric in the usual (Mundellian) sense, i.e. whether it affects all countries (of the world/of Europe/of the EMU/of the EA) or (as is assumed here, following *Breuss/Roeger*) only some of them. The last issue, though important, must remain outside of our considerations here, but we can dare at a first attempt to evaluate the SGP in terms of its macroeconomic effects by looking at the simulations described before. Evaluation means that we need a measure of macroeconomic performance. We are very much aware of the problems related to this question, and to the definition, specification and interpretation of a macroeconomic objective function, especially if it tries to measure something like "social welfare". Nevertheless, the task may be worthwhile, at least to get some starting point for further research about possible welfare effects of rules like the SGP.

In the present context, we proceed as follows: To define a normative measure of the economic outcomes of different simulation runs, we calculate economic "welfare losses" caused by various shocks under the two fiscal arrangements by assuming an additively separable quadratic "welfare loss function". The "welfare losses" in each period are equal to the sums of the weighted quadratic differences between the actual values and the optimal values for each of the target variables. Next, the "welfare losses" in each future period are discounted to their present values (using a rate of time preference attributed to the policy makers, which is assumed to be 10 percent) and summed up over the time horizon (infinity in theory, 100 years in the simulations) to obtain the measure of total "welfare loss".

The countries/regions for which a "welfare loss" (objective) function is specified are those of the EA: Germany, France, Italy, Austria and REA. We assume as target variables the rate of inflation, employment, real GDP and the budget deficit of the public sector. All target weights are set to 0.25, producing an equally weighted standardised objective function. The baseline values (simulated values without any shocks) of the target variables are considered as their optimal values. This makes sense because this reference simulation run represents a stable path towards a long-run equilibrium of the model. European objective function values are calculated as weighted averages of the respective country-specific values, with weights derived from values of GDP at market prices.

When interpreting the values of this objective function ("welfare loss function"), extraordinary care has to be taken, because the values should mainly be understood as indication for the order of preference of the policy scenarios under consideration within a specific type of shock. The absolute magnitudes of the resulting numbers give a rough feeling for the size of the welfare effects, but must not be overvalued with respect to quantitative comparisons. Moreover, for different shocks the absolute values of the objective function cannot be compared either. What can be done – and this is the main task of this exercise – is a systematic comparison of the welfare effects of shocks on the EA with and without the SGP. As the SGP is an institutional feature mainly relevant for the EA, this justifies the neglect of other countries and regions.

The results of these calculations are summarized in Table 1. Higher numbers mean higher "welfare losses", hence lower numbers are "better" than higher ones.

Table 1: "Welfare Results" for the EA

	Type of Shock	TFP (Supply) Shock		Demand Shock	
	Duration	Permanent	Temporary	Permanent	Temporary
Institution	No SGP	23.93	9.46	10.09	4.44
	SGP	21.14	9.29	15.05	9.27

The main result from this comparison is the following: When the three economies of France, Germany and Italy are subject to an unfavourable supply (TFP) shock, it is better for the EA to stick to the SGP. If they are hit by a negative demand shock, the EA does better without the SGP. It does not make much difference whether the respective shock is temporary or permanent. Instead, it is the type of the shock (supply or demand) that counts.

As already said, this result must be treated with great caution. It certainly depends on the specification of the objective function in a non-trivial way. For instance, if we raise the rate of time preference (making the policy-maker evaluating the results more impatient) sufficiently (in our case, weighting each period's "welfare losses" by one tenth of those of the previous period), the SGP will never be advantageous. On the other hand, if we introduce public debt instead of the deficit as argument in the objective function, the SGP will always be advantageous. A lot of additional sensitivity analyses can be imagined to explore whether the SGP comes out more often as advantage or as disadvantage. Nevertheless, we consider our result as not completely arbitrary, because previous analyses with the same model but fairly different simulations have nearly always shown the superiority of fixed rules under supply shocks and of more flexible rules under demand shocks.[4] The present result fits into this picture and may therefore be regarded as a (preliminary) indicator of the circumstances under which fiscal policy in the EA works better with the SGP than without it.

---

4 E.g., *R. Neck / G. Haber / W. J. McKibbin* (2005) Global Macroeconomic Policy Implications of an Enlarged EMU, in: *F. Breuss / E. Hochreiter* (eds.), Challenges for Central Banks in an Enlarged EMU, Vienna 2005, Springer, pp. 235–257.

VI. Conclusions

We have shown that most of the results regarding the SGP fiscal rule as compared to a scenario without that rule, which were derived by *Breuss/Roeger* simulating European shock scenarios with the QUEST Model, also hold when using the MSG2 Model. We extend these results by distinguishing between temporary and permanent supply and demand shocks. A preliminary "welfare" analysis indicates that the SGP rule may be advantageous when a negative supply shock hits the economies under consideration. On the other hand, a negative demand shock seems to be better dealt with by letting automatic stabilisers work irrespective of the SGP deficit limit. Unfortunately, the practical value of this insight is limited as many shocks in reality contain supply and demand elements and the nature of a shock cannot always be recognized in advance. Therefore more research on the nature of the shocks affecting Europe and their macroeconomic impacts is required before a comprehensive evaluation of the SGP can be attempted.

List of Authors

Univ.-Prof. Dr. *Fritz Breuss*, Europainstitut, Vienna University of Economics and Business Administration and ECSA Austria.

Director *Marco Buti*, DG Economies of the Member States, European Commission, Brussels.

Prof. *Paul De Grauwe*, Faculty of Economics and Applied Economics, University of Leuven.

Univ.-Ass. Dr. MMag. *Gottfried Haber*, Department of Economics, University of Klagenfurt.

Prof. *Andrew Hughes Hallett*, School of Public Policy, George Mason University, Virginia, USA.

Univ.-Prof. Dr. *Wilhelm Kohler*, Department of International Economic Relations, Eberhard Karls University Tübingen.

Prof. *Jean-Victor Louis*, Emeritus professor of the Free University of Brussels (ULB), Honorary general counsel of the National Bank of Belgium.

Univ.-Prof. Dr. *Reinhard Neck*, Department of Economics, University of Klagenfurt.

Univ.-Prof. Dr. *Ewald Nowotny*, Department of Economics, Vienna University of Economics and Business Administration and CEO of BAWAG, Vienna.

Dr. *Werner Roeger*, Deputy Head of the Econometric Modelling Unit of the Directorate General for Economic and Financial Affairs (DG ECFIN) at the European Commission in Brussels.

Prof. *André Sapir*, ECARES, Université Libre de Bruxelles and Senior Fellow and Research Scholar at BRUEGEL, Brussels.

Dr. *Waltraud Schelkle*, European Institute, London School of Economics and Political Science, London.

Paul van den Noord, PhD, Head of the European Union Desk, Organisation for Economic Co-operation and Development (OECD), Paris.

Springer-Verlag and the Environment